Information Technology and Organizational Transformation

Solving the Management Puzzle

Information Technology and Organizational Transformation

Solving the Management Puzzle

Suzanne Rivard, Benoit A. Aubert, Michel Patry, Guy Paré and Heather A. Smith

ELSEVIER
BUTTERWORTH
HEINEMANN

AMSTERDAM BOSTON HEIDELBERG LONDON NEW YORK OXFORD PARIS
SAN DIEGO SAN FRANCISCO SINGAPORE SYDNEY TOKYO

Elsevier Butterworth-Heinemann
Linacre House, Jordan Hill, Oxford OX2 8DP
200 Wheeler Road, Burlington, MA 01803

First published 2004

British Library Cataloguing in Publication Data
A catalogue record for this book is available from the British Library

Library of Congress Cataloging in Publication Data
A catalog record for this book is available from the Library of Congress

ISBN 0 7506 6202 6

For information on all Elsevier Butterworth-Heinemann publications visit our website at http://elsevierbooks.com

Typeset by Charon Tec Pvt Ltd., Chennai, India
Printed and bound in Great Britain

Contents

Preface

The origins of this book go back to a research project at CIRANO and HEC Montréal on new organizational forms. We were then studying the deployment of information technology (IT) in large and small firms and the changes in the networking of firms. It soon became clear that the dramatic developments in IT and the strategic changes that were associated with these: outsourcing, e-commerce, business process reengineering, etc., were all interconnected. These paved the way to many organizational innovations.

We wanted to know what role IT plays in the development of organizational innovations. We then decided to investigate a few well-documented cases of organizations, which were profoundly transformed, reinvented in a sort, as a result of the process of embedding IT in new governance structures. *Information technology and organizational transformation: solving the management puzzle* synthesizes our findings.

We do not claim that the cases here presented are representative in any ways, or that these show us the way ahead. Instead, we hope that our framing of the issues and our analyses of the cases shed light on organizational transformations. We hope that this book will show that there are many ways to reinvent an organization. In fact, each case illustrates a particular path, and a particular strategy.

These cases, and others that we know of, at first presented themselves to us as puzzles. Soon, however, it became apparent to us that these puzzles had common features. This is how we came up with our own way of framing that mass of information: we called it *The management puzzle*. The management puzzle is itself framed by social, technical, and business environmental forces upon which managers have little or no control at all. But managers do have an influence on four fundamental puzzle pieces: strategy, structure, information technology, and leadership. Our aim has been to help managers and analysts put the pieces of the management puzzle together. We thus tried to find answers to questions such as: What role does each piece play in transforming an organization? How do these pieces fit together? Which piece – if any – plays a central role? etc.

The book is divided in four parts:

- The first part presents the puzzle frames and describes the features of the organization of the twenty-first century. In it, the many faceted waves of change that confront all organizations are reviewed in detail and the major shifts and trends are clearly identified.

- The second part dissects the four fundamental management puzzle pieces: strategy, structure, information technology, and leadership. Each piece of the management puzzle is then examined. Its shape is related to the changes in the environment of the new economy, as well as to the other pieces.

- The third part examines three very different and equally interesting experiences of organizations with untraditional organizational forms: *Progressive Insurance*, *Oticon*, and *Li & Fung* are examples of performing enterprises with very untraditional organizational structures. Their analyses show that each experience rests on a different set of innovations – and puzzle pieces – as pivotal elements. The paths to organizational innovations are numerous and varied. Yet, a few key lessons can be drawn from these analyses.

- The fourth part precisely draws a number of managerial lessons from our analysis. We call that part *The management challenge*, and divided it into four major sections: people management, IT management, knowledge management, and change management.

We hope this book will be useful for managers who have to cope every day with the barrage of changes raining down on them and who must lead their organizations into uncharted territory. We also hope that our analysis will inspire analysts and researchers who, like us, try to understand how organizations – large and small – cope in the current environment and how managers reinvent these organizations to improve their efficiency and serve society. Recognizing that our book is one among several pieces of work on this complex topic, we have provided a bibliography that includes the main sources of information that we used in writing this book.

We are very grateful to the organizations that have sponsored this book. First among these are HEC Montréal and CIRANO whose continuous support has been vital to the realization of this book. We also want to thank Industry Canada and Queen's University for their contribution. Finally, we would like to thank our families who pretended to understand that our research was worth sacrificing many private moments with our spouses and children. We cannot overstate our appreciation to all the members of our families.

Suzanne Rivard
Benoit A. Aubert
Michel Patry
Guy Paré
Heather A. Smith

PART I

Management in the twenty-first century organization

You cannot pick up a newspaper or book these days without hearing about some aspect of the new economy and its implications for business. There are new paradigms, new business models, new technologies, new trends for managers to monitor and, most importantly, new minefields for managers to navigate on a daily basis. A manager's job in the twenty-first century organization is not easy. Not only do today's managers have to cope with the barrage of changes raining down like shrapnel, they must also lead their organizations through this uncharted territory, all the while trying to carry on their firms' business. Needless to say, these days managers face a great deal of uncertainty in almost every aspect of their working lives.

Twenty-first century managers live in a world in which they are told to abandon the tried and true assumptions about business and the tools and practices which have been developed carefully over time. Meanwhile, new fads are coming and going at the speed of light, and the media, vendors, and consultants hype ideas and technologies before they are fully developed. Often, it is unclear just *why* all this is happening and how it all fits together. Thus, many managers today must feel as if they are facing a table full of jigsaw puzzle pieces with no idea of the size, shape, or outline of what they are supposed to accomplish. Somehow, they must put together a coherent picture of what *their particular* organization will look like but with so many pieces, and no picture to guide them, the task seems Herculean.

This book is designed to help managers to find the right pieces and to put them together so that they make sense. The first chapter begins the process by building the frames of the puzzle so that managers will be able to see the size and shape of the task awaiting them. Subsequent chapters will examine the individual puzzle pieces that have to be put together – strategy, structure, information technology, and leadership. In addition, they will present the cases of three firms that were equally successful in putting these pieces together, while choosing pieces with dramatically different forms and adjusting them in radically different ways. These cases illustrate that there is no single best way of assembling the pieces. They show that firms can be quite successful in their adaptation to their environment, yet follow their very own trajectory.

Chapter 1

The puzzle frames

The world is changing. At the beginning of the new century, it is clear to almost everyone that new technology, new enterprise models, a new business environment, and a new geopolitical environment are converging and recreating almost everything we have traditionally understood about organizations. Three responses to the changing environment are possible. Firms can anticipate change and flourish. They can react to change and struggle to survive. Or, finally, they can ignore change and face the likelihood of going under.

Why is change happening? To understand this, we must understand the key role played by technology and information in business transformation. Change at all levels is being driven by the transformation of our society from an industrial to an information economy. Networked, modular and open (i.e. interconnectable) technology is leading to an increasingly freer exchange of information among people, businesses, and nations. This, in turn, is leading to increasingly interconnected global economic development, new economic alliances and rules, and the liberalization of developing economies, commonly referred to as *globalization*. Together, information technology (IT) and globalization are reinventing marketplaces, threatening regulatory environments, challenging the traditional ways of conducting business, driving deregulation of industry, and creating instability in the old political order.

Faced with these new conditions, businesses have little choice but to change both internally and externally. Internally, the advent of massive amounts of information and technology has meant that organizations *must* engage in information analysis or risk being swamped by data. However, *as soon as a company takes the first tentative steps from data to information, its decision processes, management structure, and even the way work gets done begin to be transformed.*[1] This transformation began slowly; the information economy is already about 40 years old and it is only just now coming to fruition with its own economic and organizational models. Until recently, technology and information networking beyond an organization's boundaries has been missing. With the advent of the Internet and other networking technologies, this is now feasible. Thus, in future, the information economy will have an increasingly revolutionary impact, as new infrastructures are developed to harness the power of worldwide information. While more traditionally-based organizational models will not collapse overnight, they are likely to decline in scope and importance and find themselves increasingly left behind. In other words, we will still need farmers, manufacturers, and other institutions of earlier economies; however, we will need progressively fewer of them and those remaining will be transformed by technology and information.

Change does not come easily to organizations. The transformations of the information age will be extremely challenging because of the speed and pace with which they are occurring. Nevertheless, managers must begin to grapple with them and their implications for how their businesses will operate. They will need a vision for what their organization will look like in the future, so they can work towards it.

The next three sections present the salient features of the environment in which business will operate over the next 20 years. The business, technology, and social changes now occurring provide the puzzle's frames. They will shape and limit the necessities and possibilities of all future organizational activity (see Figure 1.1).

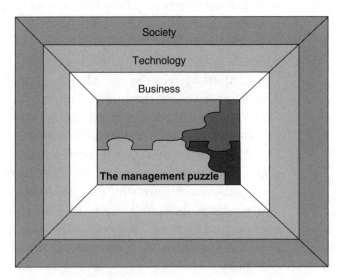

Figure 1.1
The management puzzle is framed by social, technical, and business changes.

While they are considered separately here, they are inextricably connected to each other and to the picture of the twenty-first century organization. Each change helps establish the dimensions of the picture. Together, they form a rather formidable border for the image that managers have to assemble. The final section of this chapter looks at how organizations are beginning to respond to these changes and will sketch the beginnings of a generic picture of the organization of the future.

The business frame

Despite considerable uncertainty about *how* to get there, there is a general consensus among organizations about what issues they will have to address and manage over the next decade. There are six broad areas in which the business border of the puzzle is changing (see Figure 1.2).

The customer edge

Customers are changing. This is not due to a sudden alteration in the gene pool but to the way in which companies compete for customers and to customers' ensuing rising expectations. IT enables companies to market and produce their products in ways radically different from those in the past. Between the 1950s and

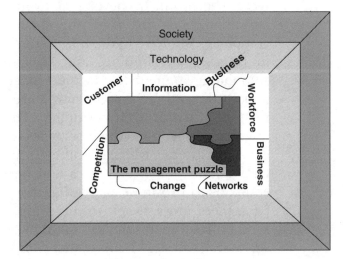

Figure 1.2
The business frame.

the 1990s, successful organizations perfected their abilities to make and sell products. They worked to forecast customer needs and to build reliable, complex goods and services, which would be inventoried and sold. The technology innovations of the last decade, however, are enabling companies to go further and discover, or even anticipate, customer needs, and to fulfill them with customized goods and services delivered rapidly. This "sense and respond" model of doing business creates new markets for a company's products, changes how it does business, both internally and with its customers, and most importantly, alters forever what customers expect from business. As experts in one-to-one marketing state: *Customers … do not want more choices. They want exactly what they want – when, where, and how they want it – and technology now makes it possible for companies to give it to them.*[2]

As companies find new ways to compete by becoming more customer-centric and responsive, their customer base will likely become considerably different from what it is today. The marketplace is becoming increasingly segmented into groups of people with similar needs. Therefore, it is becoming less stable and uniform and more volatile and variable. Organizations have already begun to respond by shifting their marketing strategies from a focus on products to meeting customer needs but they still know relatively little about how to sense or anticipate them.

In the twenty-first century, a company's success will be even more driven by the extent to which it can target its products to specialized customer needs. Thus, over time, many companies will evolve to become customer-driven businesses. *Market-mapping* is, therefore, going to be a key organizational capability. While new technologies will be developed to help companies understand customer needs and to identify their best customers, successful companies will have to do more. They will have to start "thinking in reverse," i.e. finding out what their customers want and responding immediately to those needs. They will also have to look at the world through "new lenses" and develop a learning relationship with each customer.[3] This relationship will be an ongoing connection, which becomes smarter as the company and customer interact with each other. Individuals will teach the company about their preferences and needs, thereby enabling the company to provide exactly what they want and, in the process, tying them more closely to the company in the long term. This form of "customer intimacy" can only be built up over time but, if successful, will yield a substantial competitive advantage.

Businesses will begin to measure the effectiveness of their plans by the benefits they bring to their customers. This means aiming for more than customer satisfaction; they will seek customer delight – the point at which customers are so completely satisfied with what a business is offering that it can retain them for many product generations. This will be done in many ways, often in conjunction with some form of IT. Some businesses will provide customers with direct access to company information. Others will concentrate on personalizing products and information for individuals. Still others will involve customers at an earlier stage in product development, making it possible for them to develop new products while customers are still defining their needs. These types of changes will reorient organizations outward and drive internal changes to help companies cope with this new focus.

As they begin to realize what is possible, individual customers also become more demanding and sophisticated. Improved quality, service, and reliability will be implicit in their needs and will become routine expectations of businesses in the near future. Quality had already become a watchword for management in the 1990s. From quality control to total quality management, companies have been using a range of techniques and methods to provide continuous improvements and to get closer to their customers. In the future, however, they will have to work even harder to meet and exceed customer expectations. As they do so, companies will increasingly come to recognize that the satisfaction, success, and happiness of their customers are integral to their own success.

Characteristics of the customer edge

More demanding customers
More segmented markets
Customer–business learning relationships
Individualized interactions

The information edge

We are rapidly becoming an information economy. Traditional economic models consider the key components of our economy to be land, labor, and capital. However, the development of intellect, innovation, and technology is rapidly becoming the key to growth for most companies, as well as industries and nations. In 2000, approximately 85 percent of all jobs in North America and 80 percent in Europe were knowledge, software, or technology based. In service industries, as well as in more traditional manufacturing and agricultural industries, intellectual processes create most of the value and competitive edge for companies. What an organization knows is already a competitive advantage in such diverse fields as consulting and oil and gas production.[4] Over the next 10–20 years, knowledge will become the new capital of society. Also known as intellectual capital, it can be broken down into three types:[5]

- *Human capital*: the capabilities of the individuals required to provide solutions to customers.
- *Structural capital*: the capabilities of the organization to share and transport knowledge to meet market requirements.
- *Customer capital*: the value of an organization's relationships with the people with whom it does business.

Thus, in the future, successful organizations will be those able to orchestrate these three types of intellectual capital to create value.

It is no surprise, then, that information is rapidly becoming the focal point of today's businesses. However, managing intellectual capital differs from managing other means of production because of four unique characteristics. First, it is not a limited resource. Unlike our forests or bank accounts, knowledge does not run out. Rather, knowledge can actually grow the more it is used and amplified with learning; it is infinitely expandable. Second, it must be developed and managed in conjunction with human resources in order to be effective. Third, it is mobile. While natural resources cannot be displaced, knowledge can be moved freely to the people who can use it. Fourth, it is costly to produce but cheap to reproduce. Typically, while the cost of producing the first copy of an information good is substantial, additional copies cost relatively little to produce. As knowledge becomes more important to a business, these characteristics will drive significant changes in how companies work and deliver value.

Technology and human beings are the packaging for intellectual capital. Technology facilitates all stages of value creation and innovation and provides the means to do more with the same amount of information. People are essential because converting data into information requires knowledge and this is the realm of specialists who have both deep vertical knowledge and strong lateral associative skills. To be successful in an information economy, therefore, organizations will need to know how to produce, acquire, disseminate, and exploit knowledge with people and technology. Structures, management, products and services, and employees will all have to adapt to an increasing emphasis on knowledge.

Businesses are essentially mechanisms for the coordination of work, materials, ideas, money, and technology to deliver value. The introduction of information technologies and electronic networks changes this process because information can be shared instantly and inexpensively among many people in many locations. As a result, company structures will no longer need rigid hierarchies and chains of command designed to assess and relay information around an organization. With knowledge in the hands of specialists, it becomes the organization's job to facilitate their work, rather than control it. Centralized decision-making and expensive bureaucracies will, therefore, become structures of the past and new organizational forms, more appropriate for managing in an information economy, will be developed.

In the future, the changing means of production will require *all* businesses to "informationalize" to survive. That is, they must learn how to put information into products and services and how to generate and sell information – no matter what business they are in at present. There will be increased emphasis on intellectual property and information goods as a source of value to the firm. Even traditional goods and services companies will find that the economic value of the information they have is much greater than that of the physical products they produce. Thus, products will become more knowledge-based and companies will need to assign a much greater importance to their existing knowledge and to value their knowledge assets more highly. Each firm's unique information assets will have to be more carefully exploited by developing branding, reputation, and packaging information and by helping people to manipulate, filter, and find the information they need. Companies will also need to develop greater depth of intellectual resources and greater capacity to integrate these resources effectively.

Our society's current lack of ability in measuring the economic value of an organization's information, knowledge, and intellectual capabilities is a significant limiting factor of the new economy. Both organizations and countries will need to find new ways of measuring and managing this value. For example, technology and knowledge diffusion have been shown to generate far greater benefits than original innovations. Company policies that fail to recognize this or try to protect intellectual property, rather than leveraging it, will miss benefits of significant value. Grasping the true value of knowledge, in all its facets, will enable organizations to change how they manage intellectual capital. This, in turn, will drive further changes in its mission and operations.

Characteristics of the information edge

Knowledge as a new source of capital
People and technology as packages for knowledge
Knowledge intensive products and services
New measures of organization value

The change edge

While change has been with us for a long time – in 500 BC, Heraclitus noted, *Nothing endures but change* – there is a general consensus that change these days is bigger, faster, and different from what it used to be. Price Pritchett points out that in the 1980s, nearly half of all U.S. companies were restructured, over 80,000 firms acquired or merged and several hundred thousand companies downsized. That is change on a grand scale! The velocity of change is different, too. A Chief Executive Officer (CEO) of a large company commented recently, *It used to be a lot of fun to work 10 years ago. You could almost cope. Today, it's almost impossible to cope because things happen at such a rapid rate.*[6]

The key drivers of change are increasing information flow, strategic discontinuities, radically changing technologies, and new business practices. Firms often face a number of significant and unpredictable changes occurring simultaneously. This results in "unrelenting complexity" and a new competitive landscape. Thus, in the future, organizations will have to be capable of anticipating and reacting to change and their ability to thrive on change will be an indicator of their competitive strength.

There are three things that are new about change these days. First, the pace of change is increasing. Businesses and customers are demanding immediate answers, anywhere, anytime. Product cycles are shrinking from years to months and days. Companies are, therefore, under pressure to deliver products faster; this means they must devise shorter development times and improved feedback loops to learn about changing market demands. Companies cannot assume that change will be steady. In many cases, changes will not be incremental, but dramatic. In a rapidly changing society, businesses must be constantly aware that a competitor can dramatically shift its business paradigm overnight.

Second, products are becoming more customized to individual customers. Customization requires changes in almost everything the organization does. Businesses must be able both to respond to customer demand and to customize products for customer needs. To do this a company must develop different relationships with its customers and its suppliers. Bill Davidow and Mike Malone, authors of *The Virtual Corporation: Structuring and Revitalizing the Corporation of the 21st Century*[7] call these "co-destiny relationships." They are based on trust and closer integration with the company and can only be achieved if traditional barriers are dropped and everything is focused on the goal at hand. Consequently, in the future, companies are likely to have fewer suppliers and they will be more closely bound together in both success and failure.

Third, the increasing importance of change in organizations will stimulate demand for better management, technology, and processes which will help people overcome their discomfort vis-à-vis change. Some organizations, notably the U.S. Army and Shell Oil, have already implemented disciplines of change, which have affected every aspect of how they operate. In short, companies must stop viewing change as the move from one stable state to another, and begin to view it as the new business environment – dynamic and continually evolving.

Dealing with change means that companies will have to develop considerable flexibility to respond quickly to changing competitive conditions, thereby developing or maintaining competitive advantage. Organizations have three main resources at their disposal for dealing with change: technology, people, and processes. Technology plays an important role in both driving and facilitating change. Technology can increase response, help coordinate actions, and make possible the development of new products and services. An organization's culture, its personnel's skills and disciplines in dealing with change, and a company's ability to deploy resources rapidly, as needed, are all essential for readiness to cope with rapid change. Finally, companies need processes and strategies in place to take advantage of change, monitor its impacts, and induce behavior changes. Altogether, the demands of change on the organization require new structures, cultures and leaders who, in addition to being able to cope with change, will thrive on it and take advantage of it.

Characteristics of the change edge

Need to anticipate and integrate change
Need to manage change
Changing relationships with suppliers and customers
Increasing change
Need for flexibility

The competition edge

In the past 10 years, a new competitive landscape has emerged. While businesses face unprecedented opportunities to tap new markets, they also face changing, shrinking, and increasingly competitive traditional markets. The number of competitors in most marketplaces has doubled and these have become increasingly voracious. Deregulation, the blurring of national borders, and lower market entry costs, has meant that many more companies are able to compete in traditionally stable markets. This increasing globalization of world markets and resources means that companies can now sell their products worldwide and access world-class expertise, regardless of where they are based, thereby increasing competition even further. The relentless restructuring of national economies is driven by advances in IT in such areas as logistics, communication, and computer aided design. In the future, competition will also come from companies which have been in a different business sector, but which see the opportunity to introduce a new business paradigm into a traditional marketplace, e.g. online booksellers. These trends suggest that over the next two decades, businesses will have to face very different competitors from their current ones:

> With markets and their players constantly changing, the possibility of enterprises establishing a sustainable competitive advantage no longer exists. No organization can afford to rest on its laurels; each must constantly innovate to compete.[8]

To cope in this global competitive marketplace, companies will need to develop new managing competencies. They will identify their strengths and use these to organize their business. Companies will also form partnerships or alliances of mutual benefit with competitors, suppliers, or other partners to take advantage of a transient competitive advantage. This will be a continual process because markets will be in constant evolution and companies will have to develop increasing flexibility in their resource deployments. Companies' operating speed will mean that strategic *thought* will replace strategic *planning*. One marketing expert put it this way: *Ten year plans are not a good enough prediction of how the competitive environment works. However good the plan is, it's going to be irrelevant if the Japanese come in next week with a better product.*[9] Strategic simulation and scenario-planning software will assist executives in managing the complexity of their competitive environment. Seen as a whole, managers will face the task of creating a balance between the stability needed to facilitate strategy development and decision-making and the instability that allows for continuous change and adaptation to a dynamic environment. This dynamic and complex environment will require flexibility, speed, and innovation.

Companies will also have to deal with increasing competition by optimizing their knowledge- and people-management. *The shift in competitiveness is to knowledge and people coming up with clever ideas*, states one expert.[10] Developing superior management skills and ways of maximizing employee skills will be more important than minimizing employee costs. Top managers will have to recruit and select top quality employees, and, at the same time, invest in training and development to build skills continuously. Managers will have to use data in different ways: traditionally, they have been using data mainly for control; in the future, they will use data for information and synchrony facilitation between areas of the firm. Furthermore, a corporate culture promoting thinking and learning must be developed.

Characteristics of the competition edge

New and changed competition
Partnerships and alliances
Competition on knowledge and people

The business network edge

As these trends develop, our concept of what constitutes a company will also change. In order to adapt to rapid change and new competition, businesses will become more fluid. New business models are already being developed to extract new forms of value. New distribution channels are emerging. Consequently, in the future, businesses will organize themselves differently. Some experts suggest that, apart from a small core of leaders, companies will look much more like movie production companies, which temporarily bring together people of diverse skills to build something and then disband. Certainly, they will be based increasingly on collaborative networks of people and technology operating without physical walls and barriers of space and time. Tapscott, Ticoll, and Lowy recently suggested that our increasing connectedness through the Internet will lead to the development of business-webs (or b-webs) that take different forms depending on the goals set by the b-web.[11] Some webs will form around a supply chain; others will take the form of a digital marketplace. Some companies will partner with others to create packages of experiences and to take advantage of the "network effect" (i.e. when use of one product is enhanced by the use of another). This trend will require what some have called a "spirit of trust" in order to enable the rapid development of true partnerships between businesses.

As businesses begin to extend themselves and look increasingly outward, internally they will also become increasingly open, networked, and entrepreneurial. In the traditional view, a business controlled all of the functions of a company's value chain. It was supported by a bureaucracy of administrators, and led by a hierarchy of managers. In the future, the use of IT will enable the elimination of the "human relays" in management, leading to less bureaucracy and flatter hierarchies. Less control of non-key parts of companies' processes will mean that organizations will be smaller and more dynamic. They will become more democratic and decentralized because knowledge will reside in their employees, not in their managers. This will lead to more team-based work allowing specialists from all parts of an organization to work together to achieve a task. Thus, there will be greater emphasis on self-discipline and individual responsibility for relationships and communications.

The trend for organizations will first be to *extend* the organization outward, then to develop a *virtual* organization and finally to evolve into a networked organization. Each of these stages offers specific challenges for management.[12] In the extended organization, value will be realized through strategic alliances, joint ventures, long-term contracts, and outsourcing. Organizations will become flatter and more decentralized as their boundaries become fluid and open. Virtual organizations take these concepts a step further and enable companies to work across time and space limitations. Technology will enable businesses to experiment with new internal structures, which had not previously been economically viable because of space or time restrictions. Companies will be able to separate some operations and people previously working together physically and to aggregate others, who had to be dispersed. This will make possible new forms of work such as telecommuting, mobile work, and virtual teamwork. Firms will be able to structure themselves to take advantage of changing time zones and to create more flexible working conditions for employees. Finally, the networked organization will combine both of these forms to create a virtual enterprise consisting of several linked businesses working together to deliver value to customers and shareholders.

Characteristics of the network edge

External collaborative networks
Open, networked, and entrepreneurial organization designs
Reduced time and space limitations

The workforce edge

The move to the new economy is a journey that begins with IT but ends with people. The reason people will become more important to the organization of the future has been summarized by Webber as follows:[13]

> The revolution in information and communications technologies makes knowledge the new competitive resource. But knowledge only flows through technology; it actually resides in people – in knowledge workers and the organizations they inhabit. In the new economy then, the manager's job is to create an environment that allows knowledge workers to learn …

Thus, while IT is the driver of the new economy, it is people – knowledge workers – whose skills and capabilities will make a company successful. Unfortunately for companies, human capital is less easy to control than other forms of capital; it can go where it is well treated and leave when it becomes dissatisfied. Organizations will, therefore, face increased competition for people. Companies will be forced to develop better ways of acquiring and retaining knowledge workers and providing them with opportunities to learn and expand their competencies. This inverts the traditional relationship between the organization and employees and will lead to a massive rethinking of how businesses are managed.

One way for companies to aim for success will be through training and development. One manager noted "In the future, people will seek out employment at companies where they can gain the most knowledge and are paid for their knowledge."[14] Workers will seek to reinvent their skills continually, since portable skills will be their entry to improved employment. Companies will have an interest in making their people more skilled as well because in doing so; they will increase the value of their knowledge assets. Some firms, such as Motorola, have begun this process by creating their own "universities," which they credit with making their employees more adaptable to change and improving the company's global market share.

Companies will also seek to provide an environment in which knowledge workers can be most productive. This means providing the information tools, which will support them and help them to apply their knowledge. As well, they will seek to eliminate distractions in the organization, which prevent knowledge workers from being productive by making sure that they are protected from traditional bureaucratic tasks such as paperwork and meetings. Since knowledge workers' decisions will constitute the company's strategy and will directly affect company performance, managers must establish the culture in which these decisions are made. This includes not only communicating the goals, vision, and values of the organization which will help them make sense of their experience, it also means establishing the emotional context in which people work. In the organization of the future, managers will have to inspire performance, rather than enforce it.

As Webber pointed out:[15]

> Managers must set a tone whereby people are secure enough to say what is really on their minds and aren't afraid to expose their ignorance or ask for help … (they must create) the emotional context in which everyone else can function effectively.

It is clear that the twenty-first century organization will depend more significantly on staff quality than in the past. With declining numbers of middle managers, workers will be increasingly empowered to make decisions and take on more responsibility in the organization. Better-educated workers will also demand changes. Workers' higher computer literacy levels, problem-solving skills, continual on-the-job learning ability and broader perspective on the organization call for a radically different organizational framework in which work will take place.

As a result, organizations will become more team-based and individuals will participate in a number of ever-shifting cross-disciplinary task-focused teams. New skills and behaviors will have to be developed to cope effectively with this mode of work. For example, leadership will likely be defined as a position on a team, rather than a job in a corporate hierarchy. Communication skills will become increasingly important in building connections between people, both within the organization and outside it.

Ultimately, management will have to be able to trust its employees to make responsible decisions and this will present the ultimate challenge. Trust is difficult to develop and can be messy, painful, and easy to violate. Interestingly, healthy conflict is a sign of trust. However, for managers, these changes will represent a loss of control and increasing vulnerability, which many will be loathe facing. All too often, fear dominates organizations and when fear is present ideas will not flow. Even when managers choose to manage on trust, *they will inhabit a world where there are no blacks and whites, only various shades of grey.*[16] Of all the changes required of management in the organization of the future, the risks of workforce development are probably the greatest due to this ambiguity.

Characteristics of the workforce edge

Emphasis on recruitment and retention
Increase training and development
Facilitating culture
Team-based work
Emphasis on quality staff

The technology frame

We often hear that science and technology will reshape society over the next 30 years, and that the convergence and ubiquity of

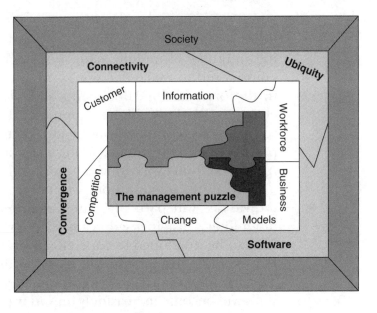

Figure 1.3
The technology
frame.

information technologies will have a huge impact on the nature of work. It would be understandable, therefore, if some managers were skeptical about the extent of these claims, given the limited impact of IT in organizations over the past 30 years. However, in the future we will see dramatic changes in technology, which will fundamentally alter what can be done with it. As we have seen above, new technological capabilities are behind most, if not all, business changes today. It is important to note that technology is facilitating these changes, not causing them. Technology changes and business changes go hand in hand, but it is *how* technology is used in business, and how people interact with and manage it, that will determine its ultimate impact. The experts suggest that there are several key trends in technology which frame how businesses will be managed in the future (see Figure 1.3).

The connectivity edge

Together, computers and telecommunications are increasingly forming a worldwide electronic infrastructure which will serve as the basis for economic transformation and growth. Just as railroads were the infrastructure of national economies in the last century, and highways of this century, technology will connect people with data, text, sounds, and images over electronic trade routes in the coming century. This new infrastructure will change the way business is conducted and enable individuals and organizations to engage in electronic commerce.

Three trends are occurring in connectivity. First, more and more people are getting connected electronically all over the world through broadband connections enabling video, voice, and data communication, and allowing them to interact remotely. Online working, shopping, voting, meeting, tax filing, and letter writing are just some of the activities which will be enabled by near universal connectivity. Second, connections are becoming wireless, resulting in greater flexibility and mobility. Once wireless communication has been firmly established, people will be able to access a wide variety of computing resources without worrying about data location and transfer. Workers will become more mobile; downloading and accessing the information they need from the field will eliminate their need to travel to a central office. Third, the Internet provides the infrastructure whereby a single individual or business can access a host of information resources instantly and dynamically. This new packaging for information goods will allow us to do more with the same information. The new infrastructure will reduce the cost and increase the value of information by vastly increasing our ability to store, retrieve, sort, filter, and distribute information. For many businesses, therefore, this opens up a new distribution channel for its products and services.

Characteristics of the connectivity edge

Electronic infrastructure
Increase capacity
Wireless
Increased ability to manipulate information

The convergence edge

To converge means to join together. In biology, the term is used to suggest that unrelated organisms have a tendency to become similar as they adapt to the same environment. It is clear that computers, telecommunications, and television are all growing together and developing similar characteristics, which will enable anyone, anytime, anyplace to communicate with and obtain access to information from a variety of devices. In this way convergence is increasingly blurring the lines between internal and external communications in companies and across time and space.

Interestingly, the telephone will remain the basis of business communication, although it will function much differently. It will become much more powerful by being integrated with computers, information, interactive voice response, the Internet, and specific telephony enhancements. Such integrated technology has already revolutionized the banking and financial services industries, as well as the customer service functions of many organizations, while significantly lowering communications costs.

Already, many workers today are message intensive, relying on phone, fax, computer, pager, and videoconferencing to keep in touch. Intel's Andy Grove predicts that the trend is towards developing single communications devices that compute, rather than computer devices that communicate. In very short order, a single device will serve as a worker's personal communicator, mailbox, fax, notebook, and secretary. In addition, it will manage and store electronic communications at a single mailbox for access, wherever the worker is. These devices will become even more powerful: they will be able to manage an individual's workflow, store and index information, relay urgent messages, and assist in report preparation.

A second trend is towards increasing richness in communications, i.e. multimedia combining voice, video, data, text, and image communication. Most knowledge workers have already found that e-mail has revolutionized their work. As connectivity increases both the scope and richness of communication between people, two things will happen. New communications paths will link people across organizational hierarchies, business boundaries, and national borders and new applications will be developed to provide increasing virtual reality.

A third trend is towards open systems. To facilitate connectivity, standards are being established enabling different types of devices from different vendors to talk to each other. Open systems (i.e. those based on industry standards) will have significant consequences for organizations: information and software will become more portable across a variety of hardware devices, reducing costs and making it more economical to develop shrink-wrapped software. Most importantly, standards are essential to create the modular, flexible and networked computing architectures that are needed for the future business environment.

```
┌─────────────────────────────────────────────────┐
│  Characteristics of the convergence edge          │
│  ───────────────────────────────────────────     │
│  Blurring between internal and external computing │
│  Integrating of devices                           │
│  Intelligent devices                              │
│  Richness of communication                        │
│  Open standards                                   │
└─────────────────────────────────────────────────┘
```

The ubiquity edge

In the near future, technology will permeate almost every business practice. It will be used increasingly to manage and connect our business and our world. Seamless interoperability between people, processes, and information repositories, regardless of location, will result in increased technological transparency. The shift towards wireless communication will reinforce this trend. It is ironic that our growing dependence on technology will ultimately lead us back to the importance of human relationships. Some businesses believe that technology will help them recover the "high touch" relationship with their customers, which they lost when they first automated.

By embedding microprocessors and sensors in materials and physical devices, companies will also be able to create objects that respond to their internal or external environment. The growing miniaturization of microchips, combined with their rapidly increasing power and decreasing cost, will make it possible for computers to be virtually anywhere. Some of the resulting applications of technology soon to be widespread are automated control and performance monitoring, self-monitoring structures, completely automated factories, and robotized devices.

As soon as technological innovations appear in one industry or sector, they usually begin to spread to others. Significantly, a single innovation can cause sales, profitability, employment, and value-added growth in a variety of indirect ways because it permits new forms of enterprise not previously possible. In this way, technology diffusion tends to generate far greater economic benefits than is first obvious. Managers must, therefore, completely rethink how they manage technological innovation. Traditionally, organizations have chosen to protect innovation rather than encourage its diffusion. However, organizations have much to gain by concentrating on leveraging, rather than limiting the diffusion of an innovation. If organizations can gain a better understanding of this effect, they will be able to develop radically different strategies for managing innovation.

Characteristics of the ubiquity edge
Embedded technology Rapid diffusion of new technology

The software edge

Two important types of software will have an impact on organizations in the immediate future. The first is groupware. This is a new class of technology designed to support communication and information sharing in a networked, team-based organization. Some groupware currently supports groups working *at the same time*, either together or across electronic networks. Others enable group work at *different times*. In the future, groupware will facilitate any-time, anyplace teamwork using a number of different interaction options, i.e. face-to-face, written, electronic. While this new technology promises to support coordination, collaboration, and team effectiveness, organizations will have to learn to harness its power appropriately to reap its benefits. The second type of software is integrated systems. Traditionally, software has been developed separately and operated independently in different parts of an organization. Unfortunately, this resulted in highly fragmented systems, which overlapped in content and function. Today, and increasingly in the future, enterprise resource planning systems (ERPs) facilitate the integration of systems to provide corporate-wide information and new competitive applications spanning more than one business unit. The first wave of integration developed common technology to control the organization's "back-end" (i.e. inventory, production, finance and control, and human resources). The second is creating "front- end" systems to manage the customer-interface parts of a business and to collect and "mine" customer information to improve company products and services.

Other types of software appearing on the near business horizon include simulation and virtual reality applications. Simulation software will allow executives to create virtual scenarios on the computer, thereby simulating different business situations free of risk. In this way, businesses will be able to advance into dynamic strategic thinking. Virtual reality will enable companies to move a step further by actually recreating real situations. Companies will then be able to develop virtual classrooms and training environments. Virtual reality technology will also become a routine part of all kinds of physical planning and product design.

Further out on the horizon, one can expect that language translation will become effective, enabling individuals speaking different languages to work together. Expert systems and artificial intelligence will also become more useful, enabling IT to supplement limited human resources and cognitive capabilities. This will lead to machines and systems capable of mimicking human learning. As they learn from their experiences, such devices will be able to adjust to the needs and working styles of individuals.

To do this, computers will need to "think" faster and differently than they do today. Two technical trends will facilitate this. Parallel processing will enable software designers to link a number of computers to help them "see" the consequences of a particular corporate action or policy change in many parts of the company at once. Fuzzy logic will enable computers to think more like people and help to develop better and more realistic simulations.

Characteristics of the software edge

Groupware
Integrated systems
Virtual reality

The social frame

A third dimension which frames the twenty-first century organization is the society in which it will operate over the next 20 years. Some of the changes occurring here will profoundly affect an organization's customer, product, and service base (see Figure 1.4).

The demographic edge

People in industrialized countries are living longer. In the future, more people will be living healthier and fuller lives to their

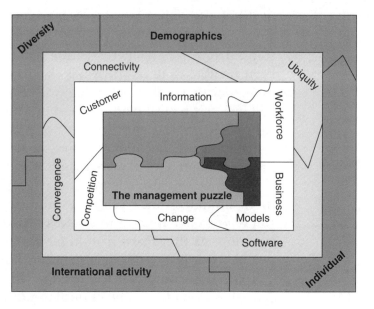

Figure 1.4
The social frame.

mid-1980s. The average age of the population will rise to about 41 and the median age of the workforce will reach 45 in 2005. Populations in the developing world, on the other hand, will be substantially younger. As older people face rising costs and the prospect of longer lives, many of them will resist retirement or return to the workforce to supplement their incomes.

Age bias is built into most organizations, particularly in their assumptions that older workers are less productive and less flexible. Companies will need to find ways of counteracting this bias so as to take advantage of the skills, understanding, and experience of older workers. Training programs and management techniques will also have to be adapted to deal with older workers' needs.

Characteristics of the demographic edge
Older population Adaptation for older workers

 ## The diversity edge

A second important social trend is the increasing workforce diversity. Over the next 10 years, 85 percent of the people entering the job market for the first time will be women and minorities.

In addition, the growth of globalization will increasingly give rise to teams composed of people who do not share the same language, assumptions, or cultural background. Cultural differences will have to be considered carefully. Indeed, it has been argued that the assumption often made that "knowledge derived in one context will have general – global significance" is flawed, and that what is considered as best practice in a given context may be quite the opposite in a different context.[17] Multicultural workgroups will need to adapt to different work expectations and communication styles and become more sensitive to the needs and perspectives of the workforce.

Characteristics of the diversity edge

More female and minority workers
Multicultural work groups

The international edge

With increasing globalization, international solutions will be required for issues such as environmental concerns, war, crime, and disease prevention. Other issues have a direct impact on business and will also need global scrutiny: design and location of business facilities, the regulation of global business, workers' rights, universal monitoring of business transactions, and business practices. One consequence of globalization and rapidly improving communications abilities is companies' increasing sensitivity to their social and environmental responsibilities. Already, companies are beginning to realize that success derives from being good corporate citizens.

Globalization represents a challenge to both organizations and nations. Companies will need to learn how to coordinate operations across many different countries. Increasingly, multinational corporations will become dominant players in the worldwide marketplace. Some futurists even suggest that large corporations will be treated as countries.[18] However, with Internet technology, even small firms can compete globally. To manage our mobility, identification cards will become international. Crime will also become supranational, focusing on economic and computer-based operations, such as business disruptions, theft, and information tampering.

Characteristics of the international edge

Increasing international scrutiny
Increasing corporate sensitivity to international issues
Need to coordinate across national boundaries

The individual edge

As the lines separating office from home and company from individual become blurred, drawing the line that divides work and personal time becomes more difficult. Increased computer literacy, will lead to people spending more time operating in electronically linked virtual communities and less time within the structure of a single business. This will give individuals more control over their careers and family lives and present organizations with new challenges for people management.

Characteristics of the individual edge

Blurring between home and office
Virtual communities
New challenges for managers

An outline of the organization of the twenty-first century

"Businesses are, in essence, mechanisms for coordination ... of work, materials, ideas, and money and the form they take is strongly affected by the coordination technologies available."[19] The hierarchical, industrial corporation of the twentieth century was designed for the technologies of the time. With the introduction of personal computing devices and networking – the technologies of the twentieth century – the mechanisms of coordination are changing, leading in turn to a change in the shape and nature of the organization of the future. When the business, technology, and social changes discussed above are taken together, they call for nothing less than a radical transformation of the workplace.

Some of the areas in which we can anticipate these changes include: size, structure, function, performance, work, and management. Researchers and practitioners agree that we do not have as clear a picture as we should of these transformations. Vogt explains that, today, we are in a similar position to that of farmers at the dawn of the industrial age: "Imagine a farming father commenting to his neighbor, 'My son says he plans to go to the city and work every day making cloth! How can he feed himself by doing something my wife spends 2 days a month doing for free?'"[20] Nevertheless, by summarizing what we do know, this section will begin to outline an image of the twentieth century organization for managers who are trying to peer into the future and prepare for it.

Size

In the near future, the ability to share information instantly and inexpensively across time and space will decrease the importance of centralized decision-making and bureaucracy in delivering value. Smaller organizations will thus become "better" because they are less expensive and more flexible. New coordination technologies will enable smaller companies to enjoy many of the benefits of larger ones without giving up the leanness, flexibility, and creativity of being small. In spite of the current spate of mergers and acquisitions, many people believe that large companies will tend to disintegrate into smaller businesses or at least semi-autonomous business units. According to James Champey, Chairman of CSC Index, companies will atomize as they attempt to focus on what they do well and get out of doing commodity-like work, which can be given away to someone else.[21]

Furthermore, as human factors become more important to the ability of firms to add value, companies will inevitably decrease in size. They will use strategic partnerships, outsourcing, and other types of alliances to concentrate on where they are adding value in the production chain, rather than trying to control the entire process. For example, Microsoft and Nintendo no longer own or manage their whole production process; rather they control critical points in the chain. Twenty-first century organizations will, therefore, tend to be more fluid and ad hoc, organized around tasks, which will be accomplished by flexible but temporary networks of individuals.

Design

Future companies will operate differently. Instead of being designed around functions, departments, and individuals, they will be organized around networks, teams, competencies, and infrastructures, both internally and across organizational boundaries. This will lead to a variety of new business models all designed to put together the capital – especially the knowledge capital – of the organization in new ways. The three primary structures of the twenty-first century organization will be: Internetworked enterprises, teams and individuals, b-webs, and industry environments.[22]

Projects will be the vehicle for carrying out the non-routine work of the organization. As the culture of individualism will detract from the productivity of the team, businesses will redesign jobs, rewards, and assessments around teams. People will shift around based on project needs and report to multiple individuals. Some will retain a few functional responsibilities, but this will not be their full-time or long-term job. Organizations will operate by naturally-developing communities of practice which arise around a task, technology, or an enterprise and can include both people who are inside and outside the organization. As one futurist explains, *Rather than saying that the organization is stable and we'll fit the projects to the organization, what you will do is fit the organization to the projects.*[23]

The b-webs will be completely new methods of doing business. They will be "distinct system(s) of suppliers, distributors, commerce service providers, infrastructure providers, and customers that use the Internet for their primary business communications and transactions."[24] The b-webs will deliver unique new value propositions, which will make the old way of doing things obsolete. They will also redefine the boundaries and the relationships of the firm. Industry environments will become increasingly important to organizations as they will define the method of competition and the standards within which the firm will operate. Companies will find themselves both cooperating and competing with their traditional competitors (i.e. "co-opetition"[25]) depending on the task at hand.

Function

Although technology will facilitate the development of new structures and enable them to draw upon needed resources, regardless of location and ownership, organizations will also have to develop a "soft" infrastructure of human and organizational factors to achieve success. Probably the most important role of the organization, both internally and externally, will be to establish the environment in which work takes place. Less direct worker supervision and increased individual decision-making responsibility puts the onus on organizations to communicate their objectives, focus, and performance expectations clearly. As knowledge workers cannot be told how to do their work, they will require clear, simple, common objectives, which translate into particular actions. Organizations and managers will help focus and coordinate the work of a variety of individuals to deliver value. In fact, the organization will "create the common vision, sense of direction, and understanding of values, ethics and standards without which individual decision-making is crippled."[26]

Furthermore, organizations will be expected to create supportive cultures fostering learning and innovation because innovation is a critical component of competitiveness. The firm will need to develop mechanisms for knowledge creation, retention, and diffusion. It will have to learn how to use and convert individual learning into specific resources and skills. And, to be better prepared to for radical innovations, it will need to foster non-linear learning (i.e. the ability to conceptualize different and contradictory forms of knowledge).

To operate effectively, networks will need standards set by organizations, and functioning as the "rules of the game." These will take many forms including: contracts, routinized processes, technical specifications, data architectures, and methods of dispute resolution. Malone notes that *the value the firm provides to its members comes mainly from the standards it has established, not from the strategic or operational skills of its top managers.*[27]

Organizations will have to evaluate their competencies and capabilities on a continuing basis. Initially, they will have to shift from the relatively narrow business strategies of the twentieth century to ones that are broader and more focused on customer satisfaction. However, competencies will not remain static. Firms will have to invest in and upgrade their competencies in order to create new strategic growth alternatives and to take advantage of new opportunities. To do this, they will have to develop their human capital in several ways. They will need to develop new abilities to manage their contingent workforce and advance the knowledge and skills of their workers. This will promote flexibility because multi-skilled staff can be deployed in a variety of ways, depending on the needs of the business.

In short, in the future, organizations will continue their role of coordinating the assets of the business, but they will do it differently than in the past by developing new strategies and competencies, and establishing new environments in which to do so. Managing and developing human capital will become relatively more important in the function of the organization, and firms will have to learn how to aggregate, disaggregate and reconfigure assets quickly in order to respond to competitive conditions.

Performance

As noted above, organizations will develop new success criteria in addition to financial measures of performance. Many of these new measures will have some connection to intellectual capital. They will monitor the value of their brainpower and knowledge assets (i.e. human capital) and will also become more interested in evaluating business results from a customer point of view (i.e. customer capital). Finally, they will assess the company's structural capital, which comprises the codified knowledge and processes residing within the organization itself, not in its people. Each of these forms of capital will be enhanced and extended by digital capital, i.e. the company's ability to create new value through digital networks. This element of company performance is and will increasingly come to be recognized by the stock markets. As well, because of the relative growing importance of human capital, companies will begin to monitor a number of other measures which contribute to their overall economic health including: quality of life, environmental considerations, research and development, and training effectiveness. Overall, companies will move towards assessing performance in a variety of ways, rather than strictly financially. Hence, they will adopt a balanced scorecard approach to performance measurement.

Work

As we move into an information economy, knowledge will become a larger part of all aspects of organizational life. This will fundamentally change the nature of work. Knowledge work has been defined as *the co-creation of new perspectives which in turn, lead to more effective actions.*[28] Much present-day professional work is already knowledge work. In the future, the sphere of knowledge work will enlarge until most workers will be responsible for contributing new insights and facilitating the implementation of new ideas. Knowledge analysis and sense-making will be key skills to leverage the company's knowledge.

New types of jobs will place a new emphasis on communication skills for all employees. Everyone will be expected to be a communicator. As computers become more intuitive, skill with particular kinds of technology will become less important and new disciplines of questioning and improving on how things are done will become more important. Information sharing and critical thinking will also be essential capabilities. A key reason for business collapse at present is that company staff do not ask the right questions. In the organization of the future *everyone in an organization should be constantly thinking through what information he or she needs to do the job and to make a contribution.*[29]

Companies will become both more flexible and available as they move closer to their customers and as customers become the focus of their work. Already common in many businesses such as banking and utilities, for instance, the "24 × 7" work environment will become even more widespread. As companies organize to enable individual employees to engage customers in the marketplace, they will also have to provide them with the authority to make decisions on the company's behalf. Thus, even organizational power structures will change and power will migrate out from the center of the organization to its periphery, i.e. where the customers are.

As employees become empowered to make decisions, increasingly, those decisions will constitute the company's strategy. One interesting benefit of the increasing use of technology in work is the natural extension of the workforce's participation in business events and decision-making. For example, the introduction of virtual technologies allows members of business units to attend appropriate meetings held in far-distant locations. Employee empowerment will most likely help harness the creativity and skills of more workers. However, involving more people in decision-making could also lead to longer and more contentious procedures. Therefore, collaborative work and decision-making skills will become more critical to work.

To facilitate new kinds of insights and questions, work will become less structured and the company organization chart will become fuzzier. People's interactions and work habits will change. Jobs will require multiple skills, tasks, and responsibilities. Competencies will change continuously. Thus, the tasks, projects, and alliances of the organization will take place in a radically different conceptual framework, in which people will be linked by what they know, rather than by their job titles or ranks.

Jobs themselves will become more transitory. As work becomes more mobile, companies will have to find ways to educate employees rapidly concerning company values and culture, and help them understand the work of the organization. While job security will diminish, previous limitations on personal freedom, creativity, initiative, talent, and skill will not be as strict as before. Companies will rely more heavily on temporary workers, part-timers, consultants, specialists, and contractors. As one HR specialist put it, *The labor market isn't likely to resemble free agency in sports, but it will reflect some of the same qualities.*[30]

Finally, work will also have to be rewarded differently. As workers won't always be physically present, companies will need to find new ways of overseeing employee productivity and measuring and compensating workers' contributions. Achievement will be rewarded more frequently than time spent or position in the corporate hierarchy. That is, performance rather than process will be assessed. Yet, for activities that still require monitoring, use of electronic monitoring and performance enhancement systems may increase. These types of systems must, however, be used appropriately or they will place employee relationships under great stress. Ultimately, companies may find that people who were successful in the traditional corporation may not be as effective in the company of the future.

Management

While business, technology, and social trends will dramatically alter the structure, function, and work of organizations and employees over the next decade, the most important changes in the organization of the twenty-first century will be found in the role of management. Drucker points out that, since the Second World War, companies have gradually come to see that *management* pertains to every aspect of bringing together people with diverse knowledge and skills to deliver value to an organization. As we move towards a more knowledgeable and empowered workforce, there will be less need for managers to direct and supervise the work of subordinates, and to analyze, digest and pass on information. Instead, different skills and perspectives for managers will be needed and valued.

First, managers will constantly need to look at the future while planning backwards into the present. Managers will have to be both visionary and transformational leaders and act continually as catalysts for change. From this vision will come their understanding of the company's needs, such as capabilities, technology and innovation. Most importantly however, managers will be expected to set the strategic environment in which the work of the organization is to be done. While much strategic decision-making will be delegated to workers, managers will retain the jobs of: setting goals for the organization; focusing the corporation on these goals; and seizing opportunities for change.

Managers will also have to create the emotional environment in which decisions are made for workers to be able to function effectively. Webber[31] points out that if decisions are made in fear and ignorance, if trust is absent, and people hesitate to disagree with each other, then individuals will not feel free to develop new knowledge, create new value and take responsibility for new ideas. Thus, trust will be a fundamental principle of management in the twenty-first century in that it takes responsibility for thinking through, setting and objectifying the firm's objectives, values, and goals.

In a complex and uncertain world, managers will have essential leadership and morale building responsibilities. With the increasing fluidity of organizations and jobs, there is a danger that staff will lose a sense of belonging to the organization. Therefore, managers will have to make sure that people feel part of the larger team. It will be their job to ensure that people are capable of joint performance. This is why management is and will be the critical determining factor in organizations. As Peter Drucker noted, *Our ability to contribute depends as much on the management of the enterprises in which we work as it does on our own skills, dedication and effort.*[32]

In the future, all managers will have to learn to manage under different circumstances, e.g. managing a remote team and managing by outputs and outcomes. New forms of work will require clear agreements with staff regarding performance expectations, priorities, communications protocols, and key supports which will be provided outside the office. Traditional status cues such as corner offices, will likely be eliminated, as will the hierarchy of "perks" for senior managers. In addition, they will have to get used to a significant lack of control. These changes will be traumatic for old-style managers because the methods and techniques, which worked for them in the past will no longer do the job. In fact, resistance from management is likely to be the biggest single reason why organizations will not change as rapidly as they would like.

While managers will lose many of their supervisory, decision-making and information processing responsibilities, they will be able to develop new competencies in managing the key assets of the organization. Their ability to manage information and IT will be especially important.

Conclusion

The picture of the twenty-first century organization is still fuzzy. While we can see the broad outlines of where organizations are going, managers still face a daunting task of trying to fill in a huge number of blank spaces and of transforming generic trends into something that works for their particular enterprise. The changes and transformations outlined in this chapter represent a significant challenge for managers in specific organizations since they will have to be interpreted for their particular needs. To do this, managers must understand the fundamental components of their particular puzzle and determine specific ways to configure these pieces to produce a coherent picture.

Part II of the book examines each of the individual pieces of the management puzzle in turn. Chapter 2 looks at the strategy piece from three perspectives. It first discusses strategy as positioning, i.e. assessment of one's environment and the exploiting it in the best way possible, sometimes by transforming it. The second perspective is strategy as capabilities, i.e. assessing one's strengths and weaknesses and building one's capabilities in order to stay ahead of the competition. Finally, the strategy as governance perspective focuses on how transactions are being allocated among various institutional arrangements and firms. Chapter 3 presents the structure piece of the puzzle, i.e. it focuses on how an enterprise is organized to accomplish its goals. After a brief overview of traditional organizational designs and forms, the chapter explores how the environmental changes presented in Chapter 1 call for a new set of success factors which, managers must consider when designing how their organizations will work. Finally, Chapter 3 suggests that today's managers need to consider both their internal (vertical and horizontal) and external structuring (external and geographic) in order to achieve their new objectives of speed, flexibility, integration, and innovation. Chapter 4 focuses on the IT piece of the management puzzle. This piece has several facets that managers need to understand, if they are to use IT effectively, and ensure appropriate assembly of the other pieces of the management puzzle. The first facet is IT strategy and how an organization develops it. The second facet concerns how IT is used within an organization to transform it. The third is the use of IT as a competitive weapon in the marketplace. The fourth facet is internal, i.e. how IT organizes itself to execute its own activities within the enterprise. Chapter 5 concludes Part II by presenting leadership, the fourth critical piece of the management puzzle. It first looks at the personal attributes, which a leader must have, which are the bedrock of leadership effectiveness. Then, it explores the essential skills of a leader and why they are needed. A third dimension of leadership is the functions, which a leader must perform in his job. Finally, the chapter looks at the new roles, which leaders are beginning to undertake within their organizations and within the larger business community.

Part III illustrates how the puzzle pieces can be put together successfully. We present and analyze the experience of three firms that arranged the four pieces of the management puzzle so that they fit closely together. The first case, Progressive delivers the unexpected – Progressive Insurance, shows how strategy and IT were codetermined, influenced each other and fed back into each other. It also shows how more permeable horizontal, vertical, and geographic boundaries gradually emerged as the outcome of business transformation. Finally, it demonstrates how the CEO's leadership abilities were of utmost importance in taking progressive from an industry gnat to a large and powerful competitor. The second case, The Organization without an Organizational Chart – Oticon, shows the importance of the CEO's vision in putting the puzzle together, and the critical role which the structure piece of the management puzzle can play. Indeed, one could almost say that the CEO's envisioned the new organizational structure before he actually formulated the firm's strategy. In this puzzle, the IT piece plays the important role of making the adjustment between structure and strategy feasible. Yet, the IT piece in itself does not have much strategic content; this once again demonstrates the utmost importance of the structure piece. The third and final case presented in Part III is that of the Virtual Value Chain – Li & Fung. This is a good example of a new structure and of a firm's adaptability to its environment. In this case, strategy is explicit, well articulated, original, and leads to tangible results. A network structure enables the flexibility and the low cost structure defined in the strategy. Similarly, IT enables the coordination of all these components, as well as the flexibility (just-in-time changes) offered to clients. In addition to these case descriptions, Part III provides a detailed analysis of the puzzle pieces for each case, and of how they were put together. The three cases illustrate the importance of each of the various pieces of the management puzzle and their mutual adjustment. They also show that there is no single way of assembling the pieces. All three firms have been quite successful in their adaptation to their environment; yet, each followed a very particular trajectory.

Part IV – *The management challenges* – examines skills, techniques and practices that enable each part of the business to connect seamlessly and present a coherent picture to the outside world. More precisely, it examines how people management, IT management, knowledge management and change management enable the strategy, structure, IT and leadership pieces to work together smoothly and effectively in a given environment.

Questions

1   Will the new forces of IT and the progress in communications favor the emergence of many smaller, specialized firms; or, to the contrary, will they foster the emergence of a smaller number of gigantic enterprises? Will the increase in the power of IT encourage more decentralization or more centralization?

2   In the context of the knowledge-based economy, the know-how and informational capabilities of firms become central to their competitiveness and long-term survival. How then will organizations cope with the mobility of their workers and the threat this represents to the organizational reservoir of know-how? How will organizations of the

twenty-first century balance the merits of employee loyalty and those of flexibility?

3   As the emerging competitive environment puts more and more value on the flexibility and agility of firms as these try to cope with a tidal wave of changes and shocks, developments in IT require the deployment of large-scale investments in infrastructure and software. Just how compatible are agility and flexibility on the one hand, and the requirements of large, sunk investments on the other? Could well-established incumbents become the victims of their own obsolete infrastructure?

4   As the deployment and mastery of IT become a key advantage for firms in the new competitive environment, the profitability of investments in IT appears very difficult to assess. This is at the source of the so-called "productivity paradox". What is the real profitability of IT investments?

5   What role should government play in the development of that new environment? What role should it play in the development of new infrastructures, in the setting of standards, and in the development of regulation to foster competitiveness and the creation on wealth? What role should it play vis-à-vis the important shifts in demography?

Endnotes

[1] Drucker, P. and Peter, F., Management and the world's work, *Harvard Business Review*, September–October 1988, 2–9.

[2] Pine II, B.J., Peppers, D. and Rogers, M., Do you want to keep your customer forever? *Harvard Business Review*, March–April 1995, 103–114.

[3] *Ibid.*

[4] See, for instance: Solomon, C., Sharing information across borders and time zones, *Workforce*, March, 1998; Browne, J. and Prokesch, S.E., Unleashing the power of learning, *Harvard Business Review*, September–October 1997.

[5] Stewart and Thomas, *Intellectual Capital: The New Wealth of Organizations*, New York, NY: Bantam Doubleday Dell Publishing Group Inc., 1999.

[6] McKeen, J.D. and Smith, H., *Management Challenges in IS: Successful Strategies and Appropriate Action*, Chichester: Wiley, 1996.

[7] Davidow, H.D. and Malone, M.S., *The Virtual Corporation: Structuring and Revitalizing the Corporation of the 21st Century*, New York: Harper Business, 1993.

[8] Tapscott, D. and Caston, A., *Paradigm Shift: The New Promise of Information Technology*, New York: McGraw-Hill, 1993.

[9] Kennedy, C., Future shock – or future success? *Director*, July, 1995, 42–46.

[10] *Ibid.*

[11] Tapscott, D., Ticoll, D. and Lowy, A., *Digital Capital: Harnessing the Power of Business Webs*, Harvard Business School Press, 2000.

[12] *Ibid.*

[13] Webber, A.W., What's so new about the new economy, *Harvard Business Review*, January–February 1993, 4–11.

[14] Greengard, Making the virtual office a reality, *Personnel Journal*, 73(9), September 1994, 66–79.

[15] Webber, A.W., *op. cit.*

[16] *Ibid.*

[17] Avgerou, C., Ciborra, C.U. and Land, F.F. (eds) *The Social Study of IT*, Oxford University Press, 2004 (in press).

[18] Vogt, *op.cit.*

[19] Malone, T.W. and Laubacher, R.J., The dawn of the E-Lance economy, *Harvard Business Review*, September–October 1998.

[20] Vogt, *op.cit.*

[21] Caldwell, B., Computer services – the new outsourcing partnership – vendors want to provide more than just services. They'll help you create a Virtual Corporation. *Techsearch Results*, June, issue 585, 1996.

[22] Tapscott *et al.*, 2000, *op. cit.*

[23] Brown, S.L. and Eisenhardt, K.M., *Competing on the Edge*, Harvard Business School Press, 1998.

[24] Tapscott *et al.*, 2000, *op. cit.*

[25] See Brandenburger, A.M. and Nalebuff, B.J., *Co-opetition*, Harvard University Press, 1996 (for a discussion of co-opetition, a new form of relationship between firms which mixes competition and collaboration).

[26] Webber, *op. cit.*

[27] Malone, T.W. *et al.*, *op. cit.*

[28] Vogt, *op. cit.*

[29] Drucker, P., The coming of the new organization, *Harvard Business Review*, January–February 1988.

[30] Greengard, *op. cit.*

[31] Webber, *op. cit.*

[32] Drucker, *op. cit.*

PART II

The puzzle pieces

Managers do their jobs in complex and uncertain business and technical environments. To compete effectively, they must develop an organization that presents a coherent response to the dynamic conditions in which their specific business operates. While a particular response can take any one of a number of forms, all managers must start with the same four pieces: strategy, information technology, structure, and leadership. Hence, organizations differ not according to the number of pieces they choose to use in completing their specific puzzle, but as a result of the different shapes of the pieces they choose. Solving the management puzzle, therefore, consists of examining the available pieces and selecting those which will both interlock effectively, presenting a harmonious and well-composed picture to the outside world, and also fill the specific frame with which their environment presents them.

While environments remained fairly stable, designing a business was rather straightforward, because enterprises knew the piece with which to begin. Strategy was always the starting point. Next came a structure to support the strategy and, finally, new management and IT systems to make the structure work.[1] In those times, "structure" and "systems" practically always followed "strategy". According to this approach, all aspects of an organization were designed to enable a particular business strategy.

Unfortunately, given the dynamic and complex nature of the environment in which businesses must operate today, it is no longer practical to proceed unthinkingly in this manner.[2] Today, as case after case suggests, it may equally be IT strategy which drives business strategy and then structure, or a response to a particular environmental condition may necessitate a particular strategy and IT infrastructure. In short, it is no longer possible, as it was in the past, to take a linear approach to organizational design and act as if a firm were operating in a closed, rational, and predictable system.[3]

Today, designing a business requires non-linear thinking that can start with any one of the four pieces and then proceed in a dynamic, interactive, and continually evolving fashion. The next four chapters examine these pieces and the different dimensions and forms which they can take. Our objective is to help managers understand the options available to them.

The following part of this book (Part III) will present three cases, which illustrate that there is no single best way of assembling the puzzle pieces. As the three cases will show, firms can be quite successful in their adaptation to their environment, yet follow their very own trajectory.

Chapter 2

The strategy piece

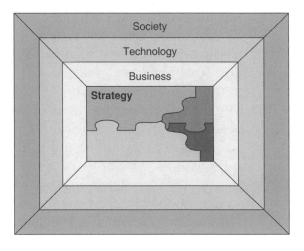

In the most general terms, a competitive strategy is an approach to doing business. At its highest level, a strategy specifies an organization's mission, vision, and goals. It can be conceived of as an overarching set of values and objectives on which more specific business strategies are built.

Two broad approaches to strategy formulation and implementation are: *strategy as positioning* and *strategy as capabilities*. The first is outward-looking, the second inward-looking. A third approach concerns *governance* issues: what should the boundaries of the firm be? How should the firm organize the network of relationships upon which a value-added solution depends? To find some answers, we will look at strategy from these three perspectives: positioning, capabilities, and governance.

Taken together, the first two strands of the literature capture the essential elements of the Harvard tradition of strategy formulation, the so-called "SWOT" model: strengths, weaknesses, opportunities, and threats. While the Porterian,[4] structuralist, "strategy as positioning" approach emphasizes the opportunities and threats faced by a business firm, the "strategy as capabilities" strand focuses on the internal strengths and weaknesses aspects.

Strategizing, implementing a strategic vision, can thus be done from three different perspectives. The first is the positioning angle, which consists in being able to assess one's environment and in exploiting it in the best possible way, sometimes by transforming it. The second is the capabilities perspective, which involves assessing one's environment followed by building one's capabilities in order to stay ahead of the competition. Finally, the governance strand looks at how transactions are allocated among various institutional arrangements and firms. It tries to answer Ronald Coase's puzzle: "Why not organize all transactions in one big firm?" The answer can be found in the existence of transaction costs: the costs of coordinating and motivating the partners to the transactions that define a firm. Governance is the way in which cooperation and control over some transactions are exercised. By appropriately choosing a firm's structure, its horizontal and vertical boundaries, and its contractual network of relationships with its stakeholders, a strategist increases the firm's efficiency. That is, its capacity to deal with uncertainty and the strategic behavior of its stakeholders. Thus, in seeking answers to "What should we do?" in the face of a rapidly changing environment, the manager must pay attention to organizational innovations that redefine a firm's scope and structure.

We thus use these three approaches – positioning, capabilities, governance – to examine our "strategy piece" of the puzzle.

Strategy as positioning

Strategy as positioning is exemplified in Porter's analysis. In essence, it implies finding a position in the market that will protect the firm against the threats of its environment arising from five market forces:

1   the intensity of industry rivalry;
2   the threat of new entrants;
3   the threat of new substitute products or services;
4   the bargaining power of suppliers;
5   the bargaining power of customers regarding quality and conditions of goods and services delivered.

A successful strategy addresses one or more of these forces in a way which is favorable to the business (e.g. limiting the ability of new companies to enter the market) which in turn, positively affects the competitive position of the firm in the industry, its profitability, and its market share. Ideally, the ways a company improves its competitive position create significant difficulties for others to copy (e.g. making it too expensive), which results in a long-term or sustainable competitive advantage, and in higher profitability. Note that while the environment is the particular arena in which a business competes, it acts as more than simply a constraining or shaping force on a business. Today, a business is no longer a passive responder to the environment, it also interacts with and helps shape its environment.

Although this perspective to strategy has come under criticism, Porter's approach still proves very useful and resilient. He argues that the rules of the game have not changed as much as the pundits of the new economy claim. Instead, Porter suggests that people are confusing operational effectiveness for strategy. He writes:

> Ultimately, all differences between companies derive from the hundreds of activities required to create, produce, sell, and deliver their products or services ... Operational effectiveness means performing similar activities *better* than rivals perform them ... In contrast, strategic positioning means performing *different* activities from rivals' or performing similar activities in *different ways*.[5]

As companies do not distinguish between these two concepts, they end up competing on the basis of operational effectiveness, resulting in a no-win situation. This trend has even been observed by proponents of the "new strategy". Mohrman *et al.*[6] comment that everyone today competes in the same four or five areas, and Rockart and Short[7] write that a number of standard corporate responses to the increasingly dynamic and competitive business environment have been initiated: time to market, service, quality, risk, cost, quality, and partnerships. Tapscott *et al.*[8] observe a number of "recurring business themes" which are a response to the current business environment including: productivity, quality, responsiveness and outsourcing, and partnering.

The problem with these responses is that, if not combined with strategic positioning, they lead to *competitive convergence* – a situation in which companies are drawn towards imitation and homogeneity. Unfortunately, because operational practices are all relatively easy to copy, they do not lead to any long-term competitive advantage in the marketplace. "The result is zero-sum competition … and pressures on costs that compromise companies' ability to invest in the business for the long term."[9]

Not all advocates of the "strategy as capabilities" approach agree with this analysis. Some, like Brown and Eisenhardt,[10] argue that it is inherently inefficient because of its lack of centralized planning. Nevertheless, this criticism highlights a significant danger of the capabilities perspective on strategy to which companies could easily fall prey.

Strategic positioning, on the other hand, is about being different from others. Managers must decide how they are going to preserve their company's distinctiveness or in which ways they are going to differentiate the firm in the many markets in which it operates. The three generic strategies offered by Porter are a starting point for the reflection: the firm may position itself as a dominant player and seek cost advantages and commanding market shares; it can differentiate and focus on innovation, sophisticated marketing strategies and on personalized and dynamic pricing; or it could entrench itself in a niche and target a group of consumers. In any case, positioning must help the firm cope with the threats posed by the competitive pressures.

Let us consider each of the five competitive forces that, according to Porter, erode a firm's competitive advantage and against which a strategy must build some defenses.

Assessing your competition

While it is true that all industries are competitive, some are more so than others. Companies in stable industries with high margins and long-lasting success formulas or which are highly regulated, are clearly in a different competitive situation than those with decreasing prices and margins, short product life and development cycles, and blurring industry boundaries.

Who is your competitor? Who will be in a few months time? These questions were easy to answer at one time, but now elicit few clear answers. Quite simply, the insulating layers which isolated and protected national industries are being degraded rapidly by a combination of factors including reductions in trade and non-trade barriers, a dismantling of many regulatory frameworks, and deployment of successful firms in technologically related markets. As a result, the traditional barriers to entry have been lowered and the threat posed by new competitors, such as Microsoft in the travel services sector, has become more significant.

Moreover, intense rivalry is all the more likely in the new competitive environment. Dominant or comfortable positions in national markets are being challenged by the winds of globalization and deregulation. Most markets are undergoing a major shake-up: a significant market share in the traditionally defined market is no longer a safeguard against the winds of fierce competition and rivalry by domestic or foreign firms. Thus, even in oligopolistic markets, the rules of the game are so altered that "cozy market equilibriums" are becoming increasingly difficult to maintain. The number and the diversity of competitors on the one hand, and the rate of innovation and its diffusion, on the other hand, sabotage market discipline and predictability.

To make things worse, in many knowledge-based sectors where information goods, such as entertainment products, news, financial services, etc., are produced, competition very often turns into a race for market dominance or innovation.[11] *Winner-take-all* markets that will likely be dominated by one or very few players are a possibility in many sectors. In such cases, important economies of scale and scope on the supply and demand sides create first-mover advantages and induce firms to invest heavily and aggressively in the early stages of the game. When many contenders make the same bets, destructive competition ensues: cutthroat competition and wars of attrition surface.

Similarly, in many information or digital goods markets, the payoffs from imposing one's standard or technology will command huge investments and aggressive behavior. *Hypercompetition*, an exacerbated form of rivalry, then develops. Low margins, unstable market shares, and very high rates of product and service innovations then become the rule.

In summary, the current phase of rapid innovation and market redefinition can be expected to reinforce the intensity of the rivalry in almost all sectors of the economy.

Assessing the threat of entry and substitutes

Assessing the threat of entry has always been difficult. As Yogi Berra famously said: "Making predictions is difficult, especially about the future!" Yet, the new environment is constantly redefining industries' frontiers. Which travel agency could have predicted, only 5 years ago, that online travel services, such as those offered by Microsoft, would represent a serious threat to its business?

More than ever, one's business position is at risk of being challenged by new opportunities and new products. These combine to reduce the "life cycles" of existing products and services, and render the threat of substitutes more vigorous. In many cases, it can be relatively easy for a new competitor to tap into a company's virtual value chain and to use this as the raw material for many new kinds of products and services.

As a result, there is now a need for firms to monitor and assess all aspects of their environment continually, so that they can reposition themselves appropriately externally and rearrange their internal infrastructure accordingly. Increasingly, the need to thoroughly understand and interact with one's business environment is seen as a critical piece of any organization's design. Mohrman *et al.* describe this ability in the following way:[12]

> The leading firms are future oriented and create the ability to satisfy the evolving needs of their customers. Then, rather than sustain current advantage, these firms move quickly … to disrupt the current advantage and … outmaneuver their competitors … The companies most likely to win are those with the ability to demonstrate flexible responses and a variety of moves over time.

In a world of continuous change, therefore, a key management piece is the ability to understand what is going on in one's business environment and to determine its relevance to the firm in order to be able to develop a coherent response. This ongoing "conversation" between the organization and its environment suggests that the environment does not "cause" organizational design, rather a set of interactions between firms and their environments leads to cycles of change as a normal part of organizational growth and development.[13] Due to this, modern firms must see exploration of the environment as both an important way to gain insight and direction about the other pieces of the puzzle and a way to help shape the environment in which they operate.

Assessing your business networks

In Porter's analysis,[14] suppliers represent an additional source of competitive pressure: depending on their bargaining power, they can capture a share of a firm's rents. This bargaining power depends on a few key factors: the number of alternative suppliers, the ease with which one can switch suppliers, the strength and size of one's suppliers, and so on. Yet, suppliers are also increasingly seen as partners or complementors as business organizations tend to create value quickly, and associate themselves more easily with strategic partners.

The new competitive environment leads many enterprises to focus more narrowly on their core competencies and outsource, contract out, and rely on partners for the provision of many intermediate goods and services. Even design and delivery of a global solution are often realized through partnerships or strategic alliances.

Hence, today, firms participate in business networks, although they might not call them this. The term "network" is used in many different ways but all meanings refer to the network of relationships, which a company has with other organizations. For example, not only do firms participate in a value chain made up of their suppliers and customers, they also compete and cooperate with different companies in different ways. Some firms provide products or services, which complement (i.e. increase the demand for) their own products or services (e.g. hot dogs and mustard). Other firms produce competitive products and services (e.g. Coke and Pepsi). However, it is not unusual these days for the same companies to compete in one sphere and cooperate in others. Thus, it is essential for a company to understand the many different dimensions along which it interacts with others.

The set of relationships with which a firm is involved can be described as its 'value network'.[15] Such a network includes five nodes: the firm itself, its traditional partners – customers and suppliers, its competitors, and its complementors, that is, those firms which offer products or services that complement the firm's own products or services. Taking advantage of the value network often requires creativity, and efforts to put aside preconceived ideas about the other nodes of the network. The case of EDS and Xerox illustrates this. In 1994, Xerox signed an IT outsourcing contract with EDS. In 2002, the firms jointly announced a strategic alliance designed to integrate EDS's IT services with Xerox's document management systems and services to provide customers with one-stop shopping and full support of their office IT infrastructure.[16] Such an agreement, wherein a firm and its supplier join forces to offer complementary services to customers, hence enlarging both firms' customer base, is in itself rather original. It is more so when such an agreement had been designed while Xerox and EDS were engaged in a major dispute regarding their IT outsourcing contract. Indeed, at the same time, EDS was suing its client alleging that it breached its contract by bringing back in-house some activities that were part of the outsourcing contract.[17] Negotiating a strategic alliance while at the same time being engaged in an extremely publicized and costly lawsuit indeed requires a new way of looking at business partnerships!

Although multifaceted relationships in which a single company is a supplier, partner, customer, and also a competitor are becoming increasingly common, most companies are unfamiliar with how to behave in such situations. Traditionally, interfirm relationships have been conducted at arms length. Today, however, more benefits may be achieved by developing long-term close relationships between firms. Companies therefore need to assess both the benefits and risks of such relationships and to determine how and where such collaboration should take place.[18]

What is the level of interdependence the firm wishes to develop with its suppliers, with its complementors, with its competitors? What alliances, partnerships, and collaborative agreements could be designed to support the desired level of interrelatedness? And what position does the firm occupy in this network? These are the crucial questions management must answer in the emerging business environment.

A network can also be a collection of physical locations that create value because of the fact that they are connected through IT (e.g. ATMs). Sharing across this type of network can increase a product's reach, the network's quality by providing different goods and services on it, and reduce the costs of setting it up. However, in these cases, a company will be affected by the decisions of other firms. Companies, therefore, need to assess both the degree and the type of their interrelatedness with other organizations in order to determine where and how cooperation and competition should take place in a physical network. This assessment must be ongoing because the benefits of a particular form of participation in a network of this type may change over time. For example, a firm may initially benefit from competition in a new market but gain more rewards from cooperation as the market matures.[19]

A third type of network in which a firm may participate is a knowledge network. This is important to the process of learning and knowledge creation. What is the firm's position in its industry knowledge network? How does the firm learn and acquire know-how? Is in-house development, learning, and R&D privileged? How does it leverage knowledge partnerships with other firms, knowledge brokers, universities, and research centers? Or is learning acquired through licenses, mergers, and acquisitions?

Many believe that learning will be the ultimate mechanism for achieving sustainable competitive advantage.[20] Knowledge networks are thought to help firms spread the costs and risks of innovation among a large number of organizations, gain access to research, and share other forms of information. Unfortunately, there is little or no evidence, to date, showing the value of these networks to the firm.[21] Nevertheless, it is important for managers to be aware of these types of activities within their organization, since a firm's long-term success may well depend on how effectively it accesses, integrates, and uses knowledge.

Understanding a company's networks is a prerequisite to understanding more about its competitive position in the environment. This helps a company evaluate its position in the value chain, understand how its strategic activities fit together, learn which channels and relationships are most profitable, and ultimately determine how the activities of the firm combine in the marketplace to create products or services which are both different and valuable.

Assessing your customers

With buyer power increasing,[22] customer orientation is becoming a much more significant shaper of organizational strategy than in the past.[23] Thus, in many cases, a customization strategy to provide customers with the specialized goods and services which will meet their particular needs and enable a company to serve many different kinds of customers can be a very good source of positioning. This strategy also allows the firm to explore the avenues of personalized or dynamic pricing, with resulting larger profit margins.

Other strategies emphasize cultivating and growing an existing customer base.[24] Developing an ongoing, interactive relationship with customers is one of the best sources of information about customers and their needs and this is particularly important when a company is seeking to uncover new sources of value.[25] Therefore, a company may initiate a thorough examination of its end customers' experiences before determining how it might transform the value proposition it offers.

With growing competition, it is becoming increasingly important to retain existing customers – preferably for life.[26] Keeping customers, especially the profitable ones, is considerably more cost-effective than seeking new ones. This is all the more important since customers are increasingly demanding and well informed. Internet and e-marketplaces, for instance, have dramatically reduced the search costs of industrial and residential customers. Customers have access to more information and are more demanding than ever before: clearly, their bargaining power has increased.

Most companies already seek to understand their customers to some extent, but to be effective in the new business environment, they will have to know a great deal more about them. First, they will need to be able to locate and identify most of their customers and to know them in as much detail as possible. Understanding customers at this level will involve people from all parts of the business.[27] At minimum, customers should be differentiated according to their needs. Companies should also recognize that their competitors and suppliers may be their customers under some circumstances.

Second, companies should seek to understand their current competitive position *vis-à-vis* their customers. Companies need to know which of their customers are most satisfied and which are the most profitable and why. Third, they need to understand the markets in which their customers operate. Interestingly, a single customer can be in different markets at different times and in different places (e.g. a person can be both a business and a vacation traveler) and these crossovers, if better understood, can provide a significant source of value to the firm.[28]

Finally, companies must understand their customers' problems so that they can reorient themselves towards solving them. This assessment not only helps companies identify their customers' recognized and unrecognized needs, it also helps them to better identify their true competition, which, as we have seen above, is not always obvious. Brandenburger and Nalebuff write:

> As people think more in terms of solving their customers' problems, industry perspective is becoming increasingly irrelevant. Customers care about the end result, not about whether the company that gives them what they want happens to belong to one industry or another. The right way to identify your competitors is ... to put yourself in the customers' shoes.[29]

They point out that companies can use this approach to identify businesses offering complementary products and services which might be used to increase the market for its own products and services. It is interesting to note that there are now IT tools which can help companies understand their customers in deeper and more meaningful ways; these should also be considered as part of any customer assessment analysis.

Overall, this approach to strategy formulation involves tailoring a company's activities to address its chosen position in the marketplace. However, to guarantee a sustainable competitive advantage, companies must also address two further issues. First, they must make trade-offs, i.e. choose what not to do, because some competitive activities are not compatible with each other. Second, they must also focus on creating a "fit" among all their activities, so that they will reinforce each other. When activities mutually reinforce each other, competitors cannot easily imitate them. Only when these things all work together effectively, is sustainable competitive advantage possible.[30]

Strategy as capabilities

However, in the last decade, with substantial upheavals in many business environments, corporate strategizing has begun to change. Many have advocated that positioning might be too simplistic a solution to the strategy formulation process. Instead, a new emphasis on the development of the capabilities and a focus on the core business of the enterprise have been suggested.

These are the foundations of the "strategy as capabilities approach". This perspective sees the firm as a bundle of assets and the strategic advantage as the capacity to deploy those assets. The core competencies are defined as the competencies that are unique to the organization, hard to replicate, and central to the organization's mission. The more difficult it is for competitors to imitate and copy one's strategy, to replicate one's competencies, the more sustainable is one's competitive advantage. Each firm is thus seen as a set of capabilities that are only partially mobile or replicable. The differences in firms' performance is thus explained by their differential abilities.

History, the combination of past decisions and luck, plays a major role in defining a firm's profile. The apparent success of the leading firms is thus hard to replicate. Furthermore, haste makes waste: replication may entail large costs. Finally, very often, the competitive advantage will result from multiple, sometimes unknown causes, which make imitation even harder.

But how could a competitive advantage imbedded in a firm's set of capabilities and history resist the tide of a turbulent environment? This is where the firm as capabilities approach leads to recognition of the central importance of serendipity, organizational learning, and core competencies.

Serendipity refers to an organization's ability to exploit opportunities intuitively and recognize the value of the intended and unintended discoveries it makes. It refers to the unplanned strategy: the emerging strategy of firms adapting quickly to changing circumstances. It builds organizational flexibility.

Organizational learning is the process by which the firm learns about its environment and about itself. Beyond what every one of its members learns, organizational learning refers to that know-how which results from the interactions of the individual within the firm, and which is often tacit in nature. Hence, the utmost importance of individual human capital development, and of the organizational know-how seen as a pool of shared resources. Much of the writing about strategy for the "new economy" is directed at companies who are making new markets with goods and services based on knowledge.[31] Certainly, firms face significantly more opportunities in these types of markets with the advent of technologies and information management capabilities. Furthermore, the ownership of intellectual capital can be an important source of differentiation for companies and can be a key starting point in determining a competitive strategy.

Following the work of Prahalad and Hamel,[32] core competencies refer to a set of interrelated skills and competencies that are fundamental for the firm. These are the skills, which help a company focus on what it does best. They are more transversal than product specific, and they generally result from a collective learning process. Identifying the core competencies at the foundation of an organization's success helps the organization by focusing on what makes it different and productive. In a turbulent environment, this allows the firm to look beyond the ephemeral shocks and think in terms of its long-term development.

The result of this approach to strategy formulation has been a relentless race to keep one step ahead of one's rivals, sometimes called "hypercompetition".[33] It has led many managers to question whether such a thing as sustainable competitive advantage any longer really exists.

This view of strategy, therefore, suggests that firms should begin to compete on the basis of one or more organizational capabilities which, if combined and adapted effectively to current environmental conditions, enable a company to create a stream of short-term advantages in such areas of new products, new market segments, new marketing channels, and new customer relationships.

Strategic advantage is thus built upon strategic flexibility which is "the capability of the firm to … respond quickly to changing competitive conditions".[34] Leaders develop strategic flexibility by first defining a vision for the business and then focusing on developing key organizational capabilities. This is done through managerial and organizational introspection, openness to change, engaging in non-linear thinking, and the adoption of a systemic view of the firm.

As a result, many business strategy experts today believe that traditional strategic planning by senior managers is no longer possible in today's unpredictable environment.[35] The careful positioning of the past must be replaced by a more dynamic and disorganized approach which emphasizes continuous strategy making over time throughout the entire organization.

Strategy as governance

The roots of this new perspective on strategy can be found in firms' improved information processing capabilities. Organizations are set up to minimize the costs of executing certain forms of transactions. As Ronald Coase[36] has suggested, as long as the cost of organizing a transaction within a firm is equal to or less than the cost of carrying out the same transaction on the open market, there will be a reason for the company to exist. Therefore, to be successful, a firm must deliver better value at a lower price than the marketplace.

As technology destroys old methods of delivering value, it also enables new structural forms for the creation of value. As this becomes apparent, companies will need to break down their traditional value propositions (disaggregate) around these new value propositions. To do this, companies will have to focus on what they do well, develop core competencies in these areas, and form partnerships and alliances to deliver the rest.[37] Tapscott *et al.* put it succinctly:

> Effective strategists (need to) honestly face the many weaknesses inherent in industrial-age ways of doing things. They (must)

redesign, build upon and reconfigure their components to radically transform the value proposition.[38]

Ultimately then, this strategic perspective sees an organization as an institutional method for organizing transactions. Hence, the advent of the Internet, for instance, signifies that the costs of using the market have been dramatically reduced. This creates opportunities for firms and entrepreneurs who will dismember and rearrange transactions in the most economical way. Again, in the words of Tapscott *et al.*:

> Thanks to Internetworking, the costs of many kinds of transactions have been dramatically reduced and sometimes approach zero. Large and diverse groups of people can now, easily and cheaply, gain near real-time access to the information they need to make safe decisions and coordinate complex activities.[39]

Thus, strategizing also consists in reshaping organizations, seeking new ways, processes, and organizational structures to deliver better business propositions to ever demanding consumers. Networks of firms, virtual firms, electronic hubs, and e-marketplaces are precisely new ways of organizing the cooperation of dispersed individuals and firms.

The rapid developments in IT are reshaping markets and challenging existing governance structures. Actually, one anomaly in the existing strategy literature is the relationship of IT strategy to business strategy. While most researchers suggest that IT strategy should result from business strategy, there is a growing body of evidence and thought that this is not always the case. With the ability of IT to create and enhance new organizational capabilities and to create new products and services which can lead to a repositioning of a firm in one or more marketplaces, IT has become more than a passive technology. This perspective suggests that it is sometimes desirable to adapt business strategy to emerging IT capabilities, and to adapt a firm's configuration to its IT environment. For example, the electronic hubs for business-to-business transactions are making new markets, which did not exist previously. Thus, to formulate an effective business strategy, managers need to understand trends in IT.

Therefore, strategy as governance implies rethinking the organizations' traditional boundaries and interfaces. It is strategy in the long run: an effort to provide definitions of "who we are" and "what we do", and consequently, to shape the dense network of relationships that define the organization.

Strategy: a final word

The three perspectives on strategy – strategy as positioning, strategy as capabilities, and strategy as governance – stress the need to maximize the coherence between a company's external strategy and its internal execution. Companies, therefore, must design an internal business strategy, which complements external strategy, and forms a focused and integrated system. "The success of a strategy depends on doing many things well … and integrating them. If there is no fit … there can be no distinctive strategy and little sustainability."[40]

The new environment poses enormous challenges to the process of strategy formulation and implementation. The cases analyzed in this book show how the managers of business firms caught in the midst of these changes reformulated their firm's strategy and in so doing, defined the position they wanted to defend, the capabilities on which they depended, and the shape of the organization that was required to deliver competitive solutions.

Questions

1   Just how compatible are the three perspectives on strategy formulation and implementation that we described: strategy as positioning, strategy as core competencies, and strategy as governance?

2   Some argue that the formal process of strategy formulation in itself has become impossible and irrelevant in such a fast-changing world. If this were true, what lessons for decision makers are left by the strategic exercise? On the other hand, if strategy formulation is still possible and useful, how should managers cope with the demands of fast-paced environments?

3   How should companies develop customer loyalty in the new environment in which clients have access to more information than they ever had and competitors have all means of reaching for them?

4   How should companies deal with and manage their networks of suppliers and complementors? To what extent should the latter be involved in the strategic process of the organization?

5   How should companies cope with the increasing demands for accountability and ethical behavior in the context of increasing networking?

Endnotes

[1] Sauer, C., Yetton, P.W. and Associates (eds.), *Steps to the Future: Fresh Thinking on the Management of IT-Based Organizational Transformation*, San Francisco, CA: Jossey-Bass Publishers, 1997.

[2] Hitt, M.A., Keats, B.W. and DeMarie, S.M., Navigating in the new competitive landscape: building strategic flexibility and competitive advantage in the 21st century, *Academy of Management Executive*, **12**(4), 1998, 22–42.

[3] *Ibid.*

[4] Porter, M.E., *Competitive Strategy*, Free Press, 1980.

[5] Porter, M.E., What is strategy? *Harvard Business Review*, November–December 1996.

[6] Mohrman, S.A., Galbraith, J.R. and Lawler III, E.E., *Tomorrow's Organization: Crafting Winning Capabilities in a Dynamic World*, Jossey-Bass Publishers, 1998.

[7] Rockart, J. and Short, J., The networked organization and the management of interpedence, in Scott Morton (ed.), *The Corporation of the 1990s*, New York: Oxford Press, 1991.

[8] Tapscott, D., Ticoll, D. and Lowy, A., *Digital Capital: Harnessing the Power of Business Webs*, Harvard Business School Press, 2000.

[9] Porter, M.E., 1996, *op. cit.*

[10] Brown, S.L. and Eisenhardt, K.M., *Competing on the Edge*, Harvard Business School Press, 1998.

[11] Shapiro, C. and Varian, H.R., *Information Rules: A Strategic Guide to the Network Economy*, Boston, MA: Harvard Business School Press, 1999.

[12] Mohrman, S.A. *et al.*, 1998, *op. cit.*, p. 3.

[13] Applegate, L.M., *Managing in an Information Age: Organizational Challenges and Opportunities*, Harvard Business School Press, 1995.

[14] Porter, M.E., 1980, *op. cit.*

[15] Brandenburger, A.M. and Nalebuff, B.J., *Co-opetition*, Currency-Doubleday 1996.

[16] Business Wire, *EDS, Xerox join forces to provide one-stop shopping for networked offices*, November 25, 2002, www.businesswire.com/webbox/bw.112502/223292145.htm

[17] Wall Street Journal, *EDS wins contract extension for Xerox project*, November 29, 2001.

[18] Carlin, B.A. *et al.*, Sleeping with the enemy: doing business with a competitor, *Business Horizons*, September–October 1994, 9–15.

[19] Brandenburger, A.M. and Nalebuff, B.J., 1996, *op. cit.*

[20] Tapscott, D., *The Digital Economy: Promise and Peril in the Age of Networked Intelligence*, New York: McGraw-Hill, 1996.

[21] Harris, K., Austin, T., Fenn, J., Hayward, S. and Cushman, A., The impact of knowledge management on enterprise architecture, *Gartner Group Strategic Analysis Report*, 25 October 1999.

[22] Hagel III, J. and Rayport, J.F., The coming battle for customer information, *Harvard Business Review,* January–Februrary 1997.

[23] Mohrman, S.A. *et al.,* 1998, *op. cit.*

[24] Davidow, H.D. and Malone, M.S., *The Virtual Corporation: Structuring and Revitalizing the Corporation of the 21st Century,* New York: Harper Business, 1993.

[25] Moon, Y., Interactive technologies and relationship marketing strategies, *Harvard Business Note #9-599-191,* 19 January 2000.

[26] Davidow, H.D. and Malone, M.S., 1993, *op. cit.*

[27] Peppers, D., Rogers, M. and Dorf, B., Is your company ready for one-to-one marketing? *Harvard Business Review,* January–February 1999, 3–12; Peppers, D. and Rogers, M., *Enterprise One to One: Tools for Competing in the Interactive Age,* Doubleday, 1999.

[28] Gilmore, J.H. and Pine II, B.J., The four faces of mass customization, *Harvard Business Review,* January–February 1997, 91–101.

[29] Brandenburger, A.M. and Nalebuff, B.J., 1996, *op. cit.,* p. 19.

[30] Mohrman, S.A. *et al.,* 1998, *op. cit.;* Porter, M.E., 1981, *op. cit.*

[31] Davis, S. and Botkin, J., The coming of knowledge-based business, *Harvard Business Review,* September–October 1994; Evans, P.B. and Wurster, T.S., Strategy and the new economics of information, *Harvard Business Review,* September–October 1997.

[32] Prahalad, C.K. and Hamel, G., *Competing for the Future,* Harvard Business School Press, 1996.

[33] Hitt, M.A. *et al.,* 1998, *op. cit.*

[34] *Ibid.*

[35] Brown, S.L. and Eisenhardt, K.M., 1998, *op. cit.*

[36] Coase, R., The nature of the firm, *Economica,* 1937.

[37] Evans, P.B. and Wurster, T.S., 1997, *op. cit.*

[38] Tapscott, D. *et al.,* 2000, *op. cit.*

[39] *Ibid.*

[40] Porter, M.E., 1996, *op. cit.*

Chapter 3

The structure piece

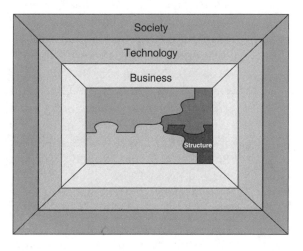

The second piece of the management puzzle – structure – pertains to how an enterprise is organized to accomplish its goals. At its simplest, structure determines how power and authority are distributed in an organization. Managers must identify who has responsibility for such things as: how decisions will be made; who will coordinate and execute activities; and how planning and control of strategy and operations will be accomplished.[1] Traditional approaches to designing an effective organizational structure[2] have, therefore, concentrated on:

- *departmentalization*: formation of departments and their respective tasks;
- *specialization*: types of people needed and their job duties;
- *authority and control*: levels of authority needed, their proper span of control and signing authority of different levels;

- *distribution of power*: decision-making units in the company (i.e. in which department, and in a centralized or decentralized fashion);
- *centralization versus decentralization*: best balance between centralization and decentralization and organization of field locations and international operations.

While these remain important objectives of structure, more recently we are beginning to realize that structure can have an important impact on how an organization functions in an increasingly challenging business environment. For example, structure can help an enterprise manage complexity; be more responsive to changing business conditions; and deal with the increasing number of interdependencies in many modern enterprises.[3,4] In addition, structures create the conditions under which innovation and change can flourish.[5] Today, because of the rapidly changing environments in which most companies operate, we also recognize that structures are critical management tools for problem solving,[6] resource allocation, and the management of intellectual assets.[7] In fact, effective structures are now being viewed as differentiating factors which can give a firm a significant competitive advantage in the marketplace.[8]

Thus, managers are becoming more aware that structure is much more tightly linked than they had previously realized with the other puzzle pieces, and even with the environment. As Von Bertalanffy points out, organizations are open systems which exist in a state of mutual communication and interdependence on the environment.[9] Managers play a significant role in choosing how this interaction takes place and organizational design is a key element of how they respond to and shape their environment. For example, structures play a central role in the interpretation of environmental stimuli and the configuration of the organization's response.[10] Similarly, structure is intimately linked with strategy; in fact it has been called "the other half of strategy," because it is the means by which strategy is carried out and monitored in the firm.[11] Today, structure increasingly interacts with technology as well. Although no causal relationships have been established between a certain type of technology and a particular form of structure, it is very clear that technology is having an ever-larger impact on the types of organization structures, which are possible and/or desirable. Technology enables different forms of controls to be used and can link people in ways which previously had not been possible. Information technology (IT) not only facilitates different forms of coordination, it creates opportunities for new levels of coordination.[12] Successful organizations take advantage of these new possibilities to design structures which improve their effectiveness in both new and traditional ways. Overall, structure is, therefore, a critical piece of the management puzzle because it plays an important role in how an enterprise responds to its environment, enables strategy, and facilitates critical organizational competencies.

This chapter will examine the structure piece from all these perspectives. First, it looks at the basics of how organizations are usually designed and outlines traditional organizational forms. The second section explores how the recent changes in the business environment are calling for a new set of success factors which, in turn, must be considered by managers when designing how their organizations will work. These factors are: speed, flexibility, integration, and innovation. The third, and last, section suggests that, today, organizations not only need to consider their internal (vertical and horizontal) structures but also their structuring outside the organization's boundaries (external and geographic) in order to achieve the objectives of speed, flexibility, integration, and innovation.

Traditional structural forms

Traditionally, organization structures have been designed to optimize productivity and reduce transaction costs.[13] Until recently, economics have favored the development of large bureaucratic organizations designed to provide a functional division of labor. The bureaucratic structure is designed to help an organization cope efficiently with doing business on a large scale. In this type of structure, the firm is broken down into units of specialization, each with a particular responsibility for a major task. These units are then further subdivided into smaller units, until every individual has detailed job responsibilities.

Organizational structures have long been designed around a focal theme. For example, a functional structure is organized according to the type of work being done (e.g. research and operations). Product structures are designed according to the types of products produced or services provided (e.g. computers and musical instruments). Market structures focus on the type of market or customer being served (e.g. retail and wholesale). Finally, geographic structures are organized around the needs of a particular geographic region (e.g. Asia and North America). Each theme has its own strengths and weaknesses, which need to be considered in its design. For example, in a product structure, each division provides its own functions, generally duplicating resources and missing opportunities for sharing. Economies of scale may also be lost.

Since the early 1980s, there has been considerable experimentation with new organizational designs. There is a widespread belief that if we could only get the structure right, many of today's organizational problems would disappear (or at least become less significant).[14] In complex organizations, for instance, designers have adopted a hybrid structure which combines two or more themes in order to get the benefits of several different structures and to minimize the weakness of the main structuring theme. Galbraith identifies four hybrid organizational structures:[15]

- *Lateral organization*: This type of structure recreates the equivalent of the top management structure at lower levels in the organization to facilitate different perspectives within the firm. For example, a functionally-structured organization may have cross-functional product and process teams working to speed products to market or improve cycle time (see Figure 3.1).
- *Front–back structure*: This type of structure focuses partially on customer segments and partially on products and services. Its front-end structure is organized around customers, customer segments, channels, industries, or

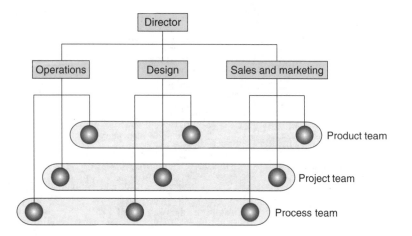

Figure 3.1
A lateral organization structure.

geographies. These units concentrate on sales and service, and the specific needs of particular customers (e.g. business and individual consumers). Its back-end structure concentrates on products (e.g. research and development, manufacturing, and marketing). Each product division interacts with each customer division. This structure enables companies to achieve both customer responsiveness and product scale (see Figure 3.2).

■ *Multi-structuring*: This type of structure creates a number of cross-functional units or teams dedicated to different market segments, customers, and channels. It enables a firm to shift its competitive focus as the need arises by creating teams for each of a company's strategic initiatives.

■ *Internal marketing*: A fourth type of hybrid structure tries to replicate market conditions internally and make all parts of the organization more responsive, competitive, and flexible. In this structure, internal service providers must compete for a company's business, offer their services at market rates, and even make a profit. Some firms even allow their business units to market their services externally.

Today it is widely agreed that traditional organizational forms now present serious problems for firms trying to do business under conditions of significant environmental uncertainty, hypercompetition, and technological complexity. They have resulted in

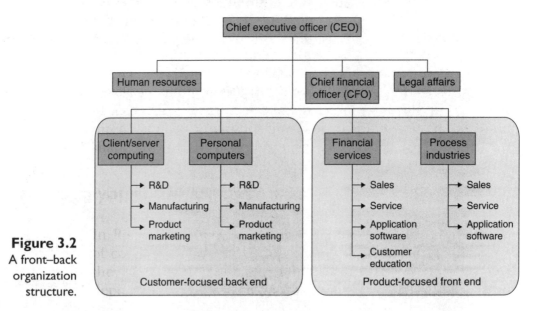

Figure 3.2
A front–back
organization
structure.

firms that are, to a large extent, organizationally incapable of carrying out the sophisticated strategies that they are developing. As a result, a functional division of labor and management hierarchies are now often seen as sources of "organizational pathology" which prevent firms from responding effectively to changing environmental conditions. What were core competencies in the past now appear to be "core rigidities" hampering the actions a firm can take.[16] In short, today hierarchical firms are, to a large degree, poorly structurally equipped to deal with new business realities.[17] However, the fact remains that few of these structures are actually in existence today. Most large organizations continue to use some aspects of the hierarchical form and experiment with modifications, which will help them operate more effectively in today's environment.

A new set of critical success factors

PAG →

Managers seek to design a structure which can carry out the strategic goals of their enterprise effectively. Their structural choices must be based not only on how to facilitate the actual work of their organization but also on how to create an entity which will foster the right conditions for their strategy to be implemented. Designers should, therefore, be cognizant of these conditions and understand how different structures can encourage or hamper their development. In short, they must approach structure in a strategic fashion[18] and, hence, consider the new reality of business. In this regard, the advent of the micro-processor, the dizzying speed of information processing and communications, and the arrival of the global economy have conspired to radically shift the basis of competitive success. To a large extent, the old success factors, namely, size, role clarity, specialization, and control have become liabilities and the new success factors look very different from the old; the new business environment calls for greater speed, flexibility, integration and coordination, and learning and innovation.[19]

This is the diff erence between carrying out orders effiently + ?

Thee new Success Factors!

① Speed

Highly successful organizations are increasingly characterized by speed in everything they do. They bring new products to market faster, respond to customers more rapidly and change strategies more rapidly than ever before. While size does not preclude speed, large companies are like tankers.[20] Indeed, larger organizations are at a disadvantage in this respect since they need more space and time in which to move. As a result, some companies are trying to be more nimble by becoming leaner and focusing on their core competencies. Others are developing structures, which enable some business units to act like smaller organizations while still remaining part of a larger firm. Such organizational arrangement is often appropriate when parts of a business face hypercompetitive conditions while others compete in a more stable market.

② Flexibility

Flexibility has been called one of the critical success factors of the organization structure of the future and is considered a key way to deal with hypercompetitive environments.[21] Flexible organization structures are characterized as highly adaptable and able to move quickly to respond to changing environmental conditions and changing business strategies. A very flexible organization is one in which employees perform multiple jobs or assume multiples responsibilities, constantly learn new skills, and willingly shift to different locations and assignments.[22] In highly flexible organizations, role clarity – the old success factor – is not desirable because it can constrain responsiveness and make people less willing to jump into the breach and do whatever is needed. Instead, these new firms revel in ambiguity, throw out job descriptions, and thrive on *ad hoc* teams that form and reform as tasks shift. Flexibility has both internal and external elements. Internally, it is the capability of the firm to adapt to the demands of the environment (e.g. creating new routines or project teams). Externally, it is the firm's capability to influence its environment, so that it becomes more sensitive to change (e.g. making arrangements with suppliers, hiring external contractors).[23]

Flexibility is a balance between responsiveness and stability. Unfortunately, it is not always clear to managers how much of each is needed in their organization. Not all organizations need the same amount of responsiveness to their environment as the organization described above. Furthermore, companies need stability to preserve their organizational identity and to maintain controllability. Responsiveness without stability results in chaos.[24]

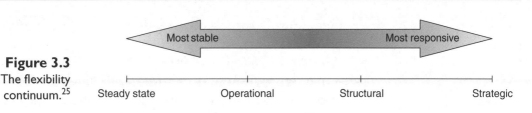

Figure 3.3
The flexibility
continuum.[25]

Some highly responsive organizations have become so flexible that they have become completely out of control. Hence, responsiveness and stability are conflicting forces, which managers must keep in equilibrium when designing for flexibility. Too much, and they risk loss of identity and control; too little can lead to loss of competitiveness and adaptability. True flexibility is, therefore, the result of an interaction between the responsiveness of the organization to its environment and the ability of management to control what it is doing.

An organization's design must provide adequate flexibility for the environmental conditions in which it operates. Clearly, the more turbulent the environment, the more flexibility is required. Different organizations have different flexibility needs or may need a different form of flexibility in different parts of their business. According to Volberda, there are four different types of flexibility. These can be viewed as a continuum from most stable to most responsive (see Figure 3.3).

■ *Steady-state flexibility*: Firms have stable throughput and relatively stable transactions; they need only a modest amount of flexibility. Changes can consist of minor improvements implemented at a moderate pace.

■ *Operational flexibility*: When the volume and mix of activities are more variable but familiar; organizations need a way to adjust quickly but in a routine fashion. They need procedures and routines to rapidly address such things as short-term fluctuations, uncertainties, or the ability to adjust the size of their workforces. In this situation, more flexibility is required but because it is predictable, it can be designed into the operations of the organization.

■ *Structural flexibility*: Organizations must deal with evolving (but not rapidly changing) business conditions; they need to be flexible in a controlled fashion. Therefore, managers, seek to create more structures and processes, such as project teams, job enlargement, and just-in-time mechanisms, which can easily be adapted to changing business needs.

■ *Strategic flexibility*: Organizations face completely unfamiliar environmental changes with far-reaching consequences and the need to react rapidly; every aspect of the firm must be flexible. Under these circumstances, designers must transform their organizations with new strategies, technologies, structures, and values, which are created to ensure extreme responsiveness to external business conditions.

How does a firm design for flexibility? Managers start with a basic structure (e.g. functional, process, and networked) and modify it to reflect their organization's need for flexibility. All types of flexibility require organizational designers to create the appropriate conditions within which they can flourish. This includes structure, culture, and technology. These ensure that all parts of an organization are working together towards the same goals. For example, when functional structures are replaced with more flexible and organic ones, reliance on formal reporting structures and planning and control systems will decline. These need to be replaced with more informal mechanisms to accomplish the same things – such as common beliefs and assumptions, training and education, technology for routine functions, improved information access, and performance-oriented structures.

③ ④ Integration and coordination

Companies that can shift directions quickly and flexibly have business processes that carry concepts of change into the institutional bloodstream, disseminating new initiatives quickly, and mobilizing the right resources to make things happen. Integrated firms focus more on how best to accomplish business or work processes and less on producing specialized pieces of work that management will pull together. In these firms, specialists are still needed, but the key to success is often the ability of those same specialists to collaborate with others to create an integrated whole.[26]

All organizational performance comes down to how well the parts of the structure are integrated and work together to create an organized whole. As traditional managerial controls are loosened in newer organization structures, the need for coordination increases dramatically.[27] In addition, research shows that there is a growing need to manage interdependencies within and between organizations.[28] The most commonly-used mechanism to do this is to overlay lateral coordinating forms on top of the base organizational structure (e.g. as in some of the hybrid organization structures discussed above). Today, with the vastly increased number of interdependencies involved in running a large-scale enterprise, no matter what type of organization structure is chosen, some of these will be necessary to ensure that all organizational constituencies are dealt with.[29] There are three different levels of coordination that organizations can use:

- *Informal*: While these occur spontaneously in organizations (e.g. person A in department X works with person B in department Y), organizational designers can improve the frequency and effectiveness of this type of coordination in a number of ways. Encouraging interdepartmental rotation of people, sponsoring interdepartmental events, supporting co-location of staff, using IT to promote communication and information sharing, and developing mirror image departments (as in the holonic structures discussed above) all make it easier to gain a consensus for action, while providing consistent reward and measurement systems promoting common goals. This level of coordination is the least expensive and the easiest one to use.
- *Formal*: More formal coordinating groups include cross-functional project teams and task forces. These have a mandate and require team building and management effort to create. As formal groups operate in addition to informal coordination, not instead of them, they are more expensive to use.
- *Integrator*: This level of coordination involves the appointment of integrators to lead the formal groups. It usually requires the hiring of several full-time people whose job is to integrate the work of others. This type of coordination is often expensive and difficult to achieve because it confuses the roles and responsibilities of the formal organization structure.

An organization designer must try to match the coordination needs of the business' strategy with the most effective mechanism to accomplish them. While informal coordination is the most desirable, for many companies this may not be enough. More formal mechanisms are needed when a leader believes that he or she should take a more active role in coordination. This could include situations in which particular issues must be addressed; coordination is needed to implement a particular strategy; or management wishes to call attention to a particular type of coordination needed.

As people-based coordination mechanisms are somewhat limited, another commonly used coordination mechanism is technology.[30] Organization-spanning technology can be used to promote the use of standards and facilitate teamwork across networks. Technology also facilitates multi-dimensional views of information, making it easier to adopt different coordination foci at different times. However, while IT can make the management of interdependence more effective, it is widely recognized that it can only enhance, not replace, the informal coordination mechanisms in the firm.

Learning and innovation

Organizations that succeed in a world of rapid change find learning and innovation essential.[31] These organizations constantly search for the new, the different, the unthinkable. They create innovative processes and environments that encourage and reward creativity, whereas in organizations that focus on control, the creative spirit and people who innovate are often stifled by systems of approvals, checks, and double-checks, because innovation threatens standard operating procedures.

There are many ways organizations can promote learning and innovation through structure. Establishing an overarching set of corporate values and priorities is an essential first step because these encourage knowledge creation. However, organizations must also design mechanisms to utilize and convert learning into specific resources, skills and actions. This can be accomplished with structures, which promote and reward creativity and take advantage of new knowledge and ideas. Flatter and more horizontal organization structures also appear to enhance innovation because there are fewer boundaries to be overcome. Cross-functional teams also help learning because they reduce the likelihood of organizational politics becoming a barrier.[32] Finally, in competitive industries, structures should have functions for intelligence-gathering and for processing the information received from the environment.

Great Description

Towards boundaryless organizations

In their quest to achieve the success factors of the twenty-first century, organizations must confront and reshape four types of boundaries: vertical, horizontal, external, and physical/global.[33] Organizations are commonly thought of first and foremost as vertical structures.[34] Vertical boundaries represent layers within a company. They shape definitions of status, rank, and career progression. Traditional elements of vertical boundaries are spans of control, limits of authority, and other manifestations of hierarchy. The classical example is the military, where clear symbolic and substantive differences exist by rank.

If vertical boundaries are floors and ceilings, horizontal boundaries are walls between rooms.[35] Horizontal boundaries are the dividing lines between divisions, departments, groups, units, and functions. The boundaries that distinguish employees within a function (e.g. hourly versus salaried employees) are also horizontal dividers, with each group having its own rules and procedures, ways of tracking time, access to buildings or files, and so on. Boundaries between functions exist in the traditional firm when each function has a singular agenda that may compete or conflict with other functional agendas.

External boundaries are barriers between firms and the outside world – principally suppliers and customers but also entities as governmental agencies, special interest groups, and communities.[36] In traditional organizations, clear differentiators exist between insiders and outsiders. Some of these differentiators are legal, but many are psychological, stemming from varied senses of identity, strategic priorities, and cultures. In such a context, business is done through negotiation, pressure tactics, withholding of information, and the like. With information technology, workforce mobility, and product standardization, physical boundaries are quickly disappearing. People work in different places, under different conditions and sometimes in different time zones, thus creating additional boundaries. Global boundaries exist when complex structured firms operate in different markets and countries.

In short, organizations have always had, and will continue to have, boundaries. The underlying purpose of these boundaries is to separate people, processes, and production in healthy and necessary ways.[37] Boundaries keep things focused and distinct. Without them, organizations would be disorganized. People would not know what to do. There would be no differentiation of tasks, coordination of resources and skills, or clear sense of direction. In essence, the organization would cease to exist.

Given the necessity of boundaries, the boundaryless behavior proposed by Ashkenas and his colleagues does not mean a free-for-all removal of all boundaries. Instead, they are talking about making those boundaries more permeable, allowing greater fluidity of movement throughout the organization. The authors compare the boundaryless organization to a living organism, which evolves and grows. Over time, the levels between the top and bottom of the organization may decrease, functions may merge together to combine skills, or partnerships may form between the firm and its partners, changing the boundaries of who does what. As the boundaryless organization is a living continuum, not a fixed state, the ongoing management challenge is to find the right balance of boundaryless behavior, to determine how permeable to make boundaries and where to place them. We now turn our attention to each of the four types of boundaries, which structure organizations.

Vertical boundaries

According to Ashkenas and his colleagues, the question that should concern companies today is not how to eliminate hierarchies but how to ensure healthy ones that meet the success requirements of speed, flexibility, integration, and innovation. Most organizations today have hierarchies designed around the old success factors of size, role clarity, specialization, and control. Several stories exist of innovation slowed down by too many approvals; of wrong decisions made because data from lower levels were not heard or considered; or of people's personal incentives not matching what made sense for the organization. All these constitute "red flags" signaling dysfunctional hierarchies. Other warning signs include slow response time (when organizations take too long to make decisions, respond to customer requests, or react effectively to changes in market conditions); rigidity toward change (when organizations continue to do things because they have always done it this way or when they expend more effort finding ways not to change than they spend on changing); internal frustration (when employees and managers feel dissatisfied with the organization, the way it works, the way it treats them); and customer alienation (when customers feel they are not being heard).

The presence of red flags such as those described above usually indicates that an organization's vertical boundaries need some degree of loosening. The extent to which this should occur is a judgment call that depends on what is needed to meet the success requirements of a particular organization or situation. In other words, permeability of vertical boundaries must be thought of as a continuum, not as an either/or duality. According to Ashkenas and his colleagues, finding the right balance of hierarchical looseness versus control is a central task of leadership and must be struck on multiple dimensions:

- *information* moves from information closely held or integrated at the top to open information sharing throughout the organization;
- *competence* moves from leadership skills exercised at senior levels and technical skills exercised at lower levels to competencies distributed through all levels;
- *authority* moves from decisions made only at the top to decisions made all along the line, at whatever points are appropriate;
- *rewards* move from rewards based on position to rewards and incentives based on accomplishments.

Rob Rodin, CEO of Marshall Industries, characterizes today's environment: *No two customers have the same need, but they all want the same thing – Free. Perfect. Now.*[38] In response, firms have adopted customer-oriented strategies that both assess and anticipate customer needs and in which mass-customization plays an important role. By doing so, firms try to achieve both greater flexibility and efficiency. These efforts have led to the emergence of several organizational structures, which increase the permeability of vertical boundaries, if not abolish them. Common to these organizational forms are the importance of the customer contact person and the use of IT to support and coordinate their work.

Among these new forms is the "infinitely flat organization" in which the potential number of people reporting to one supervisor is much higher than in traditional organizational forms.[39] This is made feasible by appropriately automating the scheduling, order-giving, and information feedback traditionally provided through the hierarchy. In these organizations, few orders are given by the line organization to the employees in the lower levels of the hierarchy. Rather, managers play the role of advisors who are responsible for helping customer contact personnel perform better rather than giving them precise instructions. An often cited example of an infinitely flat organization is Mrs. Fields' Cookies, which employed 8000 people, 140 of which were in staff positions at the company's head office.[40] An important part of Mrs. Fields' knowledge about the business and its products was embedded in a sophisticated information system that helped individual store managers in their day to day activities. On the basis of each individual store characteristics, the system advised store managers how many cookies to be made during the day, the number of batches to mix and when to mix them. If sales appeared low during the day, the system would suggest preparing samples and offering them to potential customers. The system also computed sales projections and generated orders for supplies. Sales reports were produced every day and were available not only to store managers but also to regional sales managers and to headquarters. The objective of the information was to free store managers from those activities and decisions that can be automated, and allow them more time to be in direct contact with the customers.

The "inverted organization" is another organizational structure that emphasizes the permeability of vertical boundaries. Marshall Industries, the fourth largest distributor of electronic components in the U.S., implemented such a structure in order to emphasize that employees were more accountable to the customer than to any supervisor in the company's hierarchy. At any given time, a customer contact person could be almost any employee in the firm. For instance, it is said that IT employees involved in the development of customer-oriented applications spend almost 50 percent of their time with customers, in order to better understand their needs.[41]

In the inverted organization, not only is the customer at the highest level of the "organizational pyramid," but the structure itself is designed in such a way that all the work performed in the organization has the objective of supporting the customer contact personnel. That is, the traditional line executives and staff personnel "work for" the customer contact person. In order to make the vertical boundaries still more permeable, Marshall Industries actually abolished the traditional line and staff functions. In addition, the traditional summit of the pyramid is occupied by the chief quality officer rather than by the president. This is not just symbolic; it is a clear message to the customer and to the employees that everybody in the firm is driven by the goal of providing the highest service quality to the customer. In order for this new structure, and its underlying organizational culture, to be institutionalized, the company adopted a new employee compensation scheme. In this scheme, **all employees are paid in the same way**, and participate in the company profit-sharing bonus pool.

To conclude, we summarize below the various signs characterizing rigid and permeable vertical boundaries in organizations.

Signs of rigid vertical boundaries

- Hierarchical organization in which roles are clearly defined and more authority resides higher up in the organization than lower down
- Numerous levels or reporting relationships exist between the first-line supervisor and the senior executive
- Hierarchical boundaries are defined by title, rank, and privilege (e.g. military)
- A major role of management is controlling the work of others to ensure they are doing the right things, in the right order, at the right time (information closely held at top)
- Creativity and innovation are driven underground because people know that new ideas will receive adverse reactions
- Slow response time and customer dissatisfaction
- Internal employee frustration
- Rewards are based on position
- Competence is specialized and focused – people do one job.

Signs of permeable vertical boundaries

- Focus is less on who has authority and rank but more on who has useful ideas
- Rank is less relevant than competence
- Good ideas from anyone are sought out
- Information moves from being closely held or integrated at the top to open information sharing throughout the organization
- Competence is widespread—people do multiple tasks as needed
- Authority moves from decisions made only at the top to decisions made all along the line, at whatever points are appropriate
- Rewards are based on accomplishments

Horizontal boundaries

While organizations need to maintain some vertical boundaries, they equally require some degree of horizontal task delineation. Today's organizations arrange themselves around such specialties as engineering, manufacturing, marketing and sales, human resources, information technology, and so on. Some organizations may have upward of 20 such departments, each forming a mini-organization with its own agenda, resources, and vertical leadership structure. Organizations with such multiple, hierarchical specialty units are often called silo, stovepipe, or chimney organizations, because they appear as a series of stacks on the organization chart.[42]

The new success factors of speed, flexibility, integration, and innovation make horizontal boundaries as problematic as vertical boundaries.[43] Moving across a maze of functional boxes inevitably creates delay, indecision, uncoordinated actions, and least-common-denominator products and services. According to Ashkenas and his colleagues, companies must take proactive steps to create permeability across the horizontal spans in order to avoid the five typical dysfunctions described below:

- *Slow, sequential cycle times*: When work flows from one function to another, each function must wait until the previous one has completed its task. In this way, the receiving function can build on the sending function's contributions. Meanwhile, weeks go by and the customer waits.
- *Protected turf*: Once horizontal boundaries become ensconced, people vie to protect their department's power and resources. Hence, departments end up spending more time protecting turf than securing or satisfying customers. This issue stems from the logic of specialization.
- *Sub-optimization of organizational goals*: This occurs when functional specialists begin to set their localized goals ahead of the organization's goals in order to optimize their own achievements and rewards.
- *The enemy-within syndrome*: This syndrome is visible in many businesses in which departments feud over resources and power. Organizations have canceled important projects because of interdepartmental conflict over design or marketing concepts, despite market demands for the product. Organizations have also canceled important information systems implementation projects because of the fear of losing power, despite the positive impacts of the system for the organization.
- *Customers doing their own integration*: As task specialization increases inside large organizations, customers commonly end up handling the integration of products and services. In such situations, accountability for customer satisfaction is spread out over many different functions.

Integration is one of the success factors for organizations because it allows them to be more responsive to customers and to react more quickly.

To create boundaryless horizontal organizations, companies must see themselves as sets of shared resources and competencies that are mobilized, in different ways at different times, to meet customer needs. Ashkenas and his colleagues provide a set of tactics, which they call *improv vehicles*, for facilitating harmonious behavior across horizontal boundaries:

- Orient work around *core processes* which, by definition, are externally customer focused;
- Tackle processes through targeted *teams*;
- Turn *vertical dimensions* (information, competence, authority, and rewards) sideways, i.e. across functions, disciplines, and product groups;
- Develop *organizational learning capability*, i.e. the organization ability to learn from the lessons of its experience and to pass those lessons across boundaries and time.

For several years now, firms have recognized the benefits associated with process orientation and business process reengineering (BPR). BPR has helped numerous firms become more profitable by eliminating non-value adding activities. Yet, according to Hammer and Stanton, the full realization of process orientation benefits requires firms to go one step further.[44] They must actually change the organizational structure by creating a process enterprise, that is, an enterprise with permeable horizontal boundaries.

Such an organizational form is made necessary by the very nature of processes. Take, for instance, the sales process, which starts with a customer order and ends with a product delivered to the customer. In an organization with rigid horizontal boundaries, several departments are involved in the process. The order-taking unit of the sales department, or the sales representative, takes the order from the customer. An important sales department objective is to sell as many as possible of the firms' products. Credit checking is the responsibility of the customer credit unit. In this unit, quality of work is assessed on the percentage of bad debts, which has to be as low as possible. The product is manufactured in a plant with its own performance objectives: high quality products, manufactured with as little waste as possible, in a manner that optimizes the resources of the plant. The product is then delivered by the delivery department that has rapid delivery as a performance objective.

While the process might be streamlined so as to eliminate non-value-adding activities, the fact that each organizational unit has its own objectives is likely to lead to sub-optimization, which could be very costly to the firm. In a large postal organization, hundreds of thousands of dollars in revenue were actually lost due to short-sightedness associated with local goals. In the operations department of this organization, great emphasis was put on speed. When customers delivered truckloads of envelopes – for instance, bills of a utility company – loading dock employees of the postal organization knew that they had to work fast. Yet, the emphasis was put on speed alone, not on profitability. This resulted in the organization discovering that bills of lading accompanying the materials delivered at the loading docks by customers were quite often forgotten for a while, if not simply lost. Indeed, the organization actually delivered the mail, yet did not bill its customers, since the transaction documents had been lost.

Since a process-based organizational structure calls for common, process-oriented goals, it is actually designed to alleviate such difficulties.[45] A process enterprise shifts organizational power away from units, toward the processes. Performance objectives are set by process, not by department. That is, all organizational members involved in a process will be evaluated on the basis of the whole process performance, not on the basis of their local objectives. Budgeting is also done by process, not by department. Sometimes, office space is even reconfigured to better accommodate the new process structure.

According to Hammer and Stanton, the presence of a process owner is the most visible difference between a process enterprise and a traditional one. Hence, choosing the right process owner is key to the successful implementation of a process-based enterprise. Process owners must not only have full responsibility for the performance of a given process, they must also have the required authority for its design, performance measurement, and employee training. While traditional line or unit managers continue to manage their own workforces, process owners have much authority on how the work is actually performed. As the very nature of process-based organizations is perceived as a threat by traditional functional managers, process owners must be selected among senior management, and their critical skill must be their ability to influence others. In such an enterprise, teamwork is of utmost importance, and coaching and development rather than control should be emphasized as management mechanisms. Finally, in a process-based organizational structure, performance must be measured on the basis of the whole process performance, and followed by compensation mechanisms. Indeed, if employees are to have a process view of their work, their compensation should be based, at least in part, on process performance.

According to Hammer and Stanton, Duke Power – an electric utility serving 2 million customers in North and South Carolina – is an exemplary process enterprise. Prior to its transformation, the company was facing deregulation; it was paralyzed by a rigid organizational structure comprising four regional profit centers and it had no designated person responsible for how the firm delivered value to its customers. Duke Power transformed itself by first identifying its core processes, assigning a process owner to each one, and having them report to the head of Customer Operations, as the regional vice-presidents did. While the regional vice-presidents continue to manage the workforce in this new organizational structure, the process owners hold the responsibility and authority over the actual operations. That is, process owners are responsible for designing their processes and for setting performance targets. Much collaboration is required between regional vice-presidents and process owners. This required collaboration between process owners and functional managers is often seen as the most fragile, and sometimes problematic, component of process enterprises. The experience at Duke Power and other firms has shown that transforming potential rivals into partners requires much tact and influence.

The various signs characterizing rigid and permeable horizontal boundaries in organizations are summarized below:

Signs of rigid horizontal boundaries

- Specialization: organization is arranged around specialties (upwards of 20 departments), each forming a mini-organization with its own agenda, resources, and vertical leadership structure. These units are often called silo, stovepipe, or chimney organizations
- Work may also be organized around products, markets, and/or geographic regions
- Organizational processes tend to be slow and sequential
- Functional units are more concerned with protecting their turf
- Sub-optimization of organizational goals (when function views its localized goals ahead of the organization's goals)

- Functional groups regard each other with suspicion, blame each other for problems, and operate as though the enemy is within the organization
- Customers are doing their own integration (accountability for customer satisfaction is spread out over many different functions)
- Employees are locked into specific roles and responsibilities and are rewarded only for those

Signs of permeable horizontal boundaries

- Organizational processes tend to be fast and parallel
- The focus of attention is always on the customer
- The customer has a single-point of contact
- Functional groups or units place greater priority on contributing to overall organizational achievements

External boundaries

While vertical and horizontal boundaries are the floors, ceilings, and internal walls of the organizational house, external boundaries describe not just outside walls but the community in which the house stands.[46] The objective of loosening internal boundaries is to create a more effective individual organization, one that is more capable of dealing with customers, suppliers, and other external entities. This is not to say that organizations should eliminate all external boundaries and form partnerships, alliances, joint ventures, and collaborations with everyone around them. That would be chaotic and counterproductive. However, by making specific external boundaries more permeable, organizations can dramatically increase speed, flexibility, integration, and innovation.[47]

As product life-cycles shrink, global competition heats up, the cost of innovation spirals upward, customers demand more, and everything moves faster, companies are realizing that they cannot keep up by working alone. They need to join forces to drive technologies, expand distribution, enter new markets, ensure sources of supply, and match end-user expectations. These structures can take a number of forms for an individual organization. Each emphasizes a different type of external relationship:

- *External sourcing and alliances*: The most widely used form of external structuring occurs along the firm's value chain with its suppliers and customers. Using technology as an interface, many companies are seeking the integration of functions, which reach beyond the organization's boundaries. Frequently, there is substantial customizing of products or services by suppliers and in return, the company makes them preferred partners guaranteeing a certain volume of work. For example, a company and its suppliers may work together closely on a product's design or develop an order fulfillment process whereby they share real time information.[48] At Dell Computer, daily demand for computer monitors is provided to another firm which fills orders and coordinates information and shipping, without ever transporting the monitors to Dell.[49] At the other end of the value chain, companies are also linking themselves much more tightly to their customers to better anticipate demand and provide improved customer service. The result is an organization which is much more responsive to its customers and more adaptable to market conditions.

This type of structure must be designed to fit an individual firm's needs. As Dell's president explains, "Figuring out how many partners we need has been a process of trial and error. ... The rule we follow is to have as few partners as possible and they will last as long as they maintain their leadership in technology and quality."[50] With external sourcing, therefore, some aspects of structure may be fairly stable while others in more dynamically evolving areas may be more volatile.

- *Partnerships and joint ventures:* A second type of external structure involves setting up an external entity with one or more partner organizations for the benefit of all the partners. Typically, this entity is focused on developing and supplying a product, a service, or a technology. The companies involved are frequently competitors who work together, sharing expertise and costs, to develop or create something they both need. A partnership often starts out as a limited-time project or special study which is co-funded and co-directed by the partners and if successful, matures into a more permanent organizational entity with equity ownership by the partners. Initially, responsibility for activities and results is usually shared between the partners who co-staff and co-lead the venture. When the external entity becomes more permanent, it will likely be more autonomous and report through a board of directors. Many companies find that partnerships and

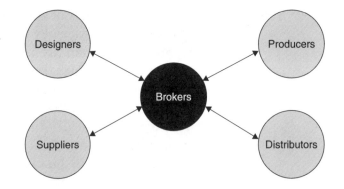

Figure 3.4
A generic network
structure.[52]

joint ventures are effective ways to share the cost of non-competitive activities or expensive research and development functions.[51]

■ *Networks*: In a network structure, common business functions typically conducted within a single organization are performed by independent organizations working in collaboration. Networks are assembled by companies, which act as brokers who play a leading role in coordinating their work. Relationships and responsibilities are outlined in a contract. Key roles in a network include: broker, designer, supplier, producer, and distributor (see Figure 3.4). Activities are coordinated by information systems and a generally-agreed structure of payment for value added. Technology also monitors performance.

Networks enable companies to focus on what they do best (i.e. their core competencies). They marry the flexibility, independence, and efficiency of market relations with the efficiency of communication channels, adaptiveness, and trust of more traditional hierarchical structures. Miles and Snow write: "the network organization in its several variations has sought to incorporate the specialized efficiency of the functional organization, the autonomous operating effectiveness of the divisional form, and the asset-transferring capabilities of the matrix organization."[53]

However, networks also have their weaknesses and are more likely to be prone to opportunistic behavior by a partner and to have less efficient transaction costs. Networks are evolving structures and companies are moving into them cautiously. Companies must pay careful attention to their role in a network or they could find themselves unable to make important decisions or have their functions taken over by other firms.

■ *Business webs*: Ultimately, as electronic communication and e-commerce become ubiquitous, networks will grow and develop increasingly complex forms. Tapscott suggests that we will increasingly see companies identify a customer value proposition and build an appropriate system of suppliers, distributors, commerce services providers, infrastructure providers, and customers to make it profitable.[54] The lead firm will control core elements of the value proposition, such as its customer relationships, value creation coordination, management processes and intellectual property. Partners will take care of everything else. Tapscott calls these structures business webs or b-webs. In the near future, he believes, companies will participate in many different b-webs, possibly taking different roles in different webs. However, he points out, "We are in uncharted territory." He suggests networks will evolve into five different types of b-webs depending on the degree of economic control and level of value integration involved:

 – *agora*: a b-web which facilitates exchanges between buyers and sellers who jointly "discover" a price for a product;
 – *aggregation*: a b-web which acts as an intermediary between producers and consumers, selecting products and services, targeting market segments, setting prices, and ensuring fulfillment;
 – *value chain*: a b-web which is structured to meet a particular customer order or market opportunity;
 – *alliance*: a b-web which provides a loosely structured value space within which participants design goods or services, create knowledge or produce shared experiences;
 – *distributive network*: A b-web which services other types of b-webs by allocating and delivering goods (e.g. information, money, and resources) from providers to users.

The structures described above are mostly ideal types or pure structural forms. As we have noted, hybrid structures are often used to acquire the advantages of more than one type of structure and to minimize the disadvantages of the dominant structural form. Managers create hybrids by considering both internal and external structures in all aspects of their organization's design. In short, successful companies in the future will be those that take a systemic, boundaryless view of their participation in the value chain. Indeed, success will come from improving the overall profitability and continuing vitality of the value chain as a whole, rather than just the companies' own bottom lines. Below we summarize the key signs of rigid and permeable external boundaries.

Signs of rigid external boundaries

- Clear differentiators exist between insiders and outsiders. Some of these differentiators are legal, but many are psychological, stemming from varied senses of identity, strategic priorities, and cultures. These differences lead most organizations to some form of we-they relationship with external partners
- Business is done through negotiation, haggling, pressure tactics, withholding of information, and the like
- When there are multiple customers or suppliers, one may be played off against another
- The traditional "every-company-for-itself" attitude
- Business partners develop strategies and plans independently
- Information sharing and joint problem solving are limited
- Rather than collaborate with other members of the value chain, a company continues to go it alone – developing its own productivity programs, competitive awards, and quick fixes for symptoms. When such companies do think of themselves as links in a value chain, their aim is to force other links to conform to what they think is needed

Signs of permeable external boundaries

- Customers or suppliers help a firm resolve its internal problems
- The company's structure includes external sourcing and alliances
- The company's structure is characterized by several partnerships and joint ventures
- The company has implemented a network structure
- Business webs (different forms of b-webs) are a key aspect of the corporate structure
- Information sharing among partners is highly valued
- Financial and human resources are shared among business partners

---

Physical and global boundaries

Information technology is enabling the development of businesses which present alternative and flexible working arrangements.

A *virtual office* is the term given to a variety of non-traditional working arrangements for employees.[55] Historically, companies have provided all their employees with a fixed office location and an extensive infrastructure. Increasingly, however, companies are recognizing that an office is expensive overhead that a lean and flexible business can no longer afford.

While not all the impacts of the virtual office are currently understood, many companies, such as Verifone, IBM, Alcoa, Proctor & Gamble, and others, are experimenting with creating new and flexible ways for their employees to interact and accomplish work. Increasingly, the "one size fits all" office is giving way to new office designs that reflect an individual or a team's specific needs at any given moment.[56]

As mentioned above, there are many types of virtual arrangements. Four of the most common ones are: the company without an office, the shared office, telecommuting, and virtual teams. These options can be used as complements to each other or separately. Each of these is briefly described below.

The company without an office

One of the most radical implementations of the virtual office is the example of a company operating without one. Although the firm may have an address, most, if not all of its employees work out of their homes or a local work space. Verifone, one of the world's largest suppliers of electronic credit card verification equipment, has 1800 employees who communicate primarily through e-mail. Staff reside in the place of their choice and meet from time to time as needed.[57] To develop new products, the company has turned geographic distance into a competitive advantage. Some members of its teams may never meet in person. Interestingly, the company has accomplished this collaboration using simple email for coordination, as opposed to videoconferencing or multimedia. With this model, Verifone feels it can stay close to its customers while being able to take advantage of expertise as quickly as needed.

Managing in this type of environment requires special skills to make it work effectively. Managers must trust their staff. They need to learn when to use particular communication tools. And they have to learn how to communicate effectively. Pape believes that almost any type of company can benefit from applying these virtual concepts to their business.[58] They signal a change in organizational philosophy and stimulate new thinking, and they help management understand which areas of decision-making can be decentralized and which need to remain centralized. These are ideas which can help any business prosper.

The shared office

Companies without any offices are still rare. A more commonly adopted model of a virtual office is some form of shared office space, sometimes called "non-territorial space" or "hoteling."[59] In this model, only people who are in the office that day are assigned space. Companies provide buildings where offices or meeting rooms can be reserved in advance, much like a hotel. Ernst & Young and Chiat/Day have both introduced this concept with their employees. When not in the office, belongings are stored in a private locker. But when they next come back, a "concierge" arranges their things on an available desk before they arrive. Their name is on the door and even their phone numbers have been forwarded.

There are several benefits to this approach. Companies who use hoteling feel that non-territorial offices tend to eliminate the office as status symbol or perk. Instead, status comes from assignment to leading-edge, highly-visible projects. Employees like it too, once they get used to this way of working. The longer they do it the less they seem to focus on the office and the more they focus on the customer. There are also considerable savings to be had.

Other forms of shared office space involve reorganizing work spaces to make them more flexible. Increasingly, companies are redesigning office space to facilitate teamwork and promote interaction. Procter & Gamble has eliminated private offices and designed its space around projects. Instead, members of teams work in open cubicles, grouped together, and can all see each other regardless of rank. Offices are designed in a modular fashion so they can be reconfigured quickly if a team needs to get bigger or smaller.

Chiat/Day management suggests that a good strategy for introducing shared or flexible officing is to "try a little of everything." In this way, employees can find out what they like and what works for them. The majority of Chiat/Day employees have found that, with training, they enjoy new ways of working. Today, most employees spend most of their time in project rooms, which are the gathering places for each particular account at the agency. The company also provides quiet rooms, a great deal of technical and human resources support and training, so that staff can be successful working in this type of environment. However, some people have found that they simply cannot be effective without access to some personal space, privacy, and quiet, and the company provides this as well.[60]

Telecommuting

Telecommuting moves work to the workers, instead of workers to the work. Through the use of telecommunications technology, such as computers, fax, and remote access, many of the physical barriers that once required workers to be in their offices have been removed. Telecommuting is growing rapidly in popularity with both large and small companies. There are many reasons for this phenomenal growth. First, it benefits the employee. Numerous studies[61] have shown that they like the increased flexibility and control, as well as the reduced commuting time, stress, and distractions involved in telecommuting. Second, it benefits the company. While many businesses have introduced telecommuting to help employees balance work and family needs, they have discovered that it has significant benefits for their bottom lines as well. Employees are demonstrably more productive. As well, a company can increase its recruiting possibilities by extending its geographic boundaries, thus making it more attractive to potential workers. Finally, telecommuting improves employee morale and therefore increases employee retention. In short, telecommuting enables companies to reduce costs and maximize their return on investment in employees.

Both managers and employees agree that there are some key critical success factors that should be followed in determining how and where telecommuting is to be used in the workplace.[62] These include:

- *Selecting the right employees*: Not all employees are well-suited to telecommuting. Some find distractions at home more of a challenge than at the office. Typically, supervisory concerns have meant that telecommuting has been limited to workers who have been with a company for some time and who are trusted.
- *Selecting the right job*: Currently, telecommuting is considered best suited for positions that require a lot of

independent work, such as sales, consulting, writing, and research. However, in the future, telecommuting will be extended to many more "information" jobs as we change our attitudes to telecommuting. For example, studies show that most people's strategic planning skills go up dramatically when they telecommute. Managing remotely can also work well with senior staff who need only "big-picture" direction, not daily instructions. It is unquestionable that in the future, more and more jobs will be able to be done by telecommuters.

■ *Designing the right work structure and incentives*: Compensation schemes must also be adjusted to support telecommuting and pay for work, not time. Procedures need to be made more flexible to accommodate work done away from a central office. Employees will need more freedom to make decisions on their own but, at the same time, companies must develop clear boundaries of behavior and accomplishment. This may be done through contractual agreements or more informally.

Virtual teams

The rise of virtual teamwork has been brought about by many of the changes identified earlier in this chapter. Organizational flattening has led to a reduction in management layers and the dispersal of human resources, both structurally and geographically, around the organization. New forms of partnerships and alliances among organizations to manage a value chain can require increasing interorganizational cooperation and sharing. Virtual teamwork also supports new forms of organizational flexibility, such as telecommuting. The shift to a knowledge economy also forces greater flexibility. Finally, the increasing globalization of business makes virtual teamwork a much more cost-effective alternative to massive relocations and travel.

Thus, today, virtual teams are becoming both a benefit and a necessity for most businesses.[63] They also enable companies to tap into their best brains for a specific project, no matter where they may be located. They enable companies to utilize resources from outside the organization. They help reduce time to market and increase competitiveness. They improve productivity and help companies to both realize the synergies of teamwork and exploit the capabilities of telecommunications and information technology.

However, there are challenges to making these teams work and most of these focus on the human, rather than the technological, issues involved.[64] A virtual team represents a radically different work environment for most people. Thus, *developing effective virtual teams goes well beyond the technical problem of linking people together ... It is imperative that such teams rebuild the interpersonal interaction necessary for organizational effectiveness.*[65] For example, miscommunication is a common problem because of the lack of visual and oral clues in electronic communication. This can lead to different assumptions being made by people with different cultural backgrounds, and different philosophies about work.[66] At the individual team member level, workers must learn how to work in a virtual environment, maintain effective communication with others from a wide variety of cultural backgrounds, and deal with shifting team membership. Participation and collaboration skills will need to be developed. Managers must learn to communicate especially clearly with team members. Their objectives and expectations must be well expressed. One manager of a virtual team noted that such groups require *more* formal communication, not less, and that informal management styles are not as effective in a virtual environment. At a company level, organizations must address such issues as compensation and evaluation in ways, which are consistent with how these teams operate.

Penetrating global boundaries has also become a necessity for the successful organization of the twenty-first century. Already, global reach is becoming a new business standard. For instance, companies have been experimenting with using globally distributed teams to develop products such as software concurrently, taking advantage of time zone differences to make faster progress on a project.[67] Other companies are seeking new markets; some are taking advantage of new cross-border trade agreements; some are exploiting new technology; some are looking for less expensive labor or new sources of capital. Many organizations will recognize at least one of the above reasons as a sufficient rationale for crossing global boundaries. The challenge, however, does not usually lie in finding something to drive globalization but in finding the right path to globalization and implementing it in a fashion that suits the organization. Among the most daunting challenges companies face when going global are: establishing a workable global structure (many global organizations struggle continually to find the right solution for gaining the global synergies and coordination they desire); hiring global supermanagers (people with a sizable knowledge and sincere appreciation of international issues, who also have basic management skills, plus advanced linguistic, cultural, and people skills); managing people for a global environment (developing global talent and ensuring mutual trust between managers and remote workers); and learning to love cultural differences (overcoming cultural paralysis).[68]

The key characteristics or signs of rigid and permeable physical/global boundaries in organizations are summarized below.

Signs of rigid physical/global boundaries

- Often stemming from national pride, cultural differences, market peculiarities, or worldwide logistics, these boundaries may isolate innovative practices and good ideas within a single country, keeping the overall company from leveraging the learning from specific countries and markets to increase company success
- Domestic (local) company (employees, partners, customers, and activities)
- Interactions between employees and with external partners occur face-to-face

Signs of permeable physical/global boundaries

- "Work anytime, anywhere" is the dominant paradigm
- Use of multi-disciplinary, transnational and/or global project teams
- Telecommuting and mobile work are widely diffused
- Virtual or shared office characterizes the working arrangement
- Activities are conducted in several countries
- Focus on global integration (total global sourcing, global design, global engineering, and global purchasing)
- Leadership positions include people from culturally diverse backgrounds
- Successful firms that work across global boundaries respect and value local differences as a source of innovation

---

Conclusion

Structure is and will continue to be a challenge for managers. Designing an organization which will increase speed effectively, balance flexibility and integration, provide for equal autonomy and control, promote learning and innovation while executing the organization's work and strategic priorities successfully is not an easy task.[69] Every organization structure has its positive and negative aspects and managers need to get beyond the hype to find the right one for their business. Key decisions have to be made about how much structural change is needed and how the organization should move towards newer forms of structure. As this chapter has made clear, structure encompasses more than simply determining how a firm should be organized to carry out work. It must also consider designing ways to promote complementary behaviors and the coordination required to ensure that all parts of the organization are able to work together effectively. Finally, designing a successful structure involves being able to challenge embedded views of what an organization should look like. In fact, overcoming mental mindsets can be one of the biggest barriers to success that managers are likely to face.

Questions

1   The recent changes in the business environment are calling for a new set of success factors, which must be considered by executives and managers when designing their organizations. Describe the new success factors and explain clearly how they look different from the old ones

2   Why is structure a critical piece of the management puzzle?

3   How and why is structure more intimately linked with strategy and the other pieces of the management puzzle today than ever before? Illustrate

4   What does it mean "to approach structure in a strategic fashion"?

5   What are the key characteristics or components of traditional structural arrangements in organizations?

6   How do the new success factors make traditional organizational structures problematic? Illustrate

7   Explain the concept of boundaryless organizations. How can information technologies make organizational boundaries more permeable? Illustrate

Endnotes

[1] Volberda, H.W., Toward the flexible form: how to remain vital in hypercompetitive environments, *Organization Science*, **7**(4), 1996, 359–374.

[2] Galbraith, J.R., *Designing Organizations: An Executive Briefing on Strategy, Structure, and Process*, Jossey-Bass Publishers, 1995.

[3] Mathews, J., Holonic organisational architectures, *Human Systems Management*, **15**(1), 1996, 1–29.

[4] Tapscott, D., *Digital Capital: Harnessing the Power of Business Webs*, Boston, MA: Harvard Business School Press, 2000.

[5] Applegate, L.M., Managing in an information age: transforming the organization for the 1990s, in R. Baskerville, S. Smithson, O. Ngwenyama, J.I. DeGross (eds.), *Transforming Organisations with Information Technologies*, North Holland, 1994.

[6] Mathews, J., 1996, *op. cit.*

[7] Venkatraman, N. and Henderson, J.C., Real strategies for virtual organizing, *Sloan Manangement Review*, **39**(5), Fall 1998, 33–48.

[8] Venkatraman, N. and Henderson, J.C., 1998, *op. cit.*

[9] Von Bertalanffy, L., The theory of open systems in physics and biology, *Science*, 1950 (cited in Applegate, L.M., 1994).

[10] Volberda, H.W., 1996, *op. cit.*

[11] Venkatraman, N. and Henderson, J.C., 1998, *op. cit.*

[12] Mathews, J., 1996, *op. cit.*

[13] Tapscott, D., 2000, *op. cit.*

[14] Galbraith, J.R., 1995, *op. cit.*

[15] Mohrman, S.A., Galbraith, J.R., Lawler III, E.E., *Tomorrow's Organization: Crafting Winning Capabilities in a Dynamic World*, Jossey-Bass Publishers, 1998.

[16] Volberda, H.W., 1996, *op. cit.*

[17] Tapscott, D., *The Digital Economy: Promise and Peril in the Age of Networked Intelligence*, New York, NY: McGraw-Hill, 1996.

[18] Venkatraman, N. and Henderson, J.C., 1998, *op. cit.*

[19] Ashkenas, R., Ulrich, D., Todd, J. and Kerr, S., *The Boudaryless Organization, Breaking the Chains of Organizational Structure*, San Francisco, CA: Jossey-Bass Publishers, 1995.

[20] Ashkenas *et al.*, 1995, *op. cit.*

[21] Volberda, H.W., 1996, *op. cit.*

[22] Ashkenas *et al.*, 1995, *op. cit.*, p. 8.

[23] Ashkenas *et al.*, 1995, *op. cit.*

[24] Volberda, H.W., 1996, *op. cit.*

[25] *Ibid.*

[26] Ashkenas *et al.*, 1995, *op. cit.*

[27] Applegate, L.M., 1994, *op. cit.*

[28] Rockart, J. and Short, J., The networked organization and the management of interdependence, in M.S. Scott Morton (ed.), *The Corporation of the 1990s*, New York, NY: Oxford Press, 1991.

[29] Galbraith, J.R., 1995, *op. cit.*

[30] Rockart, J. and Short, J., 1991, *op. cit.*

[31] Hitt, M.A., Keats, B.W. and DeMarie, S.M., Navigating in the new competitive landscape: building strategic flexibility and competitive advantage in the 21st century, *Academy of Management Executive*, **12**(4), 1998, 22–42.

[32] Hitt *et al.*, 1998, *op. cit.*

[33] Ashkenas *et al.*, 1995, *op. cit.*

[34] Miles, R. and Snow, C., Organizations: new concepts for new forms, *California Management Review*, **28**, 1986, 62–73.

[35] Ashkenas *et al.*, 1995, *op. cit.*

[36] *Ibid.*

[37] *Ibid.*

[38] El Sawy, O., Malhotra, A., Gosain, S. and Young, K.M., IT-intensive value innovation in the electronic economy: insights from Marshall Industries, *MIS Quarterly*, **23**(3), September 1999, 310.

[39] Quinn, J.B., Baruch, J.J. and Zien, K.A. (eds.), Beyond teams: independent collaboration, in *Innovation Explosion: Using Intellect and Software to Revolutionize Growth Strategies*, New York, NY: The Free Press, 1997, pp. 107–140.

[40] Ostrofsky, K., Mrs. Fields' Cookies, Harvard Business School, Case #9-189-056, September 14, 1993.

[41] El Sawy *et al.*, 1999, *op. cit.*

[42] Hammer, M. and Champy, J., *Reengineering the Corporation, A Manifesto for Business Revolution*, New York, NY: Harper Business, 1993.

[43] Ashkenas *et al.*, 1995, *op. cit.*

[44] Hammer, M. and Stanton, S., How process entreprises really work, *Harvard Business Review*, **77**(6), 1999, 108–118.

[45] *Ibid.*

[46] Ashkenas *et al.*, 1995, *op. cit.*

[47] *Ibid.*

[48] Rockart, J. and Short, J., 1991, *op. cit.*

[49] Magretta, J., The power of virtual integration: an interview with Dell Computer's Michael Dell, *Harvard Business Review*, March–April 1998, 73–84.

[50] Magretta, 1998, *op. cit.*, p. 75.

[51] Galbraith, J.R., 1995, *op. cit.*

[52] Miles, R. and Snow, C., Organizations: new concepts for new forms, *California Management Review*, **28**, 1986, 62–73.

[53] Miles, R.E. and Snow, C.C., Causes of failure in network organizations, *California Management Review*, **34**(4), Summer 1992, 57.

[54] Tapscott, 2000, *op. cit.*

[55] Apgar, M., The alternative workplace: changing where and how people work, *Harvard Business Review*, May–June 1998, 121–136.

[56] *Ibid.*

[57] Galal, H., *Verifone: The Transaction Automation Company (A)*, Harvard Business School, Case #9-195-088, July 12, 1995.

[58] Pape, W.R., Becoming a virtual company, *Inc*, **17**(17), 1995, 29–31.

[59] Davenport, T.H. and Pearlson, K., Two cheers for the virtual office, *Sloan Management Review*, Summer 1998, 51–65.

[60] Flynn, G., An ad agency pitches for the virtual office, *Workforce*, **76**(11), November 1997, 56–63.

[61] Examples of studies include: Brown, D., Telework not meeting expectations – but expectations were "nonsense", *Canadian HR Reporter*, **16**(4), 3, 11; Whithouse, G., Diamond, C. and Lafferty, G., Assessing the benefits of telework: Australian case study evidence, *New Zealand Journal of Industrial Relations*, **27**(3), October 2002, 257–268.

[62] Niles, J.M., *Managing Telework: Strategies for Managing the Virtual Workforce*, New York, NY: John Wiley & Sons, Inc., 1998.

[63] Dubé, L. and Paré, G., The multifaceted nature of virtual teams (Chapter 1), in D.J. Pauleen (ed.), *Virtual Teams: Projects, Protocols and Processes*, Idea Group Inc., 2004, 1–39.

[64] Townsend, A.M., DeMarie, S.M. and Hendrickson, A.R., Virtual teams: technology and the workplace of the future, *The Academy of Management Executive*, **12**(3), August 1998, 17–29.

[65] Townsend *et al.* 1998, *op. cit.*, p. 22.

[66] Geber, B., Virtual teams, *Training*, **32**(4), 36–42.

[67] Dubé, L. and Paré, G., Global virtual teams, *Communications of the ACM*, **44**(12), December 2001, 71–73.

[68] Ashkenas *et al.*, 1995, *op. cit.*

[69] *Ibid.*

Chapter 4

The information technology piece

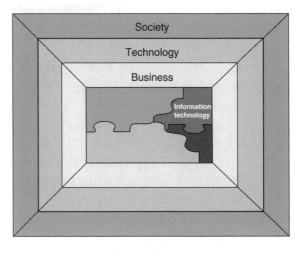

So much has been written about information technology (IT) in the past few years, it would be truly astonishing *not* to find a manager who was confused about this piece of the puzzle. Writers always seem to be predicting that organizations will be fundamentally transformed by technology and that they must adopt these new forms of IT at once or be doomed to failure.[1] But neither the technology nor the process of change is simple and most researchers have found that there is no one-to-one correspondence between the IT an organization uses (or invests in) and its impact. In other words, IT is only part of the puzzle. It is not solely the initial determinant of what the business will look like or do, nor is it always a response to the shape of the other pieces. Instead, it interacts with those pieces to create something that is unique to a particular organization.

The IT piece has several dimensions that all managers need to understand, not only to use IT effectively, but also to ensure that

Table 4.1
The dimensions of the IT piece

IT strategy development	IT as a competitive weapon
As a support to business strategy	Creating virtual value
Interactive with business strategy	Leveraging customer relationships
Vectors of virtuality	Customization of products and services
	Creating new organizational roles and market structures
	Leveraging intellectual assets
IT as a transformational tool	**The IS organization**
Process redesign	Strategy execution
Improved coordination	IS skills
Improved collaboration	IS processes
Improved information use	IT architecture
Improved research and learning	IS flexibility

the other pieces of the management puzzle are selected and assembled appropriately. The first is IT strategy and how an organization develops it. A second dimension explores how IT is used within an organization to transform it. Third, is IT used as a competitive weapon in the marketplace. The fourth dimension applies to IT internal structure, namely how IT organizes itself to execute its own activities within the enterprise. Table 4.1 summarizes these dimensions.

IT strategy development

It should not come as a surprise that a shift is taking place in how IT is viewed in organizations. IT has become a competitive necessity, essential to the survival of virtually every enterprise.[2] This shift is paralleled by a change of focus within the information systems (IS) department from a primarily internal orientation to a strategic one.[3] Today, IT not only supports the structure and functions of an organization, it has also become a critical component of business strategy. As IT has the potential to change how firms compete, it can completely change how markets and industries function.[4] Furthermore, within organizations themselves, IT is rapidly expanding from a backroom resource to a front office competitive weapon for marketing and sales.[5] In short, IT will never again be an afterthought that is applied *after* the enterprise's strategy is formed and its processes designed.

A very good example of an industry changed by technology is the banking industry. Twenty years ago, banks were managing money (bills and coins), financial documents, and all these had to be secured physically. They dealt with their clients face to face, or through the intermediary of paper, bonds, coupons, certificates, checks, and so on. Now, banks are managing information. Their documents are virtual and their security is concerned with access to networks and servers. They deal with their clients and with other banks electronically, exchanging data with all of them, without the support of paper.

The industry is changed in every aspect of the business. Tasks are different, rules are different, key elements leading to strategic advantage are different. Location went from being a strategic advantage to a disadvantage. Banks now consider their imposing buildings as liabilities. These former images of stability are useless in the new marketspace.

However, although the Gartner Group predicts that by 2003, the primary competitive differentiator of enterprises will be that they are enabled by IT, our current models of developing IT strategy are "woefully inadequate" to meet the challenges of the information age.[6] In fact, one of the main obstacles for obtaining the full value of IT in an organization is that most managers still think about IT as an investment with limited implications outside traditional cost-cutting impact. They do not yet have a clear idea of the role of IT in increasing organizational effectiveness or facilitating business transformation.[7]

There are two ways of viewing IT strategy development: IT as a support to business strategy, and IT as a critical driver of business transformation.

IT as a support to business strategy

The traditional view of IT is as a support to the organization which can help make a firm's performance faster, cheaper, and more accurate. This perspective sees IT strategy development as a separate activity from business strategy development and as responsive to both business strategies and processes.[8] From this point of view, business strategy is clearly the driver of the organization and the role of IS management is that of strategy implementer. That is, IT strategy is about selecting the best technology to effect business strategy. Managers must then design and implement the necessary infrastructure and processes to do this efficiently and effectively.[9] For example, when you implement a track-and-trace system to optimize your routing and delivery times in a courier company, you may reduce your costs and increase the quality of your service. This may improve your strategic positioning. However, the sole implementation of this system does not change the rules of the industry.

However, if the organization wishes to transform the way it does business – either internally or externally – then this approach to IT strategy will be inadequate because it severely constrains the possibilities of what IT can accomplish for an organization.

IT as a critical driver of business strategy

A newer way to view IT strategy, therefore, is to see it as a critical driver of business transformation.[10] Since IT has the potential to change both how a business works internally and to identify new ways of competing, this perspective argues that IT strategy must be equal to or even sometimes become the driver of business strategy.[11] It suggests that neither business nor IT strategy should always be considered dominant, rather that the links between the two should be dynamic, so as to allow the firm to continually assess trends in both areas and position itself appropriately in the external environment. Henderson and Venkatraman write: "The potential for IT impact is so varied and complex that the executive must consider these perspectives as alternative conceptual lenses and be prepared to continuously make adaptations."[12]

Going back to the track-and-trace system described earlier, a strategic change could be induced by integrating the system with a wider range of applications, as many courier companies (such as Fedex and UPS) have already started doing. First, by making the system available to clients on the web, they can let the client enter the details of the delivery and print the bar code immediately (see http://www.fedex.com/us/). In doing so, they transfer former employee activities to their clients. The clients are also happy because this self-service enables them to get the service when and where they want. Integration can be extended further by linking the system to the client's systems. When the client's products are ready for delivery, a signal is sent to the courier firm. The finished product, already provided with its bar code, is taken by the courier company when exiting the production line. The track-and-trace system warns the intended recipient that its order is on the way. On delivery, another signal is sent to the producer, conforming delivery. By automating the exchanges linked to the courier service, the courier company becomes virtually integrated with its commercial partners and creates barriers to new entrants.

Virtuality vectors affecting strategy

Today, the main thrust of a transforming IT strategy is to make an organization more "virtual." This means using information and technology as substitutes for people, places, activities, and objects. While this term is often used to suggest the appearance of an organization which, while appearing to be a company to customers, is actually a collection of different resources, the concept of "virtualness" can be applied much more broadly. It is, in reality, a strategic characteristic applicable to many parts of an organization. Virtualness provides a guide and context for designing IT strategy for a twenty-first century enterprise.[13] There are three distinct, yet interdependent, vectors of virtualness which, together, can fundamentally change what an organization does and how it does it. Each places IT at its center, giving IT strategy an important role in designing the core elements of any business.

Electronic retailers, such as amazon.com, are already using IT to customize their offerings and advice to each customer. Small details such as these increase customer loyalty. With fidelity programs and a simple computer system, hotels, such as Delta (www.deltahotels.ca), instantly recognize their customers. They know what type of room the client prefers, which configuration is favored, what newspaper should be delivered, etc., without having to ask the client a single question. This enables them to give perfect service to each client, even if the client is a first-time guest at that specific Delta hotel.

Customer interaction

This vector of virtualness deals with company-to-customer interactions. IT enables customers to experience products and services differently than in the past. At its simplest level, virtualization along this vector enables customers to experience products and services remotely, e.g. real-time monitoring of stock portfolios or online shopping. More complex applications of virtualness enable customers to customize products and services dynamically and to create virtual communities of customers. Today, many companies are actively trying to build remote experiences for their customers and the Gartner Group estimates that in 2003, 70 percent of enterprises in many leading industries will be competing on their ability to customize their products and services. Other strategic aspects of this vector include: creating mechanisms to provide sales and service to customers 24 h a day, 7 days a week; enabling companies to interact virtually with customers at a variety of levels; and developing a philosophy of dealing with customer communities.

Business network

A second vector focuses on building a business network to support the organization, rather than having all functions performed within the enterprise. IT is used for business-to-business transactions to enable a company to build a portfolio of relationships which can assemble and coordinate assets for delivering value to customers. Initially, a company's usual strategy is to try and determine what assets it can obtain from outside without a loss of competitive advantage (i.e. outsourcing). As it matures along this vector, however, a firm may begin to integrate its business processes with those of its partners. Finally, it may develop resource coalitions, which actually blur the boundaries of the enterprise by integrating a number of partners across a value chain. Michael Dell of Dell Computer calls this a "direct business model." He explains that whereas in the past companies have had massive structures to produce everything that was needed for a product, this new method of asset configuration enables companies to focus on how to coordinate activities in ways which will create the most value for a customer.[14] These networks are everywhere. The two airline groups, One World and Star Alliance, provide seamless service to their customers, integrate facilities, and enable clients to deal with all the companies of the group as if they were dealing with only one company.

Knowledge leverage

A third vector of virtualness focuses on opportunities for leveraging expertise within and outside of the organization. Managing information, knowledge, and intellectual assets effectively is a huge challenge for organizations these days.[15] Companies need to be able to identify their assets in this area and find ways to collect, access, and link them in order to leverage what they know, first within work groups, and then across the organization, and with partners. Knowledge needs to be managed in such a way as to increase the capabilities of the individuals and functions of an organization. It should also be used to develop timely and accurate business intelligence about customers and markets and as a base for the creation of new products, services, channels, and products.[16] For example, at Dell Computer information is used as a substitute for inventory to reduce the physical cost of shipping goods. It is also used to look at individual business units, geographic regions, and customer groups to enable the company to develop a deeper understanding of its customers and find ways to identify opportunities and economies unique to customer groups and to forecast demand.

In each of these vectors, IT is creating new capabilities for organizations, enabling them to work in new ways, and gain a better understanding of their markets and customers. A common technology platform and two-way information links are key to all of these strategies. In this way, companies are also using IT to create new roles for themselves, such as becoming value-adding intermediaries. Finally, managers can manage their businesses differently by using IT to monitor key metrics, and to enhance and improve organizational effectiveness continually.

The capabilities of current technology mean that managers can use it for more than simply improving organizational productivity. Therefore, today, IT strategy means understanding how technology can be effectively integrated into business strategy to create new opportunities and possibilities for an organization. IT strategy development is thus the outcome of a *dialogue* between business needs and technology potential. It identifies a combination of products and services unique to an organization which, ideally, will lead to a sustainable advantage over its competition and facilitate new ways of working within the organization which make it possible. The next two sections examine these two aspects of IT strategy in more detail.

IT as a transformational tool

It is widely accepted that IT plays an important role in organization change – that it can make business processes more efficient, work groups more effective, and enable more effective decisions to be made. However, there is little agreement on exactly how IT should do this and which key technologies are involved. A review of the available material on how IT is being used to transform organizations suggests that there are atleast four different ways this can be done.

Process redesign

In recent years, a great deal of attention has been paid to how IT can radically change business processes. Often called reengineering or business process redesign (BPR), IT is an essential element of this type of transformation because it permits removal of redundant steps, interconnects work as it is being accomplished, and removes constraints from where it can be located. As part of process redesign, IT makes information and knowledge more available to others in the organization and connects workers and information across organizational boundaries.

Process redesign is likely to lead to changes in structure and decision-making. Research suggests that there is no single direction on how IT will affect work.[17] However, process redesign with IT makes new ways of work possible, practical and frees organizations to make design decisions based on what is most important to them, rather than on spatial, functional, or temporal considerations. For example, since work no longer has to be organized around functions, IT can enable new structures to be created focusing around products, services, and clients. Similarly, when workers have access to the same information as their boss, there is much more scope in how and where decisions can be made. As IT can connect people across organization levels and traditional boundaries, decisions no longer have to be made in local offices or headquarters for the sake of expediency or control. Instead, they can be made where they make the most sense. In some cases, expert systems can be used to guide decisions.

Improved coordination

IT can be used to support or enable coordination between autonomous business units or partners. This is especially important for global or multinational firms. IT coordination can often be used as a substitute for more formal structures.[18] As a result, it enables businesses to organize themselves in radically different ways. Many companies are now experimenting with different forms of coordination using IT. For example, some firms are focusing on efficiency, and are taking a highly centralized approach to managing operations, no matter where they are located. Others are developing networked regional units to increase their responsiveness to local conditions. Still others are emphasizing the transfer of knowledge between business units.[19] Technology is used as the "glue" to link organizational units in a logical fashion. In short, because it transcends geographical boundaries and can facilitate coordination in a virtual, rather than a hands-on fashion, IT can be used to develop a variety of innovative organizational designs, which would not have been possible without it.

Enterprise resources planning (ERP) systems are great facilitators in that they enable many units to share information about every single activity of the company in real time. They improve coordination and support all processes. These systems link all units and ensure that information entered anywhere in the organization is taken into account everywhere else in the operations and in their management.

Customer relationship management (CRM) systems are also contributing to increased coordination. By supporting all the activities associated with the interactions with the customers, they ensure that all the information is available, and that all actions taken by any member of the organization with respect to a client is traced and known to someone subsequently dealing with the same client. Therefore, the client gets personalized service and seamless interaction with the organization.

Improved collaboration

IT enables work and workers to be interconnected in a variety of ways, thus facilitating new ways of working together. Internetworking and groupware promote communication and information sharing across hierarchical, departmental, and organizational boundaries. Software also enables people to work together in teams without being in the same location. IT can support the use of dispersed work teams and enable parallel task execution and learning from the expertise of others. Language translation software can be used to help team members who do not share the same linguistic backgrounds to work together effectively.[20] While none of these is a complete solution to virtual collaboration, the fact remains that with IT, collaboration across distance and culture is rapidly becoming easier.

This easy collaboration across boundaries and continents is in evidence with the offshore outsourcing market. Companies locate their activities without being constrained to remain on one continent. Firms such as Tata, in India, have become major players in the IT field, offering their services to a multitude of clients all over the world. SAP, a German software company, is another example. Its customer service is scattered on three different continents. One office is in Germany, one in California, and the third in India. When a customer calls, the call is directed to one of the three sites, depending on the hour of the day (the sites are conveniently located in complementary time zones). It does not matter which center takes the call. All of them will have information about the client and its system, and will be able to log directly onto the client's system to handle the call. The service is totally transparent for the client.

However, all forms of technology are not equal, nor can they always be substituted for all forms of personal interaction. A key management skill is the ability to understand the strengths and weaknesses of each collaboration medium. Some media will work for some tasks and not for others. For example, while teleconferencing or videoconferencing are much richer than asynchronous media such as e-mail, they require high levels of commitment, flexibility, and discipline on the part of several team members. In addition, open standards, reliability, and accessibility in technology are all fundamental to the effective use of IT for collaboration.[21] Finally, collaborative technology must be designed to be extremely robust. It must be able to deal with a constant churn of participants who have varying degrees of technological sophistication, and it must provide considerable functionality to make learning its application worthwhile.[22]

Improved information use

IT can give organizations a clearer understanding of their own business. It can provide them with a comprehensive picture of their organizational dynamics and help managers find a variety of ways to improve the operations of their business. There are four key ways in which IT can be used to do this:[23]

1   *Information access*: IT can provide detailed information on every aspect of a business' value chain. This information can be used to improve decision-making, predict demand more effectively, manage inventory more efficiently, and become more responsive to external market needs.

2   *Information management*: Information can be structured around the stable elements of a business (e.g. customers, suppliers, and products), and stored in a data warehouse, thereby allowing flexibility of use. Technology can also be used to integrate data from a variety of sources and provide both predictable and one-off business information for managers.

3   *Communications management*: IT can provide a corporate-wide network accessible to all employees, thereby giving them access to the information they need, when and where they need it. The advent of wireless devices is making this a greater presence in the field. Mobile communications enable more up-to-date data collection and provide staff with the information they need to make on-the-spot decisions.

4   *Presentations*: Finally, tools and templates can be used to provide user-friendly and graphic representations of information, thus facilitating improved understanding of trends and providing key metrics needed to manage the business.[24]

Improved research and learning

IT can also transform both how organizations develop and bring to market new products, and how they learn new things. Software is especially being used to transform companies' innovation processes. Every aspect of research and development – from basic to applied research, and design and engineering – can be affected. By eliminating steps in the innovation process, enabling others to be performed simultaneously, and providing a disciplined framework for complex team interactions, technology is rapidly reducing the time and cost it takes to bring a product to market. IT also facilitates experimentation and can identify subtle trends as potential problems or opportunities long before personal observation might do so. Finally, IT enables the diffusion of knowledge across a much wider area than in the past and ensures that it is transferred with higher accuracy, greater consistency and more performance reliability. In short, technology is becoming essential for organizational learning and innovation diffusion.

Boeing was able to develop the new Boeing 767 virtually, relying on computer models instead of building a series of physical prototypes as they had done in the past. In the development process, all engineers and researchers had access to the information linked with all the teams participating in the development. When a change was made, every sub-team affected was warned and could react accordingly. This enabled faster development, with fewer costly errors and greater product integrity.

Software can also enable innovations which would not otherwise have been possible.[25]As a result, managing innovation and learning software has become much more important to organizations. Managers must ensure that effective interfaces are in place so systems can work together and users can access data for their particular purposes. Overall, care must be taken to ensure that software used for innovation does not impose its own limitations on what can be done.

Taken together, these changes show that IT can dramatically transform how organizations work. However, it should be noted that technology alone does not make changes. Managers must thoroughly understand what they are trying to accomplish with technology, in order to use it effectively. Today, there are any number of organizations with a plethora of IS which have had little impact, and only a few which have a productive information environment.[26] Managers are only just beginning to realize that the effective use of IT to drive organizational transformation depends as much on the organizational context as it does on technology. Thus, today, many organizations are finding that "people issues" such as values, culture, behavior, and politics are playing a large role in how well technology is used. Managers should, therefore, be aware that if they are to use technology effectively, they must see it as part of a much larger strategy for transforming their businesses and ensure that incentives, behaviors, and culture are all consistent with what the technology is being designed to accomplish.[27]

IT as a competitive weapon

A third dimension of the IT piece is its use as a competitive weapon. Today, IT is a critical lever differentiating a business from its competitors.[28] A firm able to leverage technology differently, and exploit its functionality continuously, will be in a very strong strategic position in the marketplace. For example, in many companies, IT is frequently the main mechanism through which product options are created or customization is enabled.[29] Thus, IT is often the means whereby a competitive business strategy is carried out. As noted above, it is also an instrument for the creation of business strategies, such as developing new opportunities or markets, which could not exist without IT support. There are several ways in which IT can be used as a strategic weapon in the marketplace.

Creating virtual value

The existence of a virtual value chain parallel to an organization's physical value chain was mentioned in Chapter 1. Traditionally, information has been treated as a supporting element of value rather than as a source of value in and of itself. Increasingly, however, companies are coming to see that there are opportunities for creating and extracting value from this information, apart from the physical goods and services with which it is associated. Just as a physical value chain takes raw material and refines it into something useful, a virtual value chain collects raw information from each stage in the physical value chain and refines it into something that is valuable to a company in and of itself. The following example illustrates the distinction between the two types of value:

> When consumers use answering machines to store their phone messages, they are using objects made and sold in the physical world, but when they purchase electronic answering services from their local phone companies, they are utilizing the virtual marketspace.[30]

Most companies must operate in both the physical and the virtual worlds. Thus, while they continue to oversee a physical value chain, managers may also decide to build and exploit a virtual value chain. The processes for creating and extracting value are different in each sphere and managers need to understand both.

The interplay between these two worlds is also crucial. This requires managing them not only as distinct entities – because the economies of each are different – but also in concert, because information from the physical world is a potential source of new revenue for the company.[31]

Mobile telephone companies, such as Vodafone (www.vodafone. com.au), provide web site services to complement and extend their mobile phone services, linking their telephones with e-mail systems, short message service (SMS), and other features. This increases the value of the Vodafone offering.

Leveraging customer relationships

Technology can be used not only to better leverage a company's information, it can also be used to develop better and longer-term relationships with its customers. Using this strategy, companies aim to grow the "mindshare" of their customers through personal communications and ongoing interactions with their customers. IT is integral to this strategy because relationship management involves learning about customers and customizing marketing. Moon writes:

> The key to any successful relationship marketing program is information. The better information that a firm has about a particular customer, the more value that firm will potentially be able to provide that customer … this doesn't necessarily mean "more" information, rather information that is accurate, timely, and relevant.[32]

This information must be built up slowly over time and over multiple interactions. It enables a company to identify different customers' needs and their value to the firm, thereby allowing the company to focus its efforts appropriately.

Ideally, a company should aim for "one-to-one" marketing, whereby customers constitute a market segment of one individual. This type of marketing involves three things: creating what customers want (customization); remembering what they want; and anticipating what they want.[33] IT can be especially effective in the last two steps. Ultimately, this cycle of learning about customers, understanding their needs, and customizing marketing creates a relationship between a customer and a business, which gets smarter and smarter with each individual interaction. As a result, it is in both parties' interest to continue the relationship, and it becomes very difficult for another firm to duplicate the personalization offered.

Customization of products and services

Customization is now a clearly established business trend and is expected to be an important frontier of business competition over the next 5 years. As noted above, this is part of a trend towards increasingly virtual interaction with customers. Ultimately this will lead to the interactive development of products and services with customers in real time, and the birth of virtual customer communities, according to Henderson and Venkatraman,[34] whose three principle of customization are mentioned below.

Customization is based on three principles:

1   *reuse*: by partitioning a product or service into independent components, it is possible to reuse them to construct customized products;
2   *intelligence*: customization must be built on information about customers needs;
3   *organization*: businesses must be designed to deliver products on a dynamic and adaptive basis.

Together, these principles allow companies to achieve flexibility, responsiveness to changing needs, short product lifecycles, and short development cycles. Companies can customize their goods and services in five different ways that involve IT in some way:[35]

1   *customization of standard products and services*: they are based on remembered customer preferences, e.g. preferences for hotel services;
2   *creation of customizable products and services*: they can be adapted to individual customer preferences, e.g. personalized Internet search services;
3   *point of delivery customization*: a product is produced at the point of sale, as directed by the customer, e.g. onsite insurance claims adjustments;
4   *quick response*: enables a value chain to react rapidly to customer requests, e.g. tracking changes in fashion;
5   *modularization*: makes it possible for individual units to be used to create a variety of customized products and

services, e.g. creating benefits modules so employees can build their own benefits packages.

IT can also be useful in helping companies tailor customer communications, offer new distribution channels for products and services, and provide personalized pricing.

Creating new organizational roles and market structures

New technologies create new opportunities to capture economic value.[36] One of the key ways they do this is by changing the costs involved in a particular type of transaction, thus making new types of value integration more economically feasible. As noted above, the new economics of transactions are leading to the breakdown (disaggregation) of traditional organizational forms into their component pieces and the recreation of firms (reaggregation) in ways, which will provide new value for customers. This will ultimately lead to the creation of networks of companies linked by IT which will parcel out the elements of value creation and delivery to an optimal set of partners. These networks will be characterized by close integration of information and a reliance on network communications and standards which enable firms to operate effectively together. New opportunities will come about through participation in these networks and the new roles that businesses play in them. Some companies will act as network leaders; others will focus on value integration, collecting information from others, and adding value to create new products and services.

These groups are currently being formed. In the AOL-Time Warner merger, the acquisition of Videotron by Quebecor, or the purchase of CTV by Bell Canada, content providers and data carriers are placing their pieces on the chess board, forging alliances and planning their strategy.

Network structures will transform how companies compete against and cooperate with one another.[37] By their very nature they will be considerably more fluid than traditional organizations. The key to making them work is the ability to share knowledge and to work together in real time.

Leveraging intellectual assets

The ownership of intellectual assets can be a starting point for competitive strategy decisions.[38] As we discussed earlier, knowledge is one of the key vectors affecting the virtuality of an organization. It enables several strategic initiatives. The recent decision by the U.S. Patent Office to allow patents of methods of doing business for IT applications has opened whole new avenues of competition for firms. For example, amazon.com recently successfully sued Barnes and Noble for copying its "one-click" method of customer check-out. Patenting new ideas for doing business online considerably broadens the concept of intellectual property rights and gives companies a significant competitive weapon. Not only can they prevent rivals from copying simple customer interfaces, they can also license these assets and hence gain a new source of revenue. They may also wish to patent intellectual assets as a defensive strategy to use if and when other companies wish to prevent them from using a particular method of doing business.

In addition to the increasing value of owning intellectual assets, companies need to understand how to manage them effectively. Classical market structures do not work well with information, and companies need to realize that information products and services generate value differently.[39] For example, information is an experience good, which means that branding and reputation are important. Thus, a distinctive appearance and logos take on increasing importance in a knowledge-intensive environment. Technology is a key feature of all information products because it is the packaging of the product. IT also enables a company to present information in different ways so it can do more with the same information. As Shapiro writes, "Content providers cannot operate without infrastructure suppliers and vice versa. The information economy is about information and the associated technology."[40]

In order to manage information assets effectively, managers must understand whether or not there are complementary products which will help the market grow more quickly. They must understand the role of timing and technology compatibility in how quickly they introduce new information products. They also need to understand the costs of switching from one technology to another and how to differentiate versions of the same information goods. Finally, they must recognize that price structures must be set according to the value the consumer places on the product, not on the cost to produce it. Overall, there are a significant number of strategic decisions, which must be made about information goods and their associated technologies in order for a company to maximize the value of its intellectual property.

The use of IT as a competitive weapon reinforces the fact that there are complex interconnections between business and IT strategy. While in some cases, it may be best to follow the classical "business strategy drives IT strategy" model, in many others IT strategy or opportunities will be the drivers of business strategy. Good business and IT managers clearly can no longer afford to work separately on strategy. Instead, they must seek to understand what each brings to the table and find ways to communicate with one another in order to develop a single integrated strategy for moving the organization forward in the external marketplace.

IS organization

The fourth dimension of the IT piece is the one which most managers have traditionally associated with IT: the internal IS organization which actually delivers IT to the rest of the firm. IS' ability to deliver the strategies, systems, and technology to the enterprise is a key element of this piece. Without it, IT cannot be used effectively to support or transform a business or to be a competitive weapon. An effective internal IS organization must manage several key elements. The technology itself is very briefly described. The elements that the organization has to master follow this description.

The technology

Every time we refer to IT, we refer to a vast array of elements, most of them interconnected in various ways. These elements include hardware, software, networks, the Internet, communication equipment, and services. While a detailed description of the technology is beyond the scope of this book, the main components are described very briefly in the following paragraphs.

Hardware

The hardware category comprises all the physical equipments used to process and transmit information: computers, screens, printers, and cables. The main component is, of course, the computer itself. From a bulky ENIAC, 150 ft long and 10 ft wide, able to process 5000 operations per second, computers have evolved to smaller, more efficient, and much cheaper machines. Computers are currently classified into three categories: mainframes, minis, and micros. These categories are getting blurred, since the smaller minis currently sold can outpace the fastest mainframes produced 5 years ago. One thing is very stable: computers process data, and do so at an ever-increasing speed. Mainframes and minis are designed to be used by several users at the same time. Microcomputers (commonly called PCs) are designed to be used by a single user.

Architecture

At a very technical level, many configurations can be observed when using computers. In stand-alone modes (often used for a PC), computers are used by one user at a time, and are not linked to other systems. In shared modes, computers (often mainframes and minis) are used simultaneously by several users, but are not linked to other systems. Client–server configuration has become increasingly popular. In client–server configuration, many computers (usually PC) are linked to a server (usually a mini or a mainframe). The latter provides all the data that has to be shared between users. Since the wide acceptance of Internet standards (1995 and later), client–server has evolved into web architecture. Instead of linking clients and servers in a closed environment, many clients and servers are loosely connected. They exchange the required information using the Internet. Most of the time, the interface (the software used to communicate with the system) is simply a web browser.

Appliances

In the last decade, many peripherals have appeared. They are bar code readers, Palm pilots, intelligent cellular phones, and other new "gadgets." These appliances can send and receive data from the traditional systems, enabling mobile workers to stay connected at all times.

Software

For any computer to be used, software is required. The software is the set of programs that makes it possible to use a computer.

Operating systems like Windows 2000 or Linux are software. Spreadsheets or accounting systems are also software, as are e-mail programs, and ERP systems such as SAP or PeopleSoft. Software has evolved tremendously, taking advantage of the advances made in hardware. Among the applications that are affecting the organizations the most, we can note the following:

- *ERP systems (SAP, PeopleSoft, etc.)*: These systems support all the business activities of the organization. They enable firms to streamline processes and to share information among organization members and units in an unprecedented manner.
- *CRM systems (Siebel, SAP, etc.)*: These systems support all the interactions with the client. CRM is the combination of sales force automation and customer support and service. It combines database technology, interactivity (web sites, call centers, etc.), and mass customization.
- *E-commerce software*: This category includes all the order processing software, payment servers, and delivery servers that enable different organizations to exchange information instantly, without human intervention, and to coordinate their activities as tightly as if they were one single organization.

Integration

Probably the most fascinating development of the last 10 years is not the individual development of any single technology or software – it is the level of integration. Components of computer systems, telephone systems, telecommunication devices, and even entertainment appliances are now able to exchange information. This creates tremendous changes. This convergence is partly due to the wide adoption of TCP/IP protocol for communications and the switch from analog information storage and transmission to digital in all fields. Years ago, most computers and appliances were operating in closed environments. This is no longer the case. Any company developing a IT component thinks about how it will be connected to the exterior world, whether through a high-speed network, telephone line, cell phone network, or any other means. It is now increasingly difficult to establish the frontier between data networks, computer systems, or telephone networks. Convergence melts all these components into a larger, integrated system.

Strategy execution

Although IT strategy *development* has become a much more inter-active process, IT is not a competitive "silver bullet." As with business strategy, an effective IT strategy includes two important aspects: formulation and execution. The internal IS organization is essential to the effective delivery of an IT strategy. As Sauer and Yetton points out, "IT will only provide sustainable competitive advantage when the organization has the distinctive ability to use it. What counts is ... the organization's cleverness in working with IT."[41] Therefore, IT strategy must be developed in a way that is consistent with a firm's ability to use it effectively.

This ability depends on a variety of conditions being in place, so that a company can take advantage of what technology has to offer. IS organizations have a responsibility to ensure that these conditions exist. Research over the past 20 years has consistently shown that it is not technology in and of itself which makes the difference to an organization's competitive position. To have a significant impact, IT strategy must be coupled with three organizational conditions, which are necessary to implement it effectively:[42]

1 *top management orientation*: senior managers must be educated in technical topics;
2 *project selection criteria*: companies must have a clear strategic direction and ability to choose projects which focus on key areas;
3 *systems and structure*: there should be a close connection between technology and business decision-making and the necessary structure for making these decisions.

In short, IS organizations must ensure that business processes and structures and IS processes and structures work together for IT strategy to be effective.[43]

IS skills

While most managers consider IS skills to be technical in nature, a broad range of technical, managerial, and political skills are, in fact, needed in IS to plan, acquire, develop, implement, operate, and control IT. Research shows that there is a clear association between a firm's IS management competencies and its success in deploying IT in support of its business strategies and work processes.[44] Management skills also contribute to a firm's ability to apply IT in an effective, efficient, and timely manner. In short, IS skills convert the "raw materials" of data, technology, business knowledge, and knowledge of how to apply IT, into new products and services, transformed business processes, enriched organizational intelligence, and flexible organization structures.

There are 10 IS management competencies which are relatively stable, regardless of technology and other environmental changes, and which represent the extent to which a company is positioned to mobilize its IT assets and investments.[45,46] Some are at the individual level, while others are organizational competencies:

1 *Business deployment*: These capabilities enable managers to explore the potential business value of new IT, develop effective working relationships between business and IS staff, create useful IT measurement systems and make appropriate IT sourcing decisions.

2 *External networking*: These are competencies in developing value-adding partnerships with a variety of external IT partners including customers, suppliers, vendors, and competitors.

3 *Line technology leadership*: These competencies represent IS' ability to cultivate a willingness among non-IT business managers to own and champion IT-based business initiatives. Line managers have to get involved in IT selection and implementation. For example, implementing an order system without the input and guidance of the sales department would most probably lead to an ill-defined system. While IS personnel and consultants will provide technical guidance and business knowledge, they must count on the involvement of line managers.

4 *Process adaptiveness*: These develop the organization's ability to restructure its business processes and understand the potential of IT to transform them.

5 *IT planning*: These capabilities provide a clear vision about the contributions of IT investments to business value and enable the integration of business and IT plans.

6 *IT infrastructure*: These competencies enable a firm to devise, implement and maintain a sound technology framework. A firm does not have to own its architecture,

nor to operate it itself. However, the array of telecommunications, data processing, and networking needs has to be available and smoothly running. The organization has to keep the ability to define this architecture and to modify it at will.

7 *Data center utility*: These are the capabilities involved in building, maintaining, and securing a firm's information processing facilities.

8 *Change management*: Many IT specialists have only a limited understanding of what it takes to facilitate organizational change. They frequently assume that technology itself *does* all the work of change instead of focusing on the broader social and organizational success factors, which are necessary to facilitate change. To promote organizational transformation, IT specialists must have the skills to facilitate and create organizational change. These skills extend far beyond the traditional technical responsibilities of IS staff.[47]

9 *Staff recruitment and retention*: In the current competitive market for IS staff, companies cannot acquire the skills they need to implement IT effectively, unless they develop competitive competencies in recruiting and retaining technical staff. Some of these include: a means of developing innovative benefits and compensation; a well-defined recruitment process; a commitment to training; hiring networks; skills management; and professional challenges and advancement.[48]

10 *Resource brokering*: IS organizations also need to develop skills in brokering resources. Increasingly, IT is being implemented through a wide variety of in-house staff, consultants, outsourcers, vendors, and long-term partners. Organizations will need strong skills in learning how and when to use each type of resource effectively, which need to be retained in-house and which can best be managed by others. These decisions will play a key role in IS' capabilities, flexibility, and effectiveness and will thus have a direct impact on the organization's ability to use IT.

Developing a platform of these managerial capabilities within an IS organization is recognized as an important step towards developing competitive agility.

IS processes

IS processes not only transform business processes and strategies, they are also frequently in need of transformation themselves. Over the past decade many IS organizations have recognized that they need to change to keep up with organizational needs.[49] There are two "meta-processes" within IS which need to be thought through and designed carefully to ensure their optimal functioning in concert with organizational needs. They are: how the organization is supplied with IT services and operations; and how application requirements and opportunities are identified. Organizations must focus on both these sets of processes in order to be effective.

There are four stages of transforming IS processes to make them more compatible with current business needs.[50]

1 *Question*: Managers need to question the value of IT and the IS functions in their organization. This involves recognizing the discontinuities between current IS processes and business needs. What are we doing? How is our current IT strategy supporting the business? How do the links we are fostering with business partners really provide a competitive advantage? These are the types of questions managers have to ask themselves constantly.

2 *Lever the existing organization*: Managers need to find ways to release and realize value from their current organization, i.e. from underemployed, outdated, or unnecessary assets. This could include activities such as rationalizing data structures, pruning the applications portfolio, eliminating redundancies, and consolidating facilities.

3 *Envision*: The third stage involves generating a more visionary direction for IS and focusing on how best to create future value. One of the most effective ways to do this is to articulate and agree on a value model which will guide IS policies, practices and resourcing in each of these processes. An IT value chain helps to clarify the ways in which IT contributes to business value. As Figure 4.1 shows, some IS processes help the business realize value, while others help to create new value.

4 *Sustain*: Finally, stage four emphasizes ways of sustaining value. This could include building partnerships with the business, examining governance structures, defining new skills and roles for IS staff, and generating ideas for

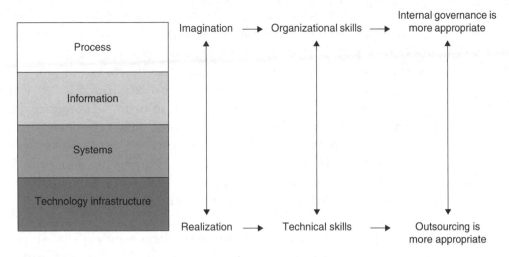

Figure 4.1
An IS value chain.[51]

exploiting IT. This stage should be seen as ongoing with IS continually learning what works and what does not, and processes and practices adapted accordingly.

IT architecture

The term *IT architecture* is often thought of as referring to technical design issues only, and, therefore, of little interest or benefit outside IS. In fact, an architecture for IT must reflect both the needs of business and the current potentialities of IT. Thus, there is a growing trend to reframe IT architecture into *enterprise architecture* to ensure that the joint influences of *both* business and technology are represented in it. IT architecture can be defined as a blueprint for a company's IT. It follows a set of principles, standards, guidelines, and technologies that describe and direct an organization's technology design for the future. It also describes to executives, business managers, IS managers, technical specialists, and vendors, in increasing levels of detail, what needs to be built. The type of business, its geographic layout, its management style, and the nature of its products and services will all affect the type of architecture a business needs, just as the type of function and location of a building dictates the architecture needed in construction. Furthermore, financial considerations, the business' stability, and its relationship to its customers and suppliers will influence the breadth and depth of technology needed. Each of these factors needs to be made explicit, so that IS will be able to properly design the appropriate type of technical architecture needed to support the business.

In addition to a technical view, there are four further views of architecture which IS must consider, in order to generate desired business results.[52] While the technical view of architecture provides the blueprint for hardware, software, and telecommunication elements, extra strata complete the picture. The other views can be seen as extra layers, each one showing the organizational implications of the IT technical architecture.

1   *business view*: a model of the future enterprise, showing it as a series of logical services linking internal and external clients;

2   *work view*: showing who will do what, where, when, and with what tools;

3   *information view*: describing the information requirements of the future organization;

4   *application view*: identifying what applications will support the work of the organization.

Designing an IT architecture is therefore not a formula, but the development of a series of principles and strategies which provide the foundation for building the organization's infrastructure and applications. For example, an important architectural principle should be that it must address the multiple technical environments to be found in their partner and customer organizations.[53]

Architecture must be considered to be a dynamic entity. Without this evolutionary dimension, it will become a static, concrete entity that will either lose its relevance or become a barrier to change. To accomplish this, many firms have established architectural advisory boards, which regularly feed new requirements, criticism, and breakthrough ideas to those responsible for the architecture.[54] It is suggested to have having a Central Architecture Committee composed of users as well as an IT Oversight Committee of IS managers to review new trends and technologies continually from both the business and IT points of view. In addition, one individual must be accountable for maintaining the ongoing integrity of the architecture. An architectural effort, which is continuous and parallel to the business change cycle, is an essential part of maintaining flexibility in IT (see below).

IS flexibility

Flexibility is a watchword for many of today's organizations and technology is a major way they seek to achieve it. While flexibility factors into almost every aspect of IT use in organizations, e.g. strategy, environmental assessment, structure, and leadership, it also applies to technology infrastructures and application architectures. Both must be designed for much greater ease of maintenance and adaptability than in the past, in order to meet the needs of business effectively. Technology based on open standards is increasingly being used to prevent "lock-in" to a particular type of hardware and software. Similarly, applications are increasingly being designed so that many aspects of the process they support can be changed by the users themselves. Internally, standards for the meaning, format and presentation of information are needed, so that applications and information can be integrated and/or easily modified.

IT organizations are building this flexibility in a number of ways. First, they are aligning their strategy development processes more closely with the business' strategic priorities, so they can become more sensitive to business needs. Second, they are looking for ways to balance the centralized guidance of IT and the benefits of shared economies of scale with the "uninhibited and rapid use of IT" often desired by local business units.[55] Third, they are developing ways to balance IT investments in systems which support the business as is and those which transform it to help the business grow and compete in new ways. Fourth, a key element of flexibility is how IS manages its own resources. Increasingly, IS organizations are using packaged software and outside resources (e.g. contractors) to deal with the wide variety of demand for IT from the business. IS' skills as a broker of resources will, therefore, significantly enhance its own abilities to respond to business needs in a flexible fashion. Finally, IS organizations must look inward to their own processes to ensure that they are enabling optimal responsiveness and flexibility of IT services.[56]

Conclusion

The changes taking place today in enterprise strategy, structure, and processes all require the enablement of technology. Building a complete picture of an organization now involves a thorough understanding of IT and its potential, and the impact and influence its different dimensions can have on the other aspects of the enterprise. As a result, IT will never again be an afterthought that is applied after the enterprise's strategy is formed and its processes and structures designed. IT is now an integral piece of the management puzzle which business leaders ignore at their peril.

Questions

1 The next step in IT is embedded technology, invisible, non-intrusive, and totally integrated with our surroundings.
   (a) What will be the new applications generated by embedded technology that will transform our organizations?
   (b) How will we differentiate work and family time once technology will have made our work environment totally portable?

2 IT increases the ease to find products anywhere in the world. At the same time, it enables companies to increase the value they provide to their customers by personalizing their offering. The first effect should lower fidelity while the second one increases it.
   (a) What are the key factors that support each effect?
   (b) In what types of market each effect is more likely to prevail?

3 How do managers evaluate technology in a context where change is constant but inter-connectivity is critical (and has to be planned for long-term relationships with business partners)?

Endnotes

[1] Robey, D., The paradoxes of transformation, in C. Sauer, P. Yetton, L. Alexander (eds.), *Steps to the Future: Fresh Thinking on the Management of IT-Based Organizational Transformation* (Jossey-Bass Business & Management Series), San Francisco, CA: Jossey-Bass Publishers, 1997, pp. 209–229.
[2] McNee, B., Percy, A., Fenn, J., Cassell, J., Hunter, R., Cohen, L., Keller, E., Goodhue, C., Scott, D., Morello, D., Magee, F., Whitten, D., Schlier, F., Baylock, J., West, M. and Berg, T., The industry trends

scenario: delivering business value through IT, *Gartner Group Strategic Analysis Report*, 30 April 1998, 83.

[3] Henderson, J.C. and Venkatraman, N., Strategic alignment: leveraging information technology for transforming organizations, *IBM Systems Journal*, **38**(2–3), 1999, 472–484.

[4] Applegate, L.M., *Managing in an Information Age: IT Challenges and Opportunities*, Harvard Business School Press, #9-196-004, 1995, 19 p.

[5] McNee, B. *et al.*, 1998, *op. cit.*

[6] Henderson, J.C. and Venkatraman, N., 1999, *op. cit.*

[7] Sauer *et al.*, *op. cit.*

[8] *Ibid.*

[9] Henderson, J.C. and Venkatraman, N., 1999, *op. cit.*

[10] Sauer *et al.*, *op. cit.*

[11] Henderson, J.C. and Venkatraman, N., 1999, *op. cit.*

[12] *Ibid.*

[13] *Ibid.*

[14] Magretta, J., The power of virtual integration: an interview with Dell Computer's Michael Dell, *Harvard Business Review*, March–April 1998, pp. 73–84.

[15] Greengard, S., Making the virtual office a reality, *Personnel Journal*, **73**(9), September 1994, 66–79.

[16] Schlier, F. *et al.*, Enterprise 2003: the technology-enabled enterprise, *Gartner Group Strategic Analysis Report*, 29 January 1998, 66.

[17] Applegate, L.M., 1995, *op. cit.*

[18] Gebauer, J., Virtual organizations from an economic perspective, in Coelho, J. Dias *et al.* (eds.), *Proceeding of the 4th European Conference on Information Systems*, 91–103, 2–4 July 1996.

[19] Boudreau, M.C., Loch, K.D., Robey, D. and Straub, D., Going global: using information technology to advance competitiveness of the virtual organization, *Academy of Management Executive*, **12**(4), 1998, 120–128.

[20] *Ibid.*

[21] Upton, D., What really makes factories flexible? *Harvard Business Review*, July–August 1995.

[22] Dubé, L. and Paré, G., Global virtual teams, *Communications of the ACM*, **12**(44), December 2001, 71–73.

[23] Applegate, L.M., 1995, *op. cit.*

[24] Magretta, J., 1998, *op. cit.*

[25] Quinn, J., *The Intelligent Enterprise*, New York: Free Press, 1992.

[26] Davenport, T.H. and Prusak, L., Technologies for knowledge management, in Schrage (ed.), *Working Knowledge*, Boston, MA: Harvard Business School Press, 1998, pp. 123–143.

[27] *Ibid.*

[28] Henderson, J.C. and Venkatraman, N., 1999, *op. cit.*

[29] Quinn, J., 1992, *op. cit.*

[30] Rayport, J.F. and Sviokla, J.J., Exploiting the virtual value chain, *Harvard Business Review*, November–December 1995, pp. 75–85.

[31] *Ibid.*

[32] Moon, Y., Interactive technologies and relationship marketing strategies, *Harvard Business Note #9-599-191*, 19 January 2000.

[33] *Ibid.*

[34] Henderson, J.C. and Venkatraman, N., 1999, *op. cit.*

[35] Pine II, B.J., Victor, B. and Boyton, A.C., Making mass customization work, *Harvard Business Review*, September–October 1993, 108–116.

[36] Bradley and Nolan, *Sense and Respond*, Harvard Business School Press, 1998.

[37] Andrews, P. and Hahn, J., Transforming supply chains into value Webs, *Strategy & Leadership*, **26**(3), 1998, 6–11.

[38] Gebauer, J., 1996, *op. cit.*

[39] Harris, K., Austin, T., Fenn, J., Hayward, S. and Cushman, A., The impact of knowledge management on enterprise architecture, *Gartner Group Strategic Analysis Report*, 25 October 1999, 22.

[40] Shapiro, C. and Varian, H.R., Recognizing lock-in, in *Information Rules: A Strategic Guide to the Network Economy*, Boston, MA: Harvard Business School Press, 1999, pp. 103–134.

[41] Sauer, C. and Yetton, P., *op. cit.*

[42] Frohman, A.L., Technology as a competitive weapon, *Harvard Business Review*, January–February 1982, 97–105.

[43] Robey, D., 1997, *op. cit.*

[44] Sambamurthy, V. and Zmud, R., At the hearth of success: organizationwide management competencies, in C. Sauer, P.W. Yetton and Associates (eds.), *Steps to the Future: Fresh Thinking on the Management of IT-Based Organizational Transformation*, San Francisco, CA: Jossey-Bass Publishers, 1997, pp. 143–163.

[45] *Ibid.*

[46] Markus, M.L. and Benjamin, R., Change agentry: the next IS frontier, *MIS Quarterly*, December 1996, pp. 385–407.

[47] *Ibid.*

[48] McNee, B. *et al.*, 1998, *op. cit.*

[49] Cross, J., Earl, M.J. and Sampler, J., Transformation of the IT function at british petroleum, *MIS Quarterly*, December 1997, pp. 401–423.

[50] Earl, M.J. and Sampler, J.L., Market management to transform the IT organization, *Sloan Management Review*, Summer 1998, pp. 9–17.

[51] Cross, J. *et al.*, 1997, *op. cit.*

[52] Tapscott, D. and Caston, A., *Paradigm Shift: The New Promise of Information Technology*, McGraw Hill, 1992.

[53] Schlier, F., 1998, *op. cit.*

[54] DeBoever, L. and Buchanan, R., Three architectural sins, *CIO*, May 1997, Vol.(10)14, pp. 124–126.

[55] McNee, B. *et al.*, 1998, *op. cit.*

[56] *Ibid.*

Chapter 5

The leadership piece

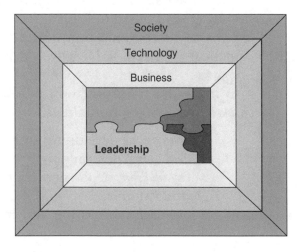

> Most people want to deal with practical things. How do I handle my account? ... How do I build this particular technology? People want to work on something that they can touch. What's left behind is my work.[1]

This quote from Franco Bernabè, the dynamic and successful chief exective officer (CEO) of Eni, Italy's large energy-focused industrial group, captures the essence of leadership in modern organizations. Leadership is chiefly about dealing with the intangibles and the most frustrating situations in the organization. While the concrete jobs can be delegated, the leader's job is to lead in the face of ambiguity and uncertainty. This has never been truer than it is today, with all of the change, which organizations are facing in their environment, strategies, organization structures, and information technology.

Just as our strategies, structures, information technology (IT), and business environments are changing, so too is what we recognize as leadership. Unfortunately, there is often a tendency to confuse leadership with management. As a result, many believe that organizations today are "over-managed and under-led."[2] Leadership is what is required for successful organizational change, innovation, breaking new ground, and creating new concepts of what works.[3] Leadership itself is changing as well. Old style leadership forms are giving way to different ones. In the past, a leader could rely on the force of his or her individual personality to drive change. Now, leaders must build organizations where transformation will occur dynamically at all levels, individual commitment to change comes from a deeply-felt understanding of the vision, and collaboration makes it happen.

In spite of the significant and rapid changes taking place in all parts of the organization, transformation does not arise automatically. It needs to be actively driven by leaders who "ignite the sparks ... fan them to keep them alive and then control the flames to make the transformation more productive."[4] Today, leaders have four key responsibilities:[5]

1   *reimaging*: developing a vision for the organization;
2   *reshaping*: determining how the organization will operate;
3   *realization*: deploying the necessary resources to realize the vision;
4   *renewal*: monitoring and improving organizational performance.

What leaders can do about each of these elements has been addressed in the other three pieces of the management puzzle (i.e. strategy, information technology, and structure). The attributes of leadership remain to be discussed, as managers attempt to accomplish these things in their organizations. While leadership is about what is left over, its value to an organization cannot be underestimated. Leaders can and do make a difference in how well organizations transform themselves, and how successful they are.[6] As Michael Dell – president of Dell Computers, points out even small things that leaders do can add up to a huge impact.[7]

There is no composite picture of a perfect leader. In fact, many of the most successful leaders do not usually fit our image of what one should be.[8] Nevertheless, we are beginning to understand that there are different dimensions of the leadership piece around which aspects of successful leadership can be explored. This chapter examines four dimensions of this critical piece of

Table 5.1
The dimensions of the leadership piece

The personal attributes of a leader	Leadership functions
Focus	Orchestrate value
Discipline	Set vision and goals
Ability to cope with ambiguity	Coordinate
Emotional stamina	Develop human capital
Leadership competencies	**Leadership in the future**
Strategic thinking	
Communication	
Technical comfort	
People management	

the management puzzle. First, it looks at the personal attributes that a leader must have. These are the bedrock of leadership effectiveness. Focus, discipline, the ability to cope with ambiguity, and emotional stamina are required to lead when the going gets rough. Then, it explores the essential skills of a leader and why they are needed. A third dimension of leadership concerns the functions, which a leader must perform in his job. Finally, we look at the new roles that leaders are beginning to undertake within their organizations and the larger business community. Table 5.1 provides an overview of these four dimensions.

Personal attributes of a leader

Of all the pieces of the management puzzle, leadership is the most dependent on the personal attributes of an individual or a small group of individuals. The characteristic most often associated with leadership is strength. For example, Porter states: "Strong leaders willing to make choices are essential"[9] for successful companies. Others write of how strong leadership is needed to drive changes in strategy, structure, and information technology.[10] In fact, strength is implicit in much of what people appear to look for in a leader. Yet, when leaders themselves are interviewed, they rarely speak about being strong. Instead they focus on a variety of different attributes which, when taken together, might contribute to a leader appearing to be strong. These include:

- *Focus*: First and foremost, leaders need focus and determination. Leaders who want to transform their organizations must be very clear about what they want to accomplish. As Bernabè points out, "If I had vacillated about my objectives and my vision for Eni, I would have been finished before I got started."[11] Several studies have shown that a key difference between companies that have successfully transformed themselves and those which have not is the leader's unrelenting attention to the end results.[12] It is all too easy to get bound up in intermediate variables, such as job skills, organization structures, or corporate politics, and to lose focus. Thus, effective leaders realize that maintaining their focus is a matter of survival.

■ *Discipline*: Leaders need mental discipline to make their vision work. They must have a clear intellectual framework for what needs to be done, then be able to use this to make the decisions about the environmental changes to which their company will respond, how it will maintain its distinctiveness, and what it will do internally to accomplish its goals. As Porter states, "Managers at lower levels lack the perspective and confidence to maintain a strategy." Leaders must say no and teach others how and when to do this. In a crisis, leaders do not react impulsively, but always think things through. Bernabè comments,

> I very carefully went through all the problems I had, analyzing them from every angle … A leader cannot take the weighted average of other people's opinions and make them his own. You have to organize the information you receive, analyze it, make your decision and then move on to the next problem.[13]

■ *Ability to cope with ambiguity*: A third attribute of strong leaders is the ability to cope with ambiguity and uncertainty. Leaders need the ability to conceptualize different scenarios and to work with different and often contradictory information. They must be able to live with a lack of ultimate answers and be comfortable with the anxiety that is generated by change. This has been described as the ability to "be roughly right and fast rather than exactly right and slow."[14]

■ *Emotional stamina*: Finally, leaders need significant personal emotional reserves. On one hand, they need to be seriously emotionally committed to the changes they are driving in the organization, on the other, they must recognize that they may receive no support for their work within the firm. In fact, they may face outright animosity. As Bernabè explains, "The more responsibility you have, the more you need to be alone."[15] While pursuing transformation, leaders frequently take large personal risks. Therefore, leaders also need to maintain some "psychological parachutes" for themselves personally, in case things do not work out. In Bernabè's case, these were knowing that if he were fired, he could work somewhere else and not be forced to change his lifestyle when he took on his new position. As a result, "These risks didn't seem that frightening (because) ... I didn't have anything to lose"[16]

Leadership competencies

In addition to personal attributes, leaders also need particular skills in order to do their job effectively. Such competencies bring out the best in their organization, regardless of the situation in which it operates. These include:

- *Strategic thinking*: The most often mentioned leadership competency is the ability to think strategically about the organization. While this means developing and communicating a long-term vision and being able to devise a sense of strategic direction for an organization, it also means developing and encouraging this type of thinking in others. Today, with strategy being increasingly perceived as part of everyone's job, leaders must be able to teach others about strategizing and promote nonlinear thinking among their subordinates. Strategic thinking is especially important when doing business in a dynamic environment. The ability to think strategically about problems under uncertain and dynamic conditions means not only identifying new approaches and business opportunities; it also means knowing when and how to set limits, so that the actions of the firm are not dissipated. Thus, this leadership skill involves both setting direction for an organization and approaching all aspects of the job from a strategic perspective.

- *Communication*: Clear communication is another frequently cited leadership competency. Effective communication to the organization as a whole is essential for obtaining its commitment to change. Such activities as changing an organization's direction, culture, values, and ways of working cannot be done by fiat. These require buy-in at all levels and in all parts of the business. Communication is a job that cannot be delegated. Leaders who have relied on their direct-report managers to pass on key messages have learned the hard way that very little actually filters down to the rest of the firm. Communication must also be direct from the leader. Written reports simply do not have the reach or the impact of personal interaction. Thus, for today's leaders, communication is most often about giving speeches to large groups within the organization. The message has to be simple (so that it does not get distorted when passed along) and it has to touch people. Bernabè explains, "To be effective, you have to tap into people's sentiments, feelings, and emotions"[17] This type of communication has been described elsewhere as the creation of "sound bites" about the vision which capture its essence and provide people with a sense of coherence and control – even if this is not completely the case.[18] While such personal communication takes a great deal of time and requires enormous patience, leaders have consistently found that it is the only way that works.

- *Technical comfort*: With IT representing such an important piece of the management puzzle, it is not surprising to find that a key leadership skill is the ability to use and understand technology. Leaders need data and systems to help them interpret their environment and to implement their vision and they must be able to process a variety of information quickly in real time.[19] Thus, technology is an extremely important tool for leaders. Research shows that the technical capabilities of the senior management team are strongly related to the effective assimilation of technology into an organization, which in turn, is a key factor in business success. Although this does not mean that all leaders in an organization must be technically knowledgeable, it is very important that solid technical skills be available somewhere in the leadership of the organization (e.g. in the chief IT executives (CIOs)).

As well, other leaders must have some degree of comfort with what technology can and cannot do, in order to make effective decisions about its use in their organization. Without this, leaders can easily misuse the potential of IT or rely on it to solve problems in inappropriate ways.[20] In fact, the increasing importance of IT in organizations has opened up new opportunities for executive leadership and CIOs who have a good blend of business and technical knowledge can provide important and valuable perspectives for other organizational leaders.

■ *People management*: Lastly, leaders need the skills to be able to draw the best from their people and to nurture talent within the organization. Increasingly, leaders are becoming teachers, mentors, and coaches and this is leading to a growing emphasis on personal leadership:

> Today, instead of driving decisions, leaders need to drive discussion and create buy-in ... to build partnerships (and) ... be empowering, coaching, counseling, encouraging, and supporting (of) their people.[21]

Leaders are called on regularly to deal effectively with conflict and with complex social, political and labor problems, all of which are exacerbated by change. The challenges of transformation often go beyond the domain of the everyday and require the leader's skills to ensure that fairness and justice prevail at times of upheaval. At this level, leadership is "fundamentally about humanity and ... about morality" and making sure that what is good for the organization is also good for the people who work there.[22]

Leadership functions

The actual work that a leader does is the most variable dimension of the leadership piece. A great deal depends on the situation in which the organization finds itself and what the leader perceives needs to be done about it. There is also a great deal of variability among the "experts" on leadership about the job of a leader. For example, some contend the primary function of the leader is to set strategy, while others believe leaders should focus more on leading at an industry level and leave strategy to their subordinates.

Clearly, leaders must use judgment about how and where they spend their time. Nevertheless, the list below represents a group of generic leadership functions, which *all* leaders must perform to a greater or lesser extent. Additional functions will vary by firm and industry situation:

■ *Orchestrate value*: All leaders have a primary job of building the value of their enterprise. This always starts with an understanding of the business environment in which it operates and where the firm provides value for its customers. Leaders need to keep their fingers on the pulse of the future, as well as the present. While they have organizational functions to help them do this, leaders never fully delegate this job. They spend time with customers, evaluate emerging trends, probe into new fields of knowledge, and assess industries – all in search of new market opportunities and sources of value. Leaders must particularly try to sense where shifts in value are coming from. As Michael Dell states,

> To lead … you have to be on the lookout for shifts in values, and if the customer declares, "Hey I don't care about that anymore, I care about this", we may have to develop new capabilities rather quickly.[23]

Today's leaders cannot assume that the value model of today will be the same tomorrow; they must never become complacent about this critical element of their business. As a result, leaders can never be satisfied with what they have achieved. Much of leadership in this area involves a willingness to disrupt current thinking within the organization in order to better align it with the marketplace. In most organizations, the job of exploring new sources of value and disrupting current sources of success belongs to the leader. If he or she does not drive this activity forward, it will likely not occur.[24] The challenge for leaders is to maintain this disruptive thinking over time as, unfortunately, it is well established that long-standing leaders are less likely to have strategies and structures appropriate to their current business environments.

■ *Set vision and goals*: Whatever the business strategy, it is the leader's job to set the vision and goals for the organization and to ensure that the enterprise is focused on them.

Leaders who have achieved successful transformations believe that it is important to set demanding goals early in the process. These establish the tone for the transformation and are essential in challenging the mindset and cherished beliefs of the organization.[25] Goals should be articulated in more than just financial terms. They could be framed as capabilities or as key indicators (e.g. employee satisfaction, customer service), which relate to their future vision for the enterprise. Leaders must have the same passion for these indicators as they have for operating numbers if they want their goals to be met or the organization will quickly tend to settle back into its comfortable routines. Once a vision and goals have been established and clearly communicated, it is the leader's job to maintain a rigorous focus on results to ensure that the organization rises to meet the occasion.

Yet, at the same time, leaders need to be open to a constant refinement of their vision and goals as the value model evolves over time. They must maintain a constant dialogue about the vision, both inside and outside the organization. This not only helps to refine the leader's understanding of the value model, the industry, and the environment, it also provides the basis for revising the organization's response in all parts of the puzzle.

■ *Coordinate*: Complex structures require intensive coordination to be effective and today, this is primarily achieved through leadership. Leaders seek to develop a top management team, which works collaboratively, yet which reflects a varied set of expertise and knowledge. Heterogeneity is strongly linked with successful strategic change and is an important resource for change. But this also means that the leader plays an important role in integrating and coordinating his or her team's diverse perspectives. The leader and the top management team then set the tone for increased coordination and collaboration throughout the organization – between headquarters and field units and across business units. Leaders must take the initiative to develop a common language for this collaboration and then "walk the talk" with communication, incentives, attention, and other actions designed to ensure that coordination is actually achieved.[26]

■ *Develop human capital*: Finally, leaders also play a critical role in developing their organization's human capital. First, they must build a superior management team whose skills and ideas they can count on. Second, they must seek to maximize their employees' skills, rather than minimizing employee costs. To do this, they must create a culture which values experience and performance over seniority and position in the hierarchy. Third, they must nurture a culture of learning in which new approaches to work and employee skills development are fostered.

At the same time, leaders also have to be prepared to make difficult human resource decisions. Senior managers may need to be replaced if they are standing in the way of change. Staff and business units may have to be outsourced to meet strategic objectives and this transition must be handled with consideration and fairness, if morale is not to be destroyed. Leaders must know how and where to deploy staff, when to use contingency workers appropriately, and how to be able to deal with the potential human costs of doing so. These include: loss of motivation, lowered morale, conflict, and loss of commitment and productivity.

Leadership in the future

Leadership is a job which is being continually reinvented. The leadership styles and skills of the late twentieth century will not be adequate for the organization of the twenty-first century. As organizations evolve, so too does leadership. The shift in emphasis from controlling and directing an organization within a stable industry to facilitating and exploring the new opportunities, structures, and management styles required by an ambiguous and constantly changing business environment is significant and frequently uncomfortable.

As organizations develop new levels of coordination, new sources of value, and new means of control and integration, new leadership opportunities are bound to emerge. One of the most important of these is the job of orchestrating businesses or parts of businesses to match the shifting mix of market opportunities. In the increasingly networked business world of the future, leaders will be adding, subtracting, merging and splitting businesses continually to match their firms' products or services more closely to market needs. Thus, a key new role for leaders will be managing a portfolio of businesses.

Networks also create new levels of integration and information, which will have to be managed. Leaders of networks will need to take greater responsibility for the execution of business strategies between organizations and for building the information and knowledge structures that will make this possible.

Finally, leaders will need to become synthesizers. As environments and strategies become increasingly complex, leaders will need to help their organizations capture the essence of strategy simply and clearly. They will need to use simplicity to build a sense of direction around an evolving strategy in a chaotic environment. To do this, leaders will need to be able to see patterns in data and across time, and to articulate the gist of complex issues clearly and succinctly.

One of the biggest challenges facing leaders will be maintaining appropriate balance. In many ways, leadership will be about living a paradox. The need for continual change will have to be balanced with the natural desire for equilibrium and stability. The desire for immediate short-term numbers must be balanced with doing the right things for the future. And the requirement for quick and visible results must be balanced against people's resistance to change. Bernabè states, "The management books tell you that big change initiatives need quick wins. In reality, it takes patience and time."[27] Leaders in the future will need to be ambidextrous – directing the present with one hand, while steering for the future with the other. They will not have an easy job but they will have an interesting and challenging one.

Questions

1 While some argue that leadership cannot be learned, and that it requires innate skills and know-how, others think that some skills can be acquired. Please discuss.

2 This chapter discussed the main attributes, competencies and functions of a leader. Technical comfort is considered one of the competencies of a leader. Elaborate on this point, identifying the extent to which you think that a top executive should be familiar with IT.

3 Dramatic changes such as reengineering endeavours profoundly affect numerous people in an organization.

In several instances, top management is not directly impacted by those dramatic changes. Please comment the following statement made by a leading consultant during a meeting of top executives in a firm where he had been mandated to accompany a reengineering project. "People in the firm have to see and feel that even top managers are impacted in their own work. If you are not willing to be, yourself, under the scrutiny of the reengineering team, I suggest that you invite someone else than myself to advise you on this project." What did this statement mean, in terms of leadership and change management?

4   Are there any of the functions of a leader that could be facilitated or supported by IT?

5   From Chapter 1's description of the changes that have taken place in the environment, how do the attributes, competencies, and functions of today's leaders differ from those required 20 years ago?

Endnotes

[1] Hill, L. and Wetlaufer, S., Leadership when there is no one to ask: an interview with Eni's Franco Bernabè, *Harvard Business Review*, July–August 1998, 80–94.

[2] Tapscott, D., *Paradigm Shift: the New Promise of Information Technology*, New York: McGraw Hill, 1993, p. 283.

[3] Tapscott, D., 1993, *op. cit.*

[4] Ashkenas, R., Ulrich, D., Todd, J. and S. Kerr, *The Boundaryless Organization, Breaking the Chains of Organizational Structure*, San Francisco, CA: Jossey-Bass Publishers, 1995, p. 326.

[5] Tapscott, D., 1993, *op. cit.*

[6] Boeker, W., Strategic change: the influence of managerial characteristics and organizational growth, *Academy of Management Journal*, **40**(1), 1997, 152–170.

[7] Magretta, J., The power of virtual integration: an interview with Dell Computer's Michael Dell, *Harvard Business Review*, March–April 1998, 73–84.

[8] Hill, L. and Wetlaufer, S., 1998, *op. cit.*

[9] Porter, M.E., What is strategy? *Harvard Business Review*, **74**(6), 1996, 61–79.

[10] Frohman, A.L., Technology as a competitive weapon, *Harvard Business Review*, January–February 1982, 97–105.

[11] Hill, L. and Wetlaufer, S., 1998, *op. cit.*

[12] Ashkenas *et al.*, 1995, *op. cit.*

[13] Hill, L. and Wetlaufer, S., 1998, *op. cit.*

[14] *Ibid.*

[15] *Ibid.*

[16] *Ibid.*

[17] *Ibid.*

[18] Brown, S.L. and Eisenhardt, K.M., *Competing on the Edge*, Harvard Business School Press, 1998.

[19] Armstrong, C.P. and Sambamurthy, V., Information technology assimilation in firms: the influence of senior leadership and IT infra-structures, *Information Systems Research* **10**(4), 1999, 304–327.

[20] Schrage, M., The real problem with computers, *Harvard Business Review*, September–October 1997, 3–7.

[21] Ashkenas *et al.*, 1995, *op. cit.*, p. 331.

[22] Hill, L. and Wetlaufer, S., 1998, *op. cit.*

[23] Magretta, J., 1998, *op. cit.*

[24] Mohrman, S.A., Galbraith, J.R. and Lawler III, E.E., *Tomorrow's Organization: Crafting Winning Capabilities in a Dynamic World*, Jossey-Bass Publishers, 1998.

[25] Cross, J., Earl, M.J. and Sampler, J.L., Transformation of the IT function at British Petroleum, *MIS Quarterly*, December 1997, 401–423.

[26] Ashkenas *et al.*, 1995, *op. cit.*, p. 338.

[27] Hill, L. and Wetlaufer, S., 1998, *op. cit.*

PART III

Putting the puzzle together

The following three chapters illustrate how the puzzle pieces can be put together successfully. To do so, we present and analyze the experience of three firms who arranged the five pieces of the management puzzle so as to fit closely together. The cases are: (1) Progressive Delivers the Unexpected – Progressive Insurance; (2) The Organization without an Organizational Chart – Oticon; and (3) The Virtual Value Chain – Li & Fung. These three cases illustrate the importance of each of the various pieces of the management puzzle and their mutual adjustment. They also show that there is no single way of assembling the pieces. All three firms have been quite successful in adapting to their environment, yet each followed a very particular trajectory.

Chapter 6 illustrates how Progressive Insurance radically transformed itself in the 1990s via a shared strategy built around the concepts of "customer delight" and "innovation," coupled with the appropriate adoption and use of emerging information technology applications. At Progressive, more permeable horizontal, vertical, and geographic boundaries emerged gradually and were an outcome of business transformation. Progressive illustrates a situation in which strategy and IT were codetermined, influenced each other, and fed back into each other. The case also describes how Peter Lewis' leadership abilities were of the utmost importance in transforming Progressive from an industry gnat to a large and powerful competitor.

Chapter 7 presents Oticon, also known as the spaghetti organization. When he envisioned the new organization structure that was to bring Oticon back on the road to prosperity, Lars Kolind, Oticon's chief executive officer (CEO), used the term "spaghetti organization." In this organizational model, traditional hierarchies, organization functions, and even actual walls, collapsed. In analyzing Oticon's case, the crucial role played by the structure piece of the management puzzle is truly striking. Indeed, one could almost say that the new organizational structure came to Kolind's mind before he actually formulated the firm's strategy. In this puzzle, the IT piece plays the important role of making the adjustment between structure and strategy feasible. Yet, by itself, the IT piece does not have much strategic content; this fact once again demonstrates the utmost importance of the structure piece.

Chapter 8 presents Li & Fung, a firm which was established in Canton in 1906, and has grown into a large organization selling consumer goods including clothing, luggage, toys, and beauty products. Li & Fung describes itself as a supply chain manager, providing a one-stop shop for customers. Li & Fung offers its clients complete services, from product design, arranging for raw material sourcing, production, product management, to shipping, and export documentation. While it does not actually perform most of these activities, Li & Fung coordinates them. It also makes sure that every step is done at the best and cheapest place in the world. It creates a web of geographically decentralized but highly coordinated activities. This organization is a good example of new structure and adaptability to the environment. In this case, strategy is explicit, well articulated, original, and leads to tangible results. The network structure makes possible the flexibility and the low-cost structure defined in the strategy. Similarly, IT enables the coordination of all these components in addition to the flexibility (just-in-time changes) offered to its clients.

In the concluding section, we provide a few key insights with regard to possible business transformation configurations and the importance of strategic alignment from our analysis of the three cases introduced above.

Chapter 6

Progressive delivers the unexpected – Progressive Insurance

Case description

It's a steamy Saturday in Houston, a day so piping hot that one would gladly consider diving into a vat of Texas chili for relief. But chili is a messy business, so instead, half the population seems to have taken refuge in their air-conditioned cars, choking Houston's freeways as a result. For Kristen Botello, all those cars mean just one thing: lots of accidents.

She's not rooting for wrecks. But she knows from experience that accidents happen. And when they do, she wants to be on the scene immediately – before the police arrive, before a wrecker tows away the cars. Why all the urgency? Because Botello, 28, settles claims for Progressive Corporation, an auto-insurance maverick that has built a prosperous, fast-growing company around speed, service, and software.

Around lunchtime, Botello's two-way radio crackles with a message. "Kristen, we've got a scene," says the dispatcher. She heads for the freeway in a Ford Explorer with the label "Progressive" emblazoned on both sides. Accidents are like mysteries, she says. And like any good detective, Botello doesn't want the scene disturbed. Sometimes she shows up so quickly that all the clues are still in place: skid marks, witnesses, cars resting in post-collision chaos. Botello inspects the vehicles, assesses the damage, does her analysis, whips out her laptop, downloads a claim file, and cuts a check on the spot. Case closed.[1]

A support to business strategy

Progressive Insurance Inc. figures among the top four auto-insurance companies in the U.S. and represents the nation's largest writer of private passenger auto insurance through independent agents. Progressive is also the number one writer of motorcycle insurance in the U.S. In business since 1937, the company provides all drivers with competitive rates and 24 h, in-person, and online services. The company sells its products (automobile, motorcycle, recreation vehicle, commercial vehicle, personal watercraft, boat, and all-terrain vehicle) over the phone, online, and through more than 30,000 independent agents[2] nationwide. Today, the company has nearly 19,490 employees in over 350 offices serving about 8 million customers.

Progressive's culture is one of high energy, continuous innovation, and dynamic growth. The corporate web site (www.progressive. com) presents some of the elements that make Progressive a unique place to work:

- *Business casual dress*: Progressive's philosophy is to allow people to dress in a style consistent with their personal tastes, but which also presents a neat appearance to customers and other contacts;
- *Art collection*: To foster creative thinking, all large Progressive offices feature works from Progressive's contemporary art collection, regarded as one of the best in the country;
- *Safety and wellness*: Most major Progressive locations feature a collegial campus setting and atmosphere, including cafeterias, Progressive-operated fitness centers and primary care facilities;
- *Innovation*: Progressive prides itself on being the technological leader in the auto-insurance industry. The company has implemented a wide variety of technologies and has received a great deal of recognition surrounding its efforts.

From its beginnings in 1937, Progressive valued innovation. It introduced the industry's first drive-in claims office. In 1956, Progressive's Safe Driver Plan lowered rates for low-risk drivers, setting an industry policy standard. More recently, the Immediate Response claims service was introduced and became the first and only 24 h, in-person claims service that serves customers when and where they need it most – at the accident scene. To complement the Immediate Response program, the Immediate Response Vehicle (IRV) was then introduced. The IRV is a specially-marked vehicle that carries trained claims professionals to wherever the customer needs them. Outfitted with the latest technology, the claim representative in an IRV is able to complete a damage estimate and write a check right on the spot. To ensure continuous innovation within the company, good ideas from anyone are always sought out. The corporate attitude is to try almost everything that makes sense and to stop it when it stops making sense. In the words of Peter Lewis, Progressive's former chief executive officer (CEO):

> We've spent a lot of money on dumb ideas, but we had the flexibility to stop it early. (…) It's ingrained in the culture to experiment, but to do so responsibly. We reward people for taking risks but punish them for not spotting bad ones early enough to pull the plug.[3]

Progressive's two largest competitors are State Farm and Allstate. State Farm Insurance insures about 20 percent of U.S. automobiles, making it the nation's leading insurer of cars. It provides auto insurance as well as homeowners, non-medical health, and life insurance. State Farm operates throughout the U.S. and Canada and has some 16,200 agents. The company also has 37,800 employees, almost half of State Farm's workforce, who deal with claims in some fashion (www.statefarm.com). Allstate Insurance, the "good hands" company is the second largest U.S. personal lines insurer behind State Farm. Its core auto lines account for 75 percent of sales; the company also sells other property/casualty (homeowners and specialty lines) and life insurance in North America and Asia. The company operates through some 13,000 exclusive agents in the U.S. and Canada (www.allstate.com).

History

Joseph Lewis and Jack Green co-founded Progressive Insurance with the objective to provide vehicle owners with security and protection. They also thought it was a good investment for a couple of lawyers who were just beginning. It was not until the end of Second World War that auto insurance became more popular, and Progressive emerged small but solid. The company grew steadily throughout the next decade, moving to new offices in downtown Cleveland, Ohio, in 1951. After the death of co-founder Joe Lewis in 1955, Jack Green became President and CEO.

Peter Lewis, Joseph's son, gets deeply emotional about insurance, in part because running Progressive is all that he has ever wanted to do. His father co-founded the company when Peter was 3 years old. As a young child, he accompanied his father to work and played on the office furniture. At age 12, he stuffed envelopes to earn his first paycheck. As a 30-something CEO, he worked 90 h a week. But Peter Lewis gets emotional about auto-insurance for another reason. In 1952, his older brother, Jon, who was 16, was driving to Canada for a fishing trip. After 12 h behind the wheel, Jon collided with an oncoming truck. His brother's death, Lewis says, "makes every car accident an emotional experience for me. I can't take them lightly."[4]

Peter Lewis began his career with Progressive shortly after graduating from Princeton in 1955. He quickly brought fresh ideas and began looking for ways to distinguish the company from its competitors. Although his duties were limited to sales, he attended the company's management meetings, where the head underwriter complained about independent agents who tried to persuade him to cover "non-standard" customers. One day, Lewis spoke up: "They're bringing us potential business. Can't we find a way to write these people?"[5] It was, he likes to say, his first great idea at Progressive. In 1957, the company wrote just $86,000 worth of policies for non-standard motorists. But over the next decade, the market took off. Lewis watched his company's premiums balloon. He had identified a niche around which he could build a big company and add to his father's legacy.

In 1965, Peter Lewis took over the reins of the company when he assumed the position of CEO, a title he still held when he celebrated his 45th anniversary with the company in 2000. After becoming a public company in 1971 and moving its headquarters to Mayfield Village, Ohio, the company experienced steady growth throughout the 1970s and 1980s. In 1987, Progressive had written $1.116 billion in premiums and the company's stock was listed on the New York Stock Exchange. Since then, the company has experienced explosive growth. The rapid pace of change at Progressive in the 1990s reflected some pressures the company had recently faced.

In the mid-80s, Allstate found itself unable to grow further in its essentially mature market due to tough competition from State Farm. As a result, Allstate decided to enter the non-standard segment. This entry had fundamentally changed the game for Progressive. Since roughly 5–10 percent of Allstate's customers turned non-standard every year, Allstate was able to grow its share very quickly without incurring large underwriting expenses, simply by retaining its customers. Progressive's management had been well aware of the threat that the entry of a large, standard insurer into the non-standard segment would pose to their positioning. Hence, there had always been the wish to put Progressive's business on a broader foundation and to find another area in which to put its skills to task. Thus, in 1986, Lewis decided to take on another non-traditional market: long-haul truck insurance, a notoriously risky but profitable market. Although Progressive did not have any expertise in this segment, it had shown its ability to develop pricing expertise in the non-standard segment and to deal with complicated claims. Yet, Progressive misjudged both the buying power of trucking companies and its own abilities to price this segment. Large claims with very long tails and sophisticated lawyers presented Progressive with an environment that turned out to be very different from their traditional one. In 1988, Allstate surpassed Progressive in the non-standard business and, until Progressive abandoned the market in 1992, the business had generated total losses of $84 million.[6]

On November 8, 1988, California voters passed Proposition 103, a referendum designed to regulate auto-insurance companies and to roll back escalating rates. In essence, customer dissatisfaction with the high automobile insurance premiums in the state had triggered this piece of legislation, which required that every insurer reduce its rates to at least 20 percent less than the rates that were in effect on November 8, 1987 unless such rollback would lead to a company's insolvency. The law was a near-fatal blow to Progressive, which had done 20 percent of its business in California. Lewis's company coughed up $60 million in refunds – and eventually reduced its workforce by 19 percent.[7]

Following Proposition 103, Lewis turned to longtime friend and Princeton classmate Ralph Nader, an outspoken supporter of the California referendum, to help him understand the animosity that consumers felt toward insurers. Nader suggested that Lewis come to Washington and meet with the heads of two-dozen state-level consumer groups. "What's wrong with auto insurance?" Lewis asked them. "It's not competitive", someone in the audience said. "Wait a minute," he replied. "There are more than 300 companies in the business. If we move our price one percentage point up or down, we get 10 percent more or 10 percent fewer applications. That's competitive." The advocates were unappeased. They insisted that Lewis worked in a non-competitive industry. That's when Lewis began to understand the extent of the industry's credibility gap.[8] Lewis calls Proposition 103 "the most frustrating experience" of his career. He also calls it "the best thing that ever happened to his company."[9] How so? Because the very legislation that threatened to put Progressive out of business also inspired its dramatic makeover in 1988. Proposition 103 was a wake-up call.

Hence, the stage was set for a period of continuous innovation in the 1990s that truly set the company apart from the competition. The company's motive was to delight the customer, even shock the consumer a little for competitive advantage. Progressive wanted to deliver the unexpected.

After 35 years, Peter Lewis retired as CEO in December 2000 and named Glenn Renwick, Progressive's chief IT officer (CIO), as his successor:

> Glenn and I share a passion for Progressive's vision of reducing the human trauma and cost of auto accidents in cost-effective and profitable ways. We have the talent in place to continue to develop innovative, consumer-focused products and services for independent agents and our direct sales choices by phone and online. Now, my role becomes that of coach and cheerleader. I've been involved with Progressive full time for 45 years, CEO for 35 years – and I'm not going anywhere.[10]

How Progressive redefined its business

Progressive reinvented its business in 1988. From Proposition 103, Lewis understood the extent of the industry's credibility gap. That is when he decided to embrace what Progressive calls "information transparency," a policy of sharing information about prices, costs, and service with customers. In 1992, Progressive brought 1-800-AUTO-PRO, a cutting-edge auto-insurance rate comparison shopping service. No longer would customers have to spend endless amounts of time calling around to compare auto-insurance rates. One phone call to AUTO-PRO would give customers a Progressive quote and comparison rates for up to three competitors. If customers were satisfied with the Progressive quote, they could buy the policy directly on the phone or locally through an independent agent. "Time and again, people don't believe we do this," says Alan Bauer, the company's Internet-process leader. "They think it's a gimmick. But it's part of information transparency. We are exposing our data to the customer."[11]

Progressive has also changed how it sells its products. Most companies either sell policies direct – over the phone or through local offices – or through captive agents representing the company (e.g. Allstate agents). Progressive, which for years had relied exclusively on a nationwide network of independent agents to sell its policies, decided to create multiple distribution channels. Now, customers wishing to purchase a policy, can do so in a number of ways: They can contact one of Progressive's 30,000 independent agents, call 1-800-AUTO-PRO, or visit Progressive on the web. Indeed, in 1997, Progressive became the first auto-insurance company to sell its products via the web. Progressive then partially transformed itself into a direct marketer that, like USAA or GEICO, avoids commissions to middlemen. The company's direct sales represent a distribution of real promise.[12] "We want to provide the information that customers need – and to provide it on their terms," concurs Alan Bauer. "We don't care if it's in person, over the phone, or online."[13]

Progressive did not become a successful auto-insurance company by doing business the way other companies did. Using multiple distribution channels has been a tremendous success, but it was Immediate Response that truly reinvented the company. Indeed, at the heart of its breakthrough business performance is immediate response, its ultra-fast claims service. Prior to Immediate Response, Progressive handled claims as any other insurance company did – inefficiently. A claim was assigned to an adjuster, who alone was responsible for interviewing the parties involved, inspecting the vehicles, and settling the dispute. As adjusters handled so many claims at once, and because they worked a conventional 9-to-5 day, claims languished in an in-basket. Rather than providing great customer service, adjusters were shuffling mountains of paper.

In 1990, the company set a new standard for customer service with a strong focus on business processes. Indeed, Progressive was one of the early adopters of the reengineering concept. For instance, the new claims adjustment process, one of the company's core processes, begins when a customer calls Progressive to report an accident. Progressive receives about 25,000 phone calls per day. Calls about existing claims are routed to the appropriate local office where representatives interview customers who have had accidents, enter data into Progressive's mainframe, and initiate Immediate Response – all in a matter of minutes. If the claimant is still at the scene of the accident, a mobile claims representative is sent in a company IRV (introduced in 1994) to begin the investigation and settlement. Today, more than 2000 of these vehicles, also called "office on wheels," are equipped with a desk, fax, printer, computer, digital camera, cellular phone, and modem as an Immediate Response tool. Progressive strives to resolve all coverage and liability issues as quickly as possible so that the claims representative is able to cut a check to the claimant during this initial meeting. Willy Graves, Texas state manager, comments, "In about 20 percent of the first Immediate Response visits, we cut a check immediately."[14]

As a result of its greater mobility, Progressive has experienced several advantages. First, by reengineering its claims adjustment process, it slashed the time required to process a collision claim from an average of 36 days to 12, cut its expense ratio from 33 to 24 percent of premiums, and increased income per employee by 70 percent.[15] Second, the company designed its processes for agility, so as to respond to every aspect of the customer's needs. This means handling calls on a wide range of issues. As shown in Table 6.1, the claims adjustment process can be reconfigured instantly to meet whatever the customer needs. Importantly, in order to respond easily and immediately to the multiple situations that clients present, Progressive has negotiated contracts with more than 400 repair facility shops covering virtually all geographical areas of Progressive's business, and has formed relationships with multiple car-rental agencies. Using a TotalProSM facility ensures fast and quality vehicle repairs for clients. Indeed,

Table 6.1
Agility of Progressive's claims adjustment process

Origin of the call	Actions to be taken
Customer calling from the accident site	Dispatch an adjuster to the site for an evaluation
Customer calling from home	In-house agent handles the call and may come see the car at the home or may have the claimant visit a claims center for an evaluation, depending on the conditions of the vehicle
Customer calling from a body shop	Progressive will work directly with the body shop to resolve the claim

customers receive priority service, warranted work, and regular reports on the status of the repairs.

Finally, the Immediate Response claims process has eliminated many defects other companies still experience. Errors occur because the damage to be repaired may not have been a result of the accident, or because claimants report problems that are not entirely accurate. Since claims representatives visit the accident site, they are able to take pictures of the damage before anything else happens to the vehicle. Likewise, they can investigate the accident while it is still fresh in everyone's mind, reducing the likelihood of loss of critical details.

Overall, Progressive clearly recognized that its Immediate Response system could only work with the right personnel. Hence it made sure that its adjusters sent to an automobile accident were thoroughly trained and empowered to make decisions. In the words of Alan Bauer:

> In most insurance companies, the ultimate responsibility for a given policy is spread among a number of people: the underwriter, the actuary, the salesperson, and the claims person. All of that ultimately rests on one person at Progressive. As Progressive adjusters wear all of these hats at the same time, they can make the trade-offs necessary. We really do give that sort of authority, and that's very frightening for a lot of people. That is not a company for everyone.[16]

Progressive hires young, blank-slate employees and invests heavily in training them, not only in insurance regulation but also in the art of negotiation and grief counseling. Its two claims adjuster training centers in Cleveland and Tampa graduate more than 1000 Progressive employees each year.

The transition to a process- and service-oriented insurance company posed some serious challenges to Progressive's executives. Bob McMillan, President of Progressive Insurance's Florida division comments:

> Like most success stories, it didn't happen overnight. When we first began the Immediate Response claims program, we didn't have any recommended structure mandated for all of our two hundred locations. All we told (representatives) was that it's not okay anymore to handle a claim in a week or ten days; from now on, we want you to do it immediately. We got two hundred approaches to solving that problem. And almost all the locations got in serious workflow difficulties for the first few months. But we kept watching them all in action until we began to observe that the ones that were working were organized on a team-based approach.

So there was nothing elegant about the entire procedure. It was simply a huge exercise in empirical research. Now we mandate team-based claims resolution throughout the company.[17]

Today, a team of 7–10 people usually carries out the claims process. A typical team has three representatives in the field, each of whom visits accident scenes and body shops or goes wherever the damaged vehicle is. Three work as inside representatives, answering the phone and managing the claims through the process. Usually, another person works as a dispatcher, sending assignments to the field representatives; and an administrative support person assists the team with administrative details. In some cases, a separate team leader functions as a quasi-supervisor. This person is responsible for quality assurance, and does on-the-job training.[18] Claims are assigned according to their complexity. Newer representatives handle single-car accidents and fender benders while more experienced representatives get multi-car accidents, often involving injuries and destroyed vehicles. One representative "owns" the claim, and other team members assist with various features. This arrangement is more efficient than having one representative do everything.

Progressive Insurance's focus on processes has largely eliminated the need for traditional management. When asked if the performers of the claims process in Ohio report to her or to the process owner of claims, Moira Lardakis, President of Progressive Insurance's Ohio division, replies, " 'Reports to' doesn't mean much around here." As Michael Hammer points out, "This Zen-like response conveys the essence of the process-centered organization."[19] The end of the organization chart does not mean the company has arrived in organizational heaven. While the process-centered organization has enabled greater flexibility, dynamism, and customer focus, this unavoidably ambiguous new arrangement brings with it contention and even conflict. As Progressive Insurance's Bruce Marlow comments, "It lacks a conventional sort of authority. There's no fixed shape, no single or total responsibility, no straight lines of command – and no simple way to make it work."[20]

How IT was used to reinvent the business

Progressive Insurance is one company that has learned how to use IT to revolutionize the business and even influence rivals.

Lewis has never been a tech-junkie. He joined Progressive almost the same day the company got its first punch-card machines. "The company was not early with computers," he says, "but the obsession my father had, and later that I had, of thinking that we could always be better, and having the freedom to experiment – to figure out how – kept my eyes open."[21]

As mentioned earlier, it took a consumer backlash in California in the late 1980s to put Progressive on its tech-driven path. In 1989, Progressive began to install a $28 million computer and nationwide voice/data system, which allowed faster communication between agents and shorter processing times for both applications and claims. By speeding up the claim processing, the new system enabled local agents to process 30 percent more claims.[22] The claims processing network, called *Progressive Automated Claims Management*, allowed local agents to download information into the central computer from their terminals. Previously, agents had to mail reports between offices and corporate or divisional headquarters, a slow and cumbersome process. More recently, the company provided its agents in the field with *ProRate*, a proprietary system, to run on their agency system. All the information the agent gathers about the policyholder is sent to Progressive electronically. Agents keep the necessary paperwork for themselves. They can electronically transfer funds. The consumer technically has a paper policy, but the process is totally electronic.

A corporate survey revealed that technology is making customer service easier for independent agents. Precisely, the survey of 865 agents revealed that 64 percent of those polled reported having more time on their hands as a result of using new technology. Of those agents who reported having more time, 43 percent of respondents said technology has enabled them to sell more business. "By offering our agents superior and easy-to-use technology, we enable them to save time, cut down on paperwork, and better serve their clients," comments Chris Garson, Agent Technology Leader for Progressive Insurance.[23]

Computer-based applications were also developed and deployed in the 1990s to support the work of claims representatives. The first stage of Immediate Response was designed to be quick and seamless, with an unbroken flow of information between the customer, Progressive's central database, and the local claims operation. Today, when a local dispatcher radios an adjuster to the scene of an accident, he will also page the corresponding claim number to him so that he can download the customer's file onto his laptop. This was not possible until Progressive's information systems department developed *Claims Workbench*, the software to do it. Early on, representatives relied on cellular phones to execute Immediate Response. They had to call dispatchers repeatedly to relay data or to retrieve coverage information from the mainframe. If representatives did not return to the office right away to update a file with their estimate, the job would not get done until the end of the day or the following morning.

Claims Workbench is an object-oriented software application developed by Progressive over 4 years. With the help of a wireless modem and a Pentium laptop, the program allows representatives to perform up to 20 separate transactions in the field – everything from entering police-report information, downloading another representative's estimate from across town, to handing out claims payments on the spot. Progressive rolled out *Claims Workbench* in September 1997. Within 3 months, the company trained 2500 representatives in 200 offices nationwide to use the software. As a result, Immediate Response became much more immediate. In 1990, claims representatives were able to inspect vehicles within 9 h of the accident report only 15 percent of the time. In 1997, the figure rose to 57 percent. "We're giving our reps the tools and information they need to do real-time decision making," says Mark Smith, head of claims for information system (IS). "They're empowered to settle claims in the field."[24] By responding quickly to a loss report, Progressive reduced other costs as well. For instance, both the number of days for which a rental car had to be supplied to the insured, and the number of days a damaged car had to be kept in storage were decreased.

Progressive has been a web believer for years. In 1995, Progressive became the first company to launch a web site. The company's web site has received, for the fourth consecutive quarter, the Gomez WebStar Award for Spring/Summer 2001 – an honor given to e-commerce companies that rank number one in their industry according to Gomez, the Internet quality measurement firm.[25] In 1996, the company introduced auto-insurance online comparison rates. In 1997, Progressive gives consumers another first: the ability to buy an auto-insurance policy in real-time online. In 1998, personal.progressive.com, the industry's most comprehensive and easy-to-use auto-insurance customer service site, was launched. The system gives customers access to their own policy information via the web. "Sometimes interacting with an insurance company is difficult for a customer. With Personal Progressive, policyholders can look up their own policy information and explore different options" comments Glenn Renwick, CIO.[26] The system allows customers to get a policy quote based on the addition of a new vehicle or other policy change, check the status of a claim, make on-line payments, and update account information.

In 2000, Progressive became the first insurance company to give policyholders access to company and account information through wireless application protocol technology (WAP). With the help of a digital cellular phone with Internet access, customers can now find a local agent by entering a zip, automatically claim service and modify their policy, access their account balance and status, and pay their bill. "We are letting people do business on their terms," says Fred Khoury, wireless Internet manager for Progressive. "Some policyholders will obviously wait until they go home, but some may want to contact Progressive instantly. WAP enables Progressive to *get onto cellular phone with a web browser*".[27] Progressive became the first auto-insurance company to receive a wireless payment from a customer using a personal digital assistant (PDA) device in 2001.

In 2000, Progressive concluded a marketing test in Texas of a product that bases auto-insurance premiums in part on when, where, and how much a vehicle is driven. The product, called *Autograph*, depends on data recorded by a device the size of a videocassette installed in the car. The data is recorded periodically and sent to Progressive using cellular communication and global positioning system (GPS) technologies. The company uses the data and other proprietary variables to calculate a monthly premium and bills the customer at the end of each month. In Houston, consumers paid an average of 25 percent less using *Autograph* than they paid using the traditional auto-insurance plan.[28]

Progressive was the only auto-insurance company to receive the prestigious CIO-100 award from *CIO Magazine* in 2001. From initiating the industry's first Immediate Response claims service, to becoming the industry's first provider of wireless Internet access in 2000, Progressive has been driven by a relentless commitment to providing unparalleled customer service and innovative ideas. As a result, it received recognition for its ingenuity and success. Progressive intends to stay one step ahead of the competition by offering customers, representatives and independent agents the innovative products and services they need, when they need them. This philosophy has made Progressive the fourth largest auto-insurance company in the country.

Case analysis

The pieces of the puzzle at Progressive

In this section, we will first present the environmental forces that have had an impact on the transformation at Progressive. Then, the nature and depth of the transformation that occurred during the 1990s will be depicted. To do so, we will examine and portray both the shape and size of each of the five pieces of the management puzzle at Progressive, namely, environment, strategy, IT, structure, and leadership.

Environment

Auto insurance proves to be a stable but competitive sector. While competition means lower rates and greater choice for insurance buyers, it may also bring confusion. The auto-insurance industry is relatively easy to enter because it has fairly low capitalization requirements. However, consumers and agents may not always know the newer market players very well, so they may be wary of doing business with these unfamiliar names.

In a mature market with little year-on-year growth, many auto-insurance companies have reclassified their business between standard and non-standard drivers. Today, non-standard policies account for only about 15 percent of the total auto-insurance market, and for many years the industry's leaders largely ignored this corner of the business, allowing Progressive to work it aggressively. The company specialized in a top-quality claims service and did not at all worry that it was a high-cost operator. This was a luxury it could afford, knowing that its customers, short of alternatives, would pay up for policies. But in the mid-1980s, giant Allstate, looking around for growth in its essentially mature market, finally focused on how much Progressive was making in its niche and, within a couple of years, outdistanced Progressive in non-standard business.

As discussed earlier, another blast came from Proposition 103, an initiative passed by California's voters in 1988, sending Lewis into a panic. This referendum was designed to regulate auto-insurance companies and to roll back escalating rates. The law was a near-fatal blow to Progressive, which had done 20 percent of its business in California. Lewis's company came up with

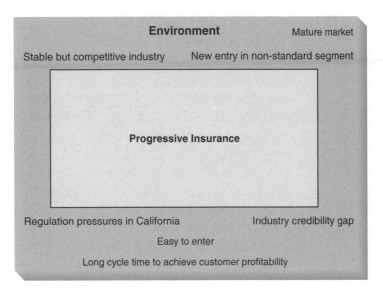

Figure 6.1
The environment
piece.

$60 million in refunds and eventually reduced its workforce by 19 percent. As explained earlier, Proposition 103 was a wake-up call for Lewis and his company.

Auto insurers, including Progressive, have become more adept, over the past few years, at holding down loss costs. In part, they have been helped by factors outside their control. Baby Boomers, a demographic group, which historically has fewer accidents, are turning 50. Airbags, seatbelt requirements, and drunk driving laws have also cut down on liability and damage claims. Auto-insurance companies have also been cutting costs by rethinking distribution models. The traditional independent or captive agent model has high commission costs, but offers better retention rates. This is important in an industry in which the average policy becomes profitable only after being in place for 18–24 months. To reduce commission costs, companies marketing through independent agencies are increasingly driving for closer, more exclusive relationships with their agents, which has increased pressure on marginal companies. Currently, the market is evenly divided between captive agents (such as State Farm and Allstate), independent agents (such as Progressive), and direct writers (such as Liberty Mutual) (Figure 6.1).

Strategy

Differentiation has always been the strategy privileged by Progressive's executives in order to cope with competition. Progressive was innovative from the start. For the first time, customers could pay their premiums in installments, an option that appealed to workers who could not afford annual premiums. They could even get drive-in claims service. Progressive wanted to make it easy for average people to protect one of their most important investments – their vehicles. The company originally focused on offering automobile insurance to blue-collar workers and property insurance on cars financed by local finance companies. In the 1950s, Progressive's executives decided to focus exclusively on the emerging non-standard segment and to fill that niche.

Increased regulation pressures and the aggressive entry of Allstate into the non-standard segment in the mid-1980s pushed Progressive to look for fresh ways to distinguish itself from its competitors. Peter Lewis then introduced Progressive to a rebuild-this-wreck period, achieving a transformation, says one competitor, "that makes you realize just how good Pete is".[29]

At that time, Lewis' vision was to get out of the car-insurance business and to get into the business of reducing the human trauma and cost of auto accidents in cost-effective and profitable ways. He, and his troops, worked to create "customer delight" for auto-insurance buyers. The company's culture of high energy and continuous innovation made everyone within the company want *to deliver the unexpected.* The company's objective was to become the No. 1 choice for auto-insurance consumers. The strategy was simply to set a new standard for customer service in the industry. Indeed, a key part of the improved experience at Progressive has been building customer trust and loyalty, which they did mostly by continually identifying new and better ways to serve customers. In short, IT-based innovative products and a relentless commitment to providing unparalleled customer service have made Progressive so Progressive in the 1990s (Figure 6.2). Willy Graves, claims-process leader, says:

> Customers expected us to deliver what they were paying for – to get their cars fixed and to cover their medical expenses. But we were spending our time putting paper into stacks. We realized that we had to treat an accident like what it is: an emergency.[30]

Information technology

Progressive has always been a technology leader in the auto-insurance industry. The company has made shopping for, buying,

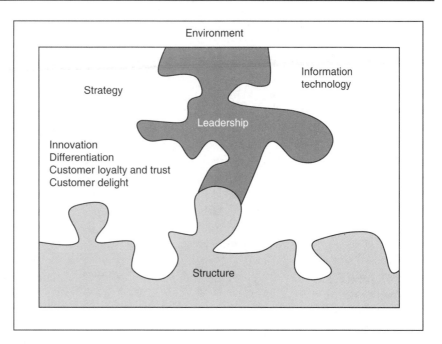

Figure 6.2
The strategy piece
at Progressive
Insurance.

and even owning auto-insurance an easy, information-rich experience for consumers. As a matter of fact, the company has been the first in the auto-insurance industry to:

- offer free auto-insurance rate comparisons (by phone and, ultimately, through Internet), making it the only company to offer "apples-to-apples" comparison rates between Progressive and up to three other companies;
- deploy a fleet of more than 2000 IRVs fitted with laptop computers, and wireless mainframe access;
- go online with a web site–progressive.com;
- sell insurance online, thereby allowing consumers to purchase auto policies in real time over the Internet;
- introduce interactive customer service on the web via personal.progressive.com;
- provide wireless access to progressive.com via cellular phones and PDAs – allowing customers to make payments, check claims history, and contact customer service;
- develop *Autograph*, a new technological device in cars which determines one's automobile insurance premium.

Altogether, these technological innovations have contributed to develop what can be called an "E-transaction model" of doing business. According to Toby Alfred, Internet site manager for Progressive, "This model creates more customer satisfaction and

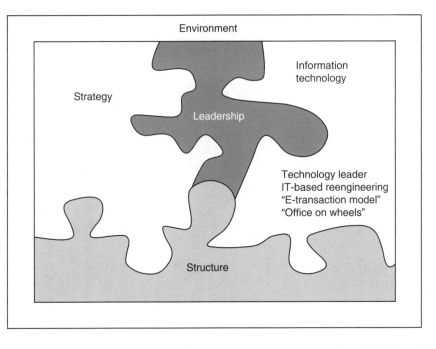

Figure 6.3
The IT piece at
Progressive
Insurance.

loyalty long-term, giving consumers greater control of their policy and personal information"[31] (Figure 6.3).

But it was Immediate Response with its fleet of 2000 offices on
wheels that really reinvented the company in the early 1990s. With
Immediate Response, Progressive set a new standard for customer
service with a strong focus on business processes. The innovation
service drastically cut the time required to process a collision
claim, enabling Progressive to get a quick, precise fix on the damage done and, in many cases, move to a quick – and lawyerless –
settlement. The new 24 h claims process was also designed for
greater agility and flexibility, so as to be able to respond easily and
immediately to every aspect of the client's needs. Nowadays, the
adjusters more or less live in Ford Explorers, taking calls from central dispatching offices and heading either to the homes of policyholders or to the accident scene itself. Lastly, Immediate Response
allowed many errors to be eliminated, since adjusters can take pictures of the damaged vehicle before anything else happens to it. In
short, the transformation which gradually occurred over the years
allowed the firm to achieve greater speed (treating any accident
like an emergency), flexibility (by allowing customers to do business with Progressive on their terms – when they want, where they
want), agility (allowing Progressive to respond to every aspect of
the customer's needs), and efficiency (eliminating undesirable
defects and errors).

Structure

The reengineering efforts deployed at Progressive, along with the adoption of emerging ITs, have had some impacts on the company's structure. Horizontal boundaries are now characterized by one-stop service for all customer needs (through sophisticated call centers) and process and team-based structures carrying ideas, resources, information, and competence with them, so that costumer needs are well met. Although team-based claims resolution is now mandated at Progressive, the company has been in different phases of evolution around the country. "In some locations we've made it all the way to a self-managed situation, but in others, teams operate in a way that's pretty traditional, and that seems to work for that location. So there's a fairly wide range, and that's fine with me, as long as it works" comments Bob McMillan, President of Progressive's Florida division.[32]

With the help of technology, not only horizontal but also vertical and geographic boundaries have become more permeable. As explained earlier, Progressive's focus on processes has largely eliminated the need for traditional hierarchy and supervision, and has transferred more power into the hands of responsible adjusters. The company redirected its focus from a person's authority and rank to an individual's useful ideas. Importantly, geographic barriers have become much more permeable over the years. Mobile work is widely diffused among claims representatives and adjusters. Bruce Marlow, Progressive Insurance's COO, observes that the company's adjusters could previously say that they were white-collar professionals who worked in a nice office park from 9 to 5 on weekdays. "But under the new situation, you can't schedule your work and you don't work 9 to 5. People work different shifts, and when a claim comes in, you go to the scene of that accident. It requires a lot of more commitment."[33] Work anytime, anywhere has become the dominant paradigm at Progressive.

Furthermore, employees' roles and skills have been adjusted in order to align with the new processes, technologies, and structures (Figure 6.4). The company has invested heavily in its workforce and the company has been reorganized annually since the early 1990s. As Lewis says:

> You can't innovate if your culture won't let you take risks or do something different, or continuously demand from you new ideas and free thinking. I have a theory that if we don't reorganize internally annually, we will probably be behind the curve. Give people

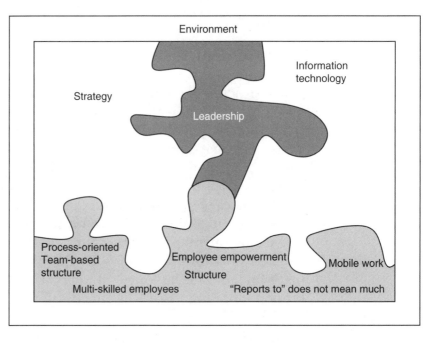

Figure 6.4
The structure piece
at Progressive
Insurance.

different functions, different jobs, different orientations, depending on the business needs and opportunities at the time – and they'll keep changing and growing as the company does. It's all about flexibility. You can't innovate without it.[34]

Leadership

When Progressive employees describe how their company approaches the auto-insurance business, they use words like "intense," "aggressive," and "unconventional." Those words also describe Peter Lewis. He is recognized as an extraordinary businessman, who, in his three decades as CEO, has taken Progressive from an industry gnat to a large, powerful competitor. Without question, Lewis was completely dedicated to making Progressive a great company, and he also brought enormous abilities to the job. His emotional attachment and relentless commitment toward his company have pushed him to make Progressive a great place to work (and live!) and one of the most regarded and respected company in North America. Lewis' entire life has been intertwined with the life of the company.

When channeled into business, Lewis' unorthodoxy spins out as creativity. He has been an instinctive challenger of assumptions and a constant generator of ideas. "Think about the world differently" is known as the Peter Lewis payoff.[35] Immediate Response was Lewis'

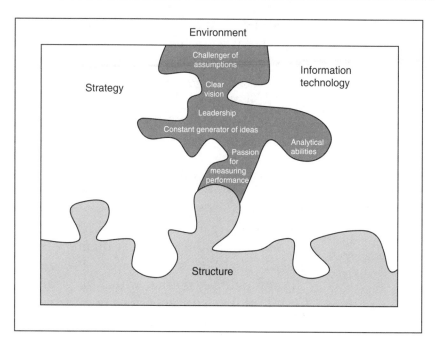

Figure 6.5
The leadership piece
at Progressive
Insurance.

second great idea – as powerful as it was simple (his first great idea was to focus on the non-standard segment). The majority of auto accidents happen before or after business hours, and on weekends and holidays, the CEO reasoned. So why shouldn't Progressive stay open around the clock? "For 3 years, people said, 'It's crazy, it's too expensive, nobody will do it,'" Lewis remarks. "And for the same 3 years, I sat here and said, "We're going to do it, no matter how much it costs and no matter how much you don't like it." Other businesses go the extra mile. Why not an auto-insurance company?"[36]

Beyond the vision are serious analytical and quantitative abilities, as well as a perfectionist's passion for testing and measuring performance (Figure 6.5). Indeed, Lewis is something of a fanatic about creating clear, measurable objectives that employees understand and agree to meet. Those who fall short do not last long in the company. Lewis explains:

> The other side of hiring good people is firing people who aren't good. We evaluate people against their objectives, which they negotiate with the company and then put in writing. If people aren't doing their job, it's good-bye. This is not a bloodthirsty place. It is a humane environment. But we do not suffer non-performance.[37]

Last, despite how much IT has been central to the reinvention of Progressive, Lewis has never been a tech-junkie. However, the obsession his father had, and that later he himself had, of thinking that things could always be better, and having the freedom to experiment, kept his eyes wide open. This has allowed him and everyone else at Progressive to learn how to use IT to revolutionize the business – and influence rivals. Today, the company uses the triple-punch of satellites, software, and the Internet to deliver on-site counseling, crash-to-cash service, and towing help.

Putting the puzzle together

In an uncertain and complex environment, managers must develop an organization that presents a coherent response to the dynamic conditions in which their specific business operates. As described earlier in this chapter, Progressive evolved in a stable, but competitive, market with little year-on-year growth. Therefore, building customer loyalty and trust constituted a critical success factor in an industry in which the cycle time to achieve customer profitability can take up to 24 months. Importantly, the rapid pace of change at Progressive in the 1990s reflected external and highly-threatening pressures the company had faced since the late 1980s, namely, the aggressive entry of Allstate into the non-standard segment, and increased regulation in California.

While a particular response to such external pressures can take any one of a number of configurations, all managers must consider the same four pieces, namely, strategy, IT, structure, and leadership. The traditional path to strategic alignment is that, in response to particular environmental conditions, a firm devises its strategy, chooses the structure and management processes that fit it, aligns IT, and ensures that individuals are appropriately trained and that roles are well designed (e.g. Scott Morton, 1991). But different paths to alignment may also lead to corporate success. For instance, Yetton *et al.* (1994) analyzed a small Australian architect firm in which business transformation occurred through the incremental adoption of IT. In that company, strategy emerged gradually and was an outcome, rather than a driver, of change.

Which path to strategic alignment was, then, adopted at Progressive? As described earlier, the company has always been a technology leader in the auto-insurance industry. Progressive has made shopping for, buying, and even owning auto insurance an easy, information-rich experience for consumers. Despite the ingenuity and innovativeness of the implemented systems and products, technology was not the sole driver of change at Progressive.

Rather, we feel that strategy and IT were codetermined, influenced each other, and fed back into each other. Indeed, the radical transformation of Progressive in the 1990s was the product of a well-defined, shared strategy built around the concepts of "customer delight" and "innovation," coupled with the appropriate adoption and use of emerging IT applications. In other words, a relentless commitment to providing unparalleled customer service through the adoption of innovative technologies has made Progressive so progressive. In most organizations, technology is just a tool, but it can be turned into a weapon against competitors if its focus is on a single mantra – in Progressive's case, *speed* – and it is kept innovative. It has worked well for Progressive and will continue to do so. In short, Progressive plans to stay one step ahead of the competition by offering customers, representatives and agents the products and services they need, when they need them. Again, this philosophy has made Progressive the fourth largest auto-insurance company in the country.

The IT-based reengineering efforts helped Progressive withstand the pressures being brought to bear on it. But they did more than just give Progressive a competitive advantage in the high-risk insurance market in which it had been operating; they converted the company from a niche player to a full-line seller. Indeed, reengineering efforts provided the company with the tools it needed to become an effective competitor in the much larger market for standard risks; a market in which it had previously had no presence and no prospects of success. Progressive discovered that if it could settle claims faster and more cheaply for bad drivers, it could do so just as well for average and good drivers.[38] This represents a good example of how IT fed back into strategy.

Lewis' leadership abilities were of the utmost importance in taking Progressive from an industry gnat to a large and powerful competitor. His emotional attachment and relentless commitment toward his company pushed him to make Progressive a great place to work and one of the most highly regarded and respected companies in North America. Importantly, Lewis' vision was essential in learning how to use IT, not only to revolutionize and reinvent the business, but also to influence close rivals and the industry as a whole. This was symbolized by Lewis' slogan: "Think about the world differently." Lewis had the same obsession his father also had, of thinking how his company could always be better, and having the freedom to experiment. Such an attitude allowed him to keep his eyes wide open constantly. "You can't have innovation that isn't technology-based today," he argued. In order to develop and realize his vision, Lewis developed a team of executives who will likely keep the company moving briskly along the path he himself has set. He is and will always be linked intrinsically and almost mystically with the company.

At Progressive, structure emerged gradually and was an outcome of business transformation. For instance, when the company initiated the reengineering process in the early 1990s, it had no recommended structure for all of the 200 locations; most sites got into serious workflow problems at the early stage of the transformation process. Only through extensive field observation and organizational learning was a team-based approach identified as the optimal structural arrangement. Ultimately the responsibility for achieving results lies with the individual professional (adjuster, for instance). Progressive's focus on process has subsequently eliminated the need for traditional or hierarchical management. Indeed, whole layers of supervisors, directors, and vice-presidents have been replaced over time by a relative handful of process owners and coaches. Today, both the process owner and the coach are supporting resources helping the individual professional accomplish his or her work, not controllers with their own agendas. More permeable geographic boundaries were also the result of a well-thought-out strategy, which consists in treating an accident like what it is: an emergency. With the help of effective use of emerging technologies such as office vans, web-based applications, and wireless technology applications, customers can do business with Progressive on their terms – when they want, where they want while Progressive employees can

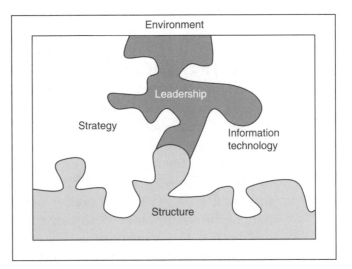

Figure 6.6
The management puzzle at Progressive Insurance.

respond instantly to every aspect of the customer's needs. In the new work environment, however, employees cannot schedule their work and they do not work 9 to 5. When a claim comes in, for instance, someone has to go to the scene of that accident.

The strategic alignment of the pieces of the management puzzle at Progressive is depicted in Figure 6.6. The radical transformation of Progressive reflected external and highly-threatening pressures the company had faced in the late 1980s. The rapid pace of change within the company was driven by a well-defined strategy, built around the concepts of "customer delight" and "innovation", coupled with IT-based reengineering efforts. Leadership was essential in aligning strategy and IT elements. Lastly, structure emerged gradually from a rather intuitive trial-and-error process and hence, was an outcome of the business transformation.

Questions

1. Was the business transformation that took place at Progressive Insurance mainly a response to particular environmental pressures or a process aimed at solving internal problems or satisfying specific needs?

2. Explain how Progressive Insurance redefined its business using the "management puzzle" described in Chapter 1. Was the transformation approach followed at Progressive Insurance linear or dynamic? Illustrate.

3. What role did IT play in the business transformation at Progressive Insurance? Was IT an "enabler" or a "driver" for change? Explain.

4. To what extent is Progressive Insurance a "boundaryless organization"? Illustrate.

5. To what extent was the business transformation at Progressive Insurance successful? Did the transformation allow Progressive Insurance to achieve greater speed, flexibility, integration, and innovation? Illustrate.

Endnotes

[1] Salter, C., Progressive makes big claims, *Fast Company*, **19**, November 1998.

[2] An independent agent is one who agrees to perform services or supply commodities under a contract. In carrying out his/her contract,

he/she is not under the control of, or an employee, of the party with whom he/she contracts.

[3] Stepanek, M., Q&A with Progressive's Peter Lewis, *Businessweek Online*, September 2000.

[4] Loomis, C.J., Sex. Reefer? And auto insurance! *Fortune*, 8 July 1995.

[5] Siggelkow, N. and Porter, M.E., *Progressive Corporation*, Harvard Business School, Case Study #9-797-109, May 14, 1998.

[6] *Ibid.*

[7] *Ibid.*

[8] Salter, C., 1998, *op. cit.*, consulted at www.fastcompany.com/online/19/progressive.html.

[9] Siggelkow, N. and Porter, M.E., 1998, *op. cit.*

[10] Progressive's press release, December 15, 2000.

[11] Salter, C., 1998, *op. cit.*

[12] Loomis, C.J., 1995, *op. cit.*

[13] Salter, C., 1998, *op. cit.*

[14] Yeh, R., Pearlson, K. and Kozmetsky, G. (eds.), Progressive Insurance: an instant execution company, in *Zero Time*, New York, NY: John Wiley & Sons, Inc., 2000.

[15] Hammer, M., *Beyond Reengineering*, New York, NY: HarperCollins Book, 1996.

[16] Siggelkow, N. and Porter, M.E., 1998, op. cit.

[17] Hammer, M., 1996, *op. cit.*

[18] Yeh *et al.*, 2000, *op. cit.*

[19] Hammer, M., 1996, *op. cit.*

[20] *Ibid.*

[21] Stepanek, M., 2000, *op. cit.*

[22] Salter, C., 1998, *op. cit.*

[23] Progressive's press release, 24 January 2001.

[24] Salter, C., 1998, *op. cit.*

[25] Progressive's press release, 8 May 2001.

[26] MacSweeney, G., Progressive inside and out, *Insurance and Technology*, **24**(10), September 1999, 13–14.

[27] MacSweeney, G., Progressive goes wireless with WAP technology, *Insurance and Technology*, **25**(13), December 2000, 14–15.

[28] Whitney, S. Think small, *Best's Review*, September 2000, 6.

[29] Siggelkow, N. and Porter, M.E., 1998, *op. cit.*

[30] Hammer, M., 1996, *op. cit.*

[31] Progressive's press release, 7 August 2001.

[32] Progressive's press release, 7 August 2001.

[33] Progressive's press release, 7 August 2001.

[34] Stepanek, 2000, *op. cit.*

[35] *Ibid.*

[36] Salter, C., 1998, *op. cit.*

[37] Hammer, M., 1996, *op. cit.*

[38] *Ibid.*

Chapter 7

The organization without an organizational chart — Oticon

Case description*

> *I sat down on New Year's Day in 1990 and tried to think the unthinkable: a vision for the company of tomorrow. It would be a company where jobs were shaped to fit the person instead of the other way around. Each person would be given more functions, and a job would emerge by the individual accumulating a portfolio of functions.*
>
> Lars Kolind, President, Oticon[1]

"Think the unthinkable." This slogan is inscribed among the classical columns framing the entry to Oticon's head office. A Danish firm with close to 1500 employees, Oticon is a world leader in the manufacture of hearing aids. It literally revolutionized the industry and, in the process, became the undisputed market leader. Oticon exports 90 percent of its production through branches and agents in over 100 countries. It maintains one of the major silicon chip research departments in Europe, as well as its own manufacturing facilities. Oticon is positioned as the most important partner in hearing aid clinics.

This success is quite recent, however, as Oticon was declaring operating losses in the late 1980s. Its market share was being eroded by large and highly diversified competitors such as Panasonic and Siemens, which could invest more in R&D and mass production, thereby gaining greater leeway to trim margins. The market for hearing aids was stagnating, and consumers were demanding a less visible product that would take full advantage of current technology. Like many companies at the time, Oticon needed to respond to new market demand while facing competition from multinationals wielding great financial and technological power. The challenge was daunting, and Oticon's survival would depend on how it responded.

---

* This case was adapted from Oticon by De Basquiat, S. and Rivard, S., and is reproduced with permission from HEC Montreal, ©HEC Montreal.

The company

Oticon was founded in Denmark by Hans Demant, whose wife had suffered a significant loss of hearing. In 1904, Mr. Demant traveled to London in search of solutions to her problem. He opened a hearing aid company in the same year, the first of its kind in the world. After Demant's death in 1910, his son William took charge and Oticon began importing and distributing products from the U.S. As the First World War broke out, the firm was well established in Denmark, the rest of Scandinavia and St. Petersburg. Oticon's network of agents expanded throughout Europe through the 1920s and 1930s. By 1940, the Second World War was interfering with supply channels, forcing Oticon to begin manufacturing its own products.

In 1957, William and his wife Ida-Emilie gave their stock holdings in the company to the Oticon Foundation, a charity dedicated to assisting people with handicaps – particularly hearing difficulties.

From 1950 to the end of the 1970s, Oticon established sales points throughout most of the world. It also revolutionized the industry by developing hearing aids worn behind-the-ear (BTE), rather than in a pocket. As electronics, silicon chips and microprocessors began to revolutionize product design, hearing aids began to employ increasingly sophisticated technology, and consumers began demanding the most from miniaturization. Beginning in the 1980s, entire hearing aids could be installed in the ear itself.

Although Oticon had, up to then, been the market leader, the technological revolution, changing consumer demand, and a stagnant market had left it vulnerable. The company was losing market share to its competitors, and by 1979 it had lost its leadership position. Firms such as Panasonic, Siemens, and Sony were covering most of the electronics markets, and were, therefore, reaping the advantages of cutting-edge research in silicon chips, miniaturization, and microprocessors. They were better positioned to gain market share by cutting their margins in spite of falling demand. In 1986, Oticon reported its first financial losses.

Oticon was no longer able to defend its product's position in the marketplace. Operations were completely inflexible, and its response time to market demand was far too unwieldy. In 1988, in the midst of this crisis, Oticon chose a new president, Lars Kolind.

Lars Kolind was a former mathematician, to all appearances quiet, shy and almost childlike in manners. Early rumor had it that because of his involvement in the scout movement, he would run the company accordingly.[2]

> In the event this was no joke. Boy scout attitudes and actions were never far away from Lars. Characteristically, within a period of 3 months after joining Oticon, he managed to acquire a nearly encyclopedic knowledge of the hearing aid business, the Oticon company, and it's staff.[3]

Yet, while being mostly gentle in his manners, Kolind could also demonstrate a strong will. He engaged in drastic cost-cutting and gave close scrutiny to any and all costs. Each expense had to be justified to him directly. He attacked unnecessary expenses, with particular attention to employee privileges. For example, when Kolind began at the firm, executives were provided with a company car from a selection of five models, based on their reporting level. He was personally offered a royal blue Jaguar XJ Sovereign 6.2, an offer he declined in favor of keeping his old Saab. Setting the example was part of Kolind's management philosophy. Collectively, these efforts took 20 percent of the price of Oticon hearing aids, and by 1989 the company was turning a profit.

Kolind soon realized that these measures would be inadequate in the face of advantages held by highly diversified competitors. The hearing aid market required a faster response time and greater flexibility than Oticon could muster. Kolind understood that Oticon could not fight a price war, and that its products would have to be positioned in an entirely different manner.

On January 1, 1990, Kolind wrote a four-page memorandum in which he set out his vision for reinventing the company. According to him, "Our company did not function thanks to the organization, but in spite of it."[4] He then proposed what he would call the "spaghetti" organization, because the image that came to his mind was of a plate of slightly overcooked spaghetti, a kind of compact interweaving of pasta, which represented the multiple roles that employees would need to take, and which were themselves interwoven.

He hoped to create an organization that would set itself apart through radical change:

> In my experience, it is impossible to change a traditional machine-like organization into building in that level of flexibility and ability to advance knowledge by any means other than revolution.[5]

Kolind's vision

One of his colleagues said of Kolind that "vision is what makes Lars tick."[6] Kolind wanted to go from "products based primarily on technology" to "products based primarily on knowledge." Oticon, which was, first and foremost, an industrial organization with very high standards for quality, would have to become a service enterprise offering physical products. This change would be the new competitive advantage that would distinguish Oticon from its competitors, which had themselves a very strong technology orientation. The final objective was clearly defined from the start: recapture market leadership by 1997.

Kolind called on the services of academics and consultants, and implemented small working groups to design the new electronic infrastructure, find a building site and choose an architect for the new head office. He wanted to begin by rethinking the organization of the head office, which he found too hierarchical, rigid, and utterly inappropriate for fostering communication.

Kolind wanted to eliminate it all: not just the titles and departments, but also the offices and all the physical constraints that impeded any kind of operational transparency. As a direct result of these changes the company came to realize that it had invented the first fully automatic hearing aid in the mid-1980s, and that the idea had never become a product because of a lack of communication between departments.

Paper and memorandums would also have to disappear if oral communication was to take its place, and all information would have to be available to everyone. Finally, employees would no longer be able to exercise a single trade, but would have to take on several, even if they had not been so qualified. Individuals would have to define their work as a function of their own qual-ities and competencies, and this new definition would evolve with their personal progress. Kolind wanted work to be adapted to the person, rather than the other way around. He firmly believed that job descriptions never fit employees; they kept employees from realizing their full potential. Above all, he thought that an employee could make use of his or her competencies in many more positions than one.

Torken Groth, an Oticon employee, says:

> You had to position yourself in the new organization, you had to create your job again, in a new context, with new relationships. Lars

told middle management that we were going to be almost obsolete in the future, that we were going to change the company from a management-driven to a project-driven organization. It would be the task that would drive the company, not those managing the tasks.[7]

Kolind even reconsidered the role of the Executive Chairman:

I don't see myself as a captain who steers the ship, I see myself as a naval architect who designs the ship.[8]

The new head office

Kolind decided to gather all employees exercising head office functions in the same building. He relocated them north of Copenhagen, in a building that had housed Tuborg's bottling operations. From the outside, the building is ordinary enough, in a turn-of-the-century style. But the interior does not resemble the traditional head office in any way. There are no private offices, only an enormous room with work tables here and there, each equipped with a computer and a telephone. But it does not look like a large warehouse, either, as is sometimes the case in companies where all offices are found in the same room. On the contrary, it is warm and inviting – wood floors, soft lighting – and each area in the building has its own character.

There are many symbols in this building, from the inscription at the entry – "think the unthinkable" – to the enormous transparent plastic tube that cuts through the cafeteria, a chute for all the paper thrown out in a day that has been placed where employees are most likely to see it. According to Kolind, the new head office should be a reflection of the collective will to change the company. Therefore, the firm sold all the furniture from the former head office to its employees within an 8-h period.[9] Kolind came to regard August 8, 1991, the day they moved into the new buildings, as a critical moment for the company.

Employees were not assigned desks. Instead, everyone was given a caddy in which a dozen files and some personal documents could be kept. The caddy was simply picked up in the morning and used through the day. Employees would set up for work according to the project they would be working on that day, and they were required to be able to relocate with a 5-min notice. Everyone rubbed elbows with everyone else; marketing with software engineers, financial managers with staff from human resources. Wanting to set an example, and in order to remain highly accessible by all employees, Kolind refused privileges. He worked in the same environment as the other employees, being easily accessible by all. If his office was needed when he was not there, his things would simply be moved out of the way.

Working in this way not only gave employees knowledge of everything going on in the company, it also created an atmosphere of mutual respect, because they got to see each other at work. Paul Erik Lyregaard, Director of R&D, says:

> It's hard to maintain "enemy pictures" in this company – they're not "those bloody fools in marketing" – You know too much about what people do.[10]

It was, in fact, Kolind's intention to have a certain amount of disorganization in the workplace. In 1995, when the whole company spent a year working on a completely digital hearing aid, Kolind noticed that employees drifted back into a departmental style of organization. One day, he had all 150 people at head office relocate within a 3-h period so that individuals in different functional roles would again find themselves working side by side.

Any and all measures were taken to encourage contact and informal communication between employees. Elevators were made inoperable so that employees would meet each other on the stairs, where they were more likely to engage in conversation. Bars were installed on all three floors where coffee was served and meetings could be organized – standing up. Rooms with circular sofas were provided, complete with small coffee tables, in order to encourage discussion.

Finally, there was the very symbolic paper room, "the only place where paper is safe."[11] A glass door closes behind anyone entering the room, showing that "it is difficult for paper to leave." All corporate mail arrives in this room, where it is scanned and destroyed. Only selected documents are retained, if only for a few days (magazines and reports) or for legal reasons.

Kolind felt that this kind of architecture and physical arrangement would create a place where: "People shift their focus from their power base and background to focus on the task, the customer, the new product."[12]

Room to work freely

Kolind and various work groups spent hundreds of hours setting out the basic values that would guide the re-organized company. These discussions led them to conclude that employees should be treated as responsible adults, but also as unique individuals. Employees would want to receive complete information and be treated as fundamentally honest. This was the point of departure for creating the new organization.

Oticon personnel have complete freedom in choosing the projects they work on, the hours they work, their vacation time and the training they need. Job offers are posted on the corporate computer system, and project managers are responsible for recruiting team members. They publicize their needs on the electronic bulletin board, and interested employees respond directly online. Work begins as soon as the team is formed. Kolind explains that even the less popular employees must find work, and when they cannot, they do not survive.

The shift from hierarchical systems to networks of experts also applied to specialized fields such as hearing, acoustics, psychology, anatomy, chip design, marketing, and finance. Employees are encouraged to develop an interest in fields other than their own by getting involved in activities for which they may have no prior qualifications. "A top chip designer who performs a marketing function in one project becomes a much better chip designer," explains Kolind, "because he sees the world stereophonically."[13]

In fact, employees are required to be active in at least three specialties, one by professional qualification and two others unrelated to the first. This allows the company great flexibility when responding to an unforeseen request in a particular domain, such as a marketing issue that arises in the midst of an important advertising campaign. In this case, individuals can be recruited freely from any work group. Everything is organized around projects, rather than tasks or departments.

Employees are responsible for creating their own competency profile. They define their own tasks and adapt activities to suit levels of knowledge and ability. Kolind considers this the best way to stimulate creativity and move beyond conventional thinking. As a result, Oticon was the first company to stop selling hearing aids as products for treating handicaps and promote them as high-technology communications systems. It was also the first to drop the standard flesh colour of its products for the silver-grey used in portable telephones.

Approximately 100 more or less important projects are under-way at Oticon at any given time. Often, they begin in a disorderly way. Many start out without any official procedure, and even when they are registered in Oticon's information system, there is no mechanism limiting the resources invested. There is a saying at Oticon that "it is easier to be forgiven than it is to get permission." Kolin adds, "If you're in doubt, do it. If it works, fine. If not, we forgive you."[14]

Each project has a project manager, who can be anyone with a good idea, and a project owner, one of the 10 people sitting on the management team (a last trace of the former hierarchical organization). The project owner must do whatever is required to make the project a success, without actually working on it. This role is one of providing advice and material support without giving instructions.

Project managers exercise a great deal of freedom. They have complete responsibility for their project, from recruitment through budgeting and determining the resources required. The only immutable requirements are with respect to deadlines. The project manager's role is to stimulate the team but not control it. The presumption is that if employees have chosen to work on a project, they must be motivated to do a good job. Directives to the team often amount to little at all. Peter Finneryp, an employee, explains:

> We were operating in a very delicate working environment because you could never see where the borders were, there were no fixed definitions. The only thing that was definite was the goal that Oticon needed to do something in this product area and "we want you to do it." That was the only job description I had nothing written. Go in and do something about it.[15]

Information and communication

Another important organizational change was giving employees free and full access to information. "Anyone can click on our strategic plan (in the computer) and see what we intend to do to: beat Siemens (…) If people know what we are doing and why we are doing it, they know exactly which project to work on."[16]

With rare exceptions, all information, including the President's mail and agenda, is accessible to all employees. Hewlett-Packard and Andersen Consulting installed software that scans all incoming mail (see The paperless office, page 191). Once scanned, the mail is promptly destroyed in the paper room. Kolind estimates that paper use has dropped 80 percent overall, for which Oticon is known as "The Paperless Company."

The team that implemented this technology interviewed employees before selecting databases and tools. Each computer has a copy of Word for word processing, a calendar, e-mail access and an electronic filing system. The filing system was one of the greatest challenges faced by the IT team. Initially, existing databases were retained unchanged and stored centrally, and employees were responsible for organizing their own files. This approach failed in short order. It became apparent that people had trouble setting up their own useable system, let alone organizing files in a way that would be transparent to others.

In the next attempt, a standardized file structure was imposed. Ten file types were determined, each corresponding to a project phase. Employees only had to give the document an appropriately evocative name and attach some key words before saving it to the right file. This system has worked well.[17]

All that is required to gain access to the central database from any workstation is an access authorization. To reduce the amount of traffic on the local area network (LAN), employees can take their computer with them when they move to another station. This allows them to continue working on the same hard disk. Mobility, therefore, presents no problems.

Under the Oticon system, all information, text, images, and drawings are digitized and available to all on a common database. This has been achieved on Plexus XDP Imaging Software from Recognition International. Although this highly evolved tool gives complete access to information, outside observers have noted that, in practice, it is not used as much as it could be. The value of the electronic filing system is in the short term: once a project is finished, it is rare that its files are accessed again. Oticon's long-term memory is oral rather than written; it is based on interaction between people.

As far as this is concerned, Kolind's position is very clear: nothing is better than oral communication. "There's absolutely no doubt that oral communication is 10 times more powerful, more creative, quicker, and nicer than writing memos."[18] The information system is there to bring people together, not stand between them. Even a tool such as Xerox's Liveboard, originally developed for facilitating the work of geographically separated team members, has been adapted for use by groups in the same room, where its large screen is used for making presentations and teaching.

Oticon uses callware to provide electronic support for brainstorming sessions and electronic blackboards for videoconferencing. Kolind believes that these tools multiply the productivity of intellectual work by a factor of five.

> We can do in 1 day what we used to do in 1 week. We use them whenever we come to a critical decision-making point. We also use groupware for collective writing of technical manuals. It's fascinating to watch 10 people working simultaneously on one document.[19]

Oticon's use of electronic systems hinges more on temporal than spatial factors. In knowledge applications, time plays a more significant role than physical location. Teams may be physically separated, but they are together when they work. Learning takes place through interaction, and the knowledge brought by each member is leveraged by a factor of five.

Limitations are even placed on communications by e-mail. Kolind himself receives only seven or eight messages per day, and is known to return them to their sender with the message, "This was a superfluous e-mail; I do not want things like this."[20]

On the other hand, telephones are used a great deal. All employees are equipped with portable phones, and telephones on desks are gradually disappearing. Employees may rarely sit at their desks, but they are often seen standing, talking on the telephone.

Managing problems

Completely changing an organization is not generally achieved without running into some problems. Kolind launched a direct attack on the organizational culture, on privileges tied to seniority and titles, and on work processes. He was very direct in his dealings with managers, knowing that they would not easily accept losing the power they derived from controlling information and owning statutory symbols. While being very persuasive either by sharing his vision or by setting example, Kolind was not afraid to use power when he felt it was necessary. He made things very clear from the start by announcing, "I am 100 percent sure that we will try this. There's enough time so that you can make a choice – whether you are going to try it with us or whether ... you find another job."[21] Nevertheless, no-one resigned during the transition period, January 1, 1991 to January 1, 1992. On the other hand, there were cuts of 10–15 percent in the secretarial pool and administrative support, as tools for managing correspondence and report writing were widely distributed among employees.

From the employees' point of view, the notion of taking on three jobs was a tough pill to swallow. Many felt that the changes brought greater social control, exercised through colleagues, rather than traditional systems. A study conducted at the end of the first year nevertheless showed that general employee satisfaction had greatly improved.

Kolind had also offered each employee a personal computer similar to the one they used at the office, so that they could take control of their own education. In response, employees formed a PC club, so that members could develop adequate computer skills. This initiative helped eliminate the tendency to count the hours worked, as individuals were free to continue working at home.

A profit-sharing plan was also introduced, with employees receiving company shares each year. The attention of the press, particularly in Denmark, was also a motivating factor. It is difficult to evaluate your company harshly when it is being touted as a model of success in work processes.

A complete success

On the cover of Oticon's 1995 annual report, Kolind wrote: "Don't be surprised. Knowledge-based organizations do work."[22] The company's objectives had, in fact, been fully attained. Even though profits fell in the first three quarters, after a year they had doubled, and Oticon reclaimed its leadership of the industry. In spite of a decline in market size in the early 1990s, Oticon sales grew 23 percent in 1992 and profits increased 25 percent. This success received wider recognition when the company was nicknamed "the first ISO 9001-certified chaos." By 1995, the company had doubled in size and profits had reached $20 million, or 10 times that of 1990. In less than 10 years Oticon had introduced 10 major product innovations.

The discovery, in 1988, that the company had already developed an entirely automatic hearing aid, allowed it to bring the product to market as Multifocus in 1991. Within the following 2 years, three other generations were invented, providing much better performance at half the size. In 1995, Oticon introduced JUMP 1, the first entirely digital product, and began the race for perfecting digital hearing aid technology. The technology, marketed in 1996 under the name DigiFocus, was available in models to be worn in or behind the ear. Oticon had shortened the product development cycle and merchandising time by 50 percent. A new product can now be designed, developed, and brought to market in less than 12 months, an exceptionally fast reaction time to consumer demand.

Lars Kolind had succeeded in achieving the challenge he had set out in the very beginning, when he said,

> ... breakthroughs require a combination of technology, psychology, and imagination. The ability to "think the unthinkable" and make it happen.[23]

Case analysis

The pieces of the puzzle at Oticon

Environment

During the 1980s, Oticon's market position and technological leadership were seriously threatened. First, the hearing aid manufacturer was faced with two dramatic technological challenges: the need to shift from analog to digital technology, and the need to develop "in-the-ear" (ITE), as opposed to BTE products. Oticon's scientific staff was very competent and knowledgeable in the area of BTE products, and all R&D efforts were devoted to perfecting the well-known products that had made Oticon's reputation. The shift in consumers' preferences in favor of ITE products, and the necessity to adapt and exploit digital technology caught the enterprise off guard. Hence, as Oticon's industrial environment became increasingly involved in the emerging knowledge-based economy, the firm's traditional responses to its environment proved inadequate.

At the same time, firms from other sectors which had developed an expertise both in digital technologies and miniaturization,

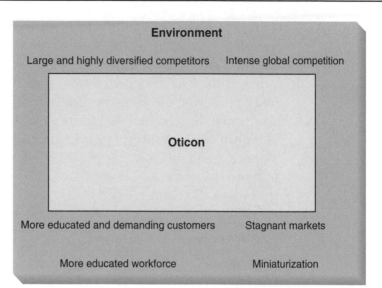

Figure 7.1
Environment.

entered the market that Oticon dominated. And these newcomers were not small start-ups: Siemens and Panasonic were large multinational firms, with solid R&D track records. Moreover, these competitors benefited from being more diversified than Oticon. Thus, a second threat to Oticon's market position was the successful entry of large diversified competitors, which benefited from significant scale economies and could tolerate low margins, at least initially. The result was a deterioration of Oticon's market share and profit margins as price competition intensified. The cozy, oligopolistic environment in which Oticon had been operating for years gave way, in a few short years, to a competitive environment characterized by a more fragmented structure and intense price rivalry.

On the demand side, a third development occurred which exacerbated competition and the battle for market shares: as global demand grew at only a modest rate, consumers became more sophisticated and asked for ever more technologically and aesthetically advanced products. The pressure on Oticon intensified accordingly (Figure 7.1).

Strategy

How did Oticon respond to these environmental challenges? The first piece of the management puzzle which Lars Kolind, Oticon's chief executive officer (CEO), used was *strategy*. After trying the classical remedy of aggressive cost-cutting to make the company profitable again, Kolind realized that doing so was not the road to success. Rather, he recognized that the firm had to reinvent itself, if it was to succeed in its new environment. He envisioned what the company ought to look like, and he described his vision in a document he drafted on New Year's Day 1989–1990. As shown in the following excerpts, the document clearly states the company's mission, sets precise goals and objectives, and draws a picture of what the business would look like, and how it would operate in the future.

Kolind's strategy[17]

The mission
To be the world's leading hearing aid manufacturer by the end of the decade

---

The goals

- To understand the customers (professional dealers) so well that we can develop products and services which are precisely on target each time, and which can be sold at high prices compared to costs
- To develop better and more production-friendly hearing aids
- To control purchasing and production, so as to respond to customers' need with minimum storage
- To support the sales companies in such a way that they become competitive in their own markets
- To administrate efficiently, simply, and as cost-effectively as possible

The objectives

- To cut 30 percent of the costs over the next 3 years.
- To improve our competitive ability by 30 percent over 3 years.

The vision

We will make Oticon's headquarters into:
A team comprising approximately 150 staff working on 500 or even 1000 tasks, all of which are continually developing. Some of the tasks are permanent, others are short term (…). Each task has a manager (…) and each belongs in a particular area. (…) Most of the staff will work on several

tasks under special project leaders (…). Departments will be replaced with groups of tasks which belong to particular areas. Memos are replaced by dialog, and all necessary written communication will take place electronically (…). The environment is open, and invites cross-disciplinary dialog. Tasks change; colleagues change; as does who sits where.

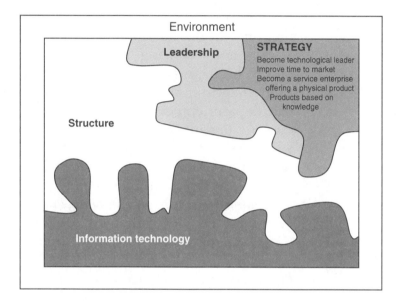

Figure 7.2
Strategy.

Kolind's vision clearly corresponds to a strategic repositioning of Oticon. In classical Porterian terms, Oticon was "stuck in the middle:" it was no longer in a position of cost leadership, and it was not sufficiently innovative. Kolind's response was to reposition Oticon as a technological leader. Its technological capacity would then enable the firm to differentiate its products and re-establish a certain degree of market control and price leadership, thus increasing its profit margin and generating the cash flows necessary to sustain its R&D strategy (Figure 7.2).

Structure

The second piece of the puzzle to come into play was *structure*, which indeed occupies the major part of Kolind's document. While during the same era other firms transformed their structure by altering their geographical and external boundaries, Oticon strictly focused on its horizontal and vertical boundaries, which were abolished. On the other hand, it introduced no significant changes to its network of external relationships or its spatial organization.

No new alliances, partnerships, joint ventures or major collaborative agreements were forged with suppliers and industry complementors. At the same time, the actual walls which, according to Kolind put people into "Rabbit Holes," simply vanished.

Prior to the transformation, Oticon's horizontal boundaries were almost impermeable. They were Kolind's first target. The two main divisions – Electronics (which was in charge of production and product development) and International (sales, marketing, and servicing subsidiaries) – communicated rather poorly. Each worked with its own set of rules, agenda, and culture. And within these divisions, work was organized around specific departments and tasks. For instance, within the Electronics division, product development was its own, closed department, and tasks were to be fulfilled sequentially, following the mass-production principles of Electronics. People were locked into specific roles and responsibilities and were rewarded only for those, to the point where, over the years, employees would execute only tasks that were clearly defined by managers; nobody took initiatives: "… people only worked with what was lying on their desk – correction: on the desk pad. That was the limit! And that's because employees got their wrists slapped if they went beyond that."[25] Moreover, "No one ever offered assistance either in their own or another department. That would be a sign that they didn't have enough to do. In other words: at the next round of lay-offs someone might be fired from your department. So you minded your own business and looked after your own job."[26]

The new structure envisioned by Kolind was to break this mold, since he suggested that: "The way we perceive our jobs has to change. We have to utilize our talents more effectively – and we can do this by creating a possibility to take on several different tasks as opposed to only one."[27] By suggesting that an employee learn, possess, and use at least three skills – for instance, that an employee from the pay office help collect sales figures in the sales department, and if artistically minded contribute to illustrate new brochures – Kolind was indeed inviting employees to cross-horizontal boundaries. As well, Oticon's project-based structure, with multi-disciplinary teams, was designed to allow for the free movement of people and ideas across fields of expertise. Teams are set up and disbanded constantly, according to the projects' evolutions. Taking initiatives was also encouraged: any employee who saw an opportunity, or knew of a problem to be solved could initiate a project.

This very fluid, organic organizational structure is not viable in a traditional, inflexible hierarchy. Hence, vertical boundaries were also among Kolind's targets. Prior to Oticon's transformation, there were six levels in the firm's hierarchy, with privileges based on rank. Not only was there a specific company car assigned to each management level, but other material signs existed. An employee hired just before the transformation mentioned: "When I came here, prestige and reward were very apparent: in the length of the curtains, the type of carpet, the arm rests on the chairs, and the size of peoples' desks. It all gave status. And that was what people strove for."[28]

The rigidity of vertical boundaries is often reflected by the importance of rules in an organization. At Oticon, "There were rules for everything, and people could – and were expected to – look everything up. (…) There were rules for the sake of rules".[29] Another sign of rigid vertical boundaries is that an organization continues to do things because they have always been done this way. At Oticon, nobody questioned procedures, or how things were done, or why they were done in a certain manner. Here is what one employee working at head office said, "Management told us that we should try to look busy, because otherwise we would be fired …".[30]

Another sign of a dysfunctional hierarchy is that creativity and innovation are driven underground because people know that new ideas will receive adverse reactions. At Oticon, product development was based on making refinements to those existing products that had made the company famous. People were not expected to do anything beyond that. In fact, trying to do anything beyond improving those existing products would be seen as somewhat of an insult by the Electronics division. "Employees had very limited opportunities to renew their skills and be creative".[31]

The new structure departed drastically from this rigid hierarchy. Hierarchy was dramatically flattened and can be summarized as follows: staff, project managers, and project owners. The staff is organized into many teams or projects headed by project managers. And each project manager reports to one of the 10 project owners, who constitute the management team of the organization.

In the new Oticon, incentive and rewards are based on achievements, on learning new skills or using previously untapped skills to help one's team or project, and on performance, rather than on rank. People are encouraged to put forth new ideas and question

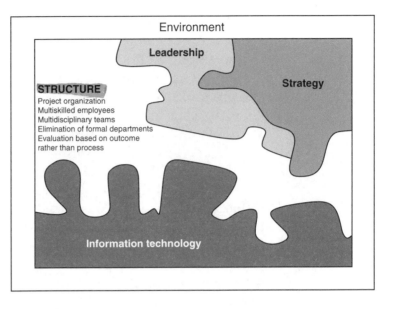

Figure 7.3
Structure.

existing ways of doing things. "Think the unthinkable" is the new motto. For example, the Multifocus system was the first product development project that used the new company structure and methods. By bringing together different people with different skills and different ideas on the same project, development time was reduced considerably, and the system was a commercial success.

In a firm with permeable vertical boundaries, competence moves from leadership skills exercised at senior levels and technical skills exercised at lower levels to competencies distributed throughout all levels. At Oticon, employees are multiskilled. The "spaghetti" structure means that employees working for three different project managers may themselves be project managers on a fourth project. It all depends on that individual's portfolio of skills. A project manager on a given project is not guaranteed to be project manager on other projects. The idea is that the most qualified person (if available) is selected to lead a project. Once a project manager has received approval, he/she sets the agenda for project work. The project manager is accountable for results. How the project reaches these objectives is of no concern for the project sponsor.[32] Hence, Kolind recognized that Oticon operated in a knowledge-based segment of the economy, where the most valuable asset is organizational know-how. By encouraging employees to develop skills, he increased the learning capability of the entire organization. And by having employees going from one project to another, he put into place the conditions for a smooth and efficient transmission and dissemination of knowledge at Oticon (Figure 7.3).

To Kolind, this alteration of horizontal and vertical boundaries was not sufficient to achieve the 30 percent improvement in competitiveness. One more step was necessary: a radical change in the physical environment, moving from "rabbit holes to an open environment."[33]

Information technology

While the third piece of the puzzle, *IT*, played an important role in Oticon's transformation, we might say that it was an enabler, rather than a driver. Kolind's strategy document actually mentioned IT as the critical component of the transformation's success. It also identifies it as the tool by which the new organizational form would become feasible, by "liberating ourselves from the idea of always working in the same place," and by helping doing away with paper "which binds us to one place." The scanning/imaging system – with its ability to incorporate images, text, and other multimedia data types into the same database – supports the "paperless office," and is a key element in rendering this part of the vision feasible. The IT infrastructure (LAN, scanning system and central database, etc.) put into place makes information available to all employees, anywhere in the headquarters. Therefore, project teams can move around and still have access to information from one of the workstations located throughout the office.

In an organization with permeable vertical and horizontal boundaries, information moves from being closely held or integrated at the top to open sharing throughout the organization. Oticon's information system was designed to give everyone access to all information, even the CEO's agenda – one of the few exceptions to this is individual salaries; as Kolind said, he had to compromise a bit on this point. If people wish to see the firm's strategic plan, it is available on the system. This way, says Kolind, if people know where the firm wants to go, they will position themselves accordingly, by choosing projects for which they feel that their skills will be most helpful in reaching the firm's objectives.

As suggested earlier in this book, IT can be used to enable a variety of "axes of virtuality:" customer interaction, business network, and knowledge leverage. In the case of Oticon, knowledge leverage

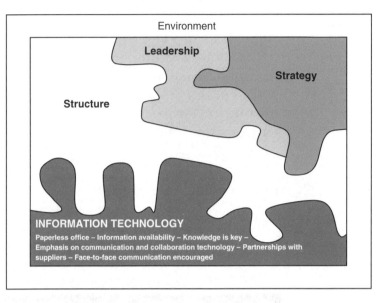

Figure 7.4
Information
technology.

was the main axis of virtuality. Information is kept in a central database, and this information is available to everyone, so that the knowledge base is continuously "fed" information. Informal, oral communication also helps to cultivate the knowledge base, which is why there are coffee bars, and "dialog" rooms sprinkled throughout the head office. Compulsory use of the stairwells (the elevator is off-limits to regular use), and the open layout at Oticon headquarters further encourages the type of exchange, which, according to Kolind, fosters innovation and value for the customer.[34]

Oticon does not have a large, formal IT organization. Oticon's document scanning system was developed in partnership with its suppliers – Hewlett-Packard and Anderson Consulting. The actual information systems group consists of six people, and, in line with Oticon's project organization, is seen as a "long-lasting project" rather than a department (Figure 7.4).

Leadership

The *leadership* piece of the management puzzle was described along four main dimensions: personal attributes of the leader, leadership responsibilities, leadership competencies, and leadership functions.

Focus, discipline, an outstanding ability to cope with ambiguity, and the strength to face adversity were used by former collaborators, employees, and partners to describe Kolind. Kolind's ability to clearly envision solutions to a problem is revealed in the strategy document he wrote in 1989. Peter Pruzan (Copenhagen Business School professor, friend, and mentor) describes how this ability was put to work during Kolind's early years at a leading edge consulting firm specializing in operations research and economic planning: "Even at the earliest stages of a potential project he always started considering how potential problem formulations could be both analytically solved and operationally implemented. It is perhaps this intuitive talent that more than any other has characterized his success in his more recent activities".[35]

Yet, without discipline, and the high level of commitment, which must accompany it, the best vision would not very likely become a realization. According to his entourage, Kolind indeed possessed a high degree of discipline and commitment. Karen Jespersen, Danish Minister of Social Affairs, worked with Kolind on a project to make Danish corporations more sensitive to social issues. She describes Kolind as being "totally committed" to whatever project he is driving.[36] Neils Jacobsen, who was named Oticon co-CEO in 1992, and eventually succeeded Kolind in 1998, said of Kolind that he was "deeply committed and absorbingly engaged".[37] Kolind's commitment to his vision went so far as having him take a "large personal financial risk by investing millions of borrowed DKK in Oticon in the early days".[38] With members of upper management who showed resistance toward change, he was firm: "I was not afraid to use power".

Kolind assumed his leadership responsibilities during the whole transformation process, from *reimaging* – developing a vision for the organization – to *renewal* – monitoring and improving organizational performance, going through *reshaping* – determining how the organization will operate, and *realization* – deploying the necessary resources to realize the vision.

The development of a clear vision of the organization was amply documented earlier in this chapter. Reshaping the organization took almost a year, during which Kolind sought inputs from consultants, academics, and employees. Groups were formed to discuss how the vision would materialize, including project organization, skill development, reward, and control systems. In order to realize the vision, Kolind created several project teams for the various elements of the transformation process. For example, an information systems project team was set up to find the appropriate solution for scanning and storing incoming paper documents. Another team was set up to oversee the design of the new work area. When the board of directors refused to finance the transformation process, Kolind mobilized his management team to invest in Oticon. He personally invested large sums of borrowed money in the company.[39] Once the new organization became a reality, Kolind continued his close monitoring. For instance, by 1991, after 2 years of profit, Oticon saw a small net loss. The problem was that, under Kolind and his transformed company, new product ideas were flowing so fast that it was difficult to keep track of the financial aspects of the company. The board was getting nervous, and convinced Kolind to seek a "co-director" who would be responsible for finance. Thus, Niels Jacobson was hired in January 1992 as Kolind's co-director. Jacobson was the opposite of Kolind: cautious, finance-oriented, "bureaucrat," etc.[40] From that point on, the company sought to improve efficiency (there were more layoffs until the summer of 1992), and increase liquidity/eliminate debt load. Here, both the board and Kolind recognized the need to monitor and improve organizational performance along different parameters after the critical part of the change process.

Strategic thinking and communication skills are strategic competencies characterizing Kolind's leadership. While his vision statement is a clear demonstration of his ability to develop and communicate a long-term vision, Kolind was also successful in developing and encouraging this type of thinking in others. The Multifocus system is an example of this ability. In 1989, Kolind created a multi-disciplinary team to develop and market a new product based on a promising but "neglected" device (neglected because few people at Oticon believed in it). This led to the very successful Multifocus system, and made employees adopt a new set of values: thinking "outside the box," persistence in the face of adverse thinking, and working alongside fellow employees with different backgrounds.[41]

Kolind's communication efforts were numerous, starting from communicating his vision to fellow managers and employees during the first few months, to the announcement of the transformation agenda made to all employees of head office, regardless of rank, in April of 1990.[42] Kolind's communication style must also be mentioned. He visited each Oticon site, and spoke to every Oticon employee in the first few months of his tenure. He ate his lunch at the employee canteen, instead of the executive dining

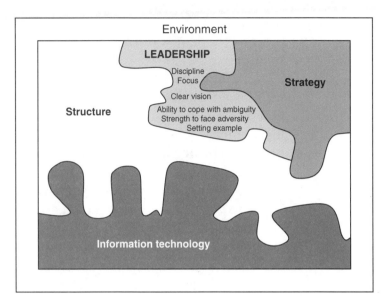

Figure 7.5
Leadership.

room, so he could continue his dialog with employees. There was also a refreshing "informality" to Kolind's style, even in written communication. A comparison of a Christmas 1981 memo written by then-CEO Bent Simonsen, with a Christmas 1988 memo written by Kolind, reveals differences between Simonsen's top-down, formal approach to Kolind's more informal, peer-to-peer attitude.[43]

As a leader, Kolind set demanding goals, early in the process. For instance, his objective for the first year was the sale of at least 12,000 units of the new Multifocus device. "Everyone shook their heads at this figure," says Jes Olsen, project manager for the Multifocus system. Oticon sold 23,000 units that year[44] (Figure 7.5).

Putting the puzzle together

Did structure followed strategy at Oticon, as in the cases of the famous industrial giants studied by Alfred Chandler, or did strategy flow from the dramatic reorganization brought about by Oticon's energetic CEO, Lars Kolind?

One thing appears certain: structure and strategy played the major roles in Oticon's story. Thus letting the sources of change from the environment as well as from technology a bit in the background. This explains why, in our representation of the five pieces of Oticon's puzzle, the structure and strategy pieces are so large.

We think that structure and strategy were co-determined, influenced each other, and fed back into each other. Once Oticon's market leadership had been undermined by an increasingly competitive and turbulent environment – to which Oticon proved to be ill adapted – and once Kolind had diagnosed the illness, it appeared clear to him that innovation and agility were the keys to the organization's survival.

It is likely that a number of elements in the desired positioning of Oticon had been identified very early. The need to get the enterprise involved in the BTE market, for instance, was seen quite early in the transformation process. Hence, strategy-as-positioning could be thought of as playing a primary role. Yet, many insights point to the direction of a *reimaging and reshaping* orientation as being the fundamental impetus.

As we saw, Kolind's intention was to transform the organization from one based on technology to one based on knowledge. Very early on, he concluded that innovation, flexibility, and agility were required if Oticon were to survive and prosper. The ideas would come later. The structure had to be changed fundamentally to liberate the spirit of innovation and encourage Oticon's employees to challenge the old way of doing things. This is symbolized in the slogan "think the unthinkable."

Thus, we are inclined to argue that, in this case, structure is as much a starting point as strategy. That is, reinventing Oticon through its structure – tearing down its internal, horizontal, and vertical walls – was equally instrumental in defining Oticon's trajectory. The market and commercial strategies that were later defined derived from the innovative capacity of the "new" organizational structure.

Of course, the very idea of reinventing Oticon's structure is intimately tied to a strategic vision: that of an agile, knowledge-based producer of technologically advanced products. This is why we say that structure and strategy were largely co-determined.

Developing such a strategic vision, envisioning a daring organizational transformation, and above all, implementing such dramatic changes hinged on and required strong leadership.

We have seen how Lars Kolind did just that. His focus, clear sense of the directions in which Oticon should be moving, and communication skills gave him what was needed to forge ahead in uncharted territory.

Consequently, we think that leadership, our third piece of the puzzle, also played an important role. It proved particularly effective in making the new structure serve the strategic reorientation of Oticon, and in making the new strategy emerge from the more innovative and fluid organization.

Implementing the new strategic vision and rendering the new organization effective required information to be shared and diffused more aggressively. It also meant that communication policies and processes be completely redesigned. ITs were used to support the transformation, but IT did not determine its trajectory, nor did it have a significant impact on the organization's transformation. The Technology piece of the puzzle was necessary, but it was not the essence of the transformation.

In Oticon's case, we think IT played a role, but that of a "supporting actor," not a lead actor. The paperless office, workflows, and shared information base represented innovations for Oticon, but they were no breakthroughs. Kolind did not use or implement very advanced and definitely innovative technologies in any critical ways. IT infrastructure, processes, and policies were enabling factors. They were necessary, but they did not confer a personality or a competitive advantage to Oticon's transformation.

As for the environment frame, it also had an impact on Oticon's transformation, but did not determine the direction or the nature of the transformation process in any way. No technological, regulatory or market-wide shocks reshaped the nature or boundaries of the industry. Entry did occur, as new and powerful competitors challenged the dominant position of Oticon. But we do not find the drivers of Oticon's organizational transformation in its environment. Naturally, the intensifying competition in the hearing aid market forced Oticon to reassess its strategy. But the organization could have taken many routes. Hence, we see the environment having an impact on the transformation of the organization, but not in a determining way.

The picture that emerges is shown in Figure 7.6. Structure dominates the landscape, along with strategy. These two are the drivers of the transformation. The fit between them is made possible by a strong and very capable leadership. Technology, particularly IT, plays a secondary role. Through its pressures, the environment motivated the change and defined the context, but

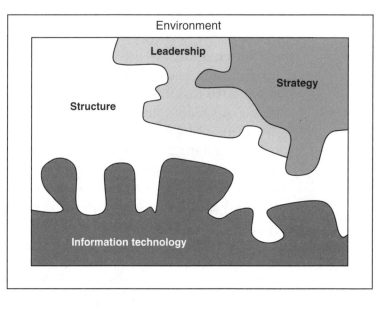

Figure 7.6
The completed
puzzle.

the shape of things that were to come at Oticon resided with the
other pieces of the puzzle.

Questions

1   Oticon has done a very good job in rendering its internal
    boundaries permeable. Yet, one might argue that it is
    somewhat impermeable to its environment, in particular
    its business partners – customers and suppliers.
    Following in Kolind's steps, what could you suggest for
    Oticon to open its external boundaries? How would you
    use IT in doing so?
2   What were the characteristics of Oticon's workforce that
    constituted together a challenge and an opportunity for
    the transformation Kolind undertook?
3   Chapter 5 discussed the attributes, competencies, and
    functions of the leader. Discuss each element with respect
    to Kolind's leadership.
4   How would you qualify the role of IT in the case of
    Oticon? Was it just accessory, and not absolutely necessary
    to make the change feasible? Was it central to Kolind's
    strategy?
5   A large insurance company launched a major project
    toward the "paperless office." Numerous task forces were

constituted. Their mandate included the identification of the main vendors and of the best practices in this domain. Numerous vendors were either visited or invited to make presentations of their highly sophisticated technology. Several firms that represented best practices were visited in order to determine the set of best practices that would be adopted by the insurance company. A 2-year, 50 million dollars project was undertaken. The technology and the accompanying systems were delivered on time, and complied with the requirements. Three years after the end of the project though everybody's desk is still inundated with stacks of papers, and the most recent statistics indicate that less than 20 percent of the technological features provided are indeed used. How would you explain this situation?

The paperless office

At Oticon, access to information is mainly through Plexus XDP Imaging from Recognition International, software based on client–server architecture.

Oticon called on the services of Hewlett-Packard (Bracknell, England) and Andersen Consulting (Chicago) for the technical component of its organizational changes, and Plexus XDP software was chosen to support the new "paperless" office.

Plexus XDP is a toolbox of several software titles as well as an optical management system that allows large quantities of documents and images to be managed on a LAN platform. The main feature of Plexus XDP is its ability to integrate images, text, and other multimedia documents in the same database. The database managing system allows control of access to both images and text, ensuring the integrity and security of data. All documents, whether they may be marketing literature, correspondence with customers, engineering drawings, or technical analyses, are scanned and entered directly into the database.

Once documents have been scanned (at a rate of 400–500 per day), they go to "in baskets" at employee workstations. Mail can be read and forwarded using HP's New Wave e-mail application. Faxes are converted into images with Plexus XLP's "fax-to-image" function and then forwarded to employees.

Searches in the database are activated with key words. When employees need to print a hard copy, they send the document to HP LaserJet printers.

Oticon's new technological infrastructure includes four scanning stations equipped with either Fuji Tsu or HP ScanJet scanners. The system uses a HP 847 server with 160 MB of memory, 10 GB of magnetic storage, a fibre optic LAN connection and 22 GB of optical storage. It all runs on a 10 MB Ethernet network, the TCP/IP protocol and LAN Manager.

HP's New Wave Office and New Wave Mail supply the graphical user interface and the e-mail interface. Two of Oticon's manufacturing facilities have been connected to the system with 1 Mbps connections, and the factory in Scotland is connected with a 64 kbps line.

The Plexus XDP system is, of course, completely integrated with the corporate system, which includes e-mail services, electronic agendas, applications such as Word and CAD/CAM systems for the graphic designers.

Endnotes

[1] Bjorn-Andersen, N. and Turner, J.A., Creating the twenty-first century organization: the metamorphosis of Oticon, in R. Baskerville, S. Smithson, O. Ngwenyama and J.I. DeGross (eds), *Transforming Organisations with Information Technologies*, North Holland, 1994, pp. 379–394 (quote p.384).

[2] Lyregaard, P.E., A colleague's view, in M. Morsing, K. Eiberg (eds), *Managing the Unmanageable for a Decade*, Oticon S/A, 1999, p. 228.

[3] *Ibid.*

[4] The revolution Oticon: creating a Spaghetti organization, *Research Technology Management*, September/October 1996, p. 54.

[5] Labarre, P., The dis-organization of Oticon, *Industry Week*, July 18, 1994, pp. 22–26.

[6] Lyregaard, P.E., 1998, *op. cit.*, p. 229.

[7] *Research Technology Management*, 1996, *op. cit.*

[8] Labarre, P., 1994, *op. cit.*

[9] Furniture sale starts culture change, *Personnel Management*, May 1993, p. 13.

[10] Labarre, P., 1994, *op. cit.*

[11] *Ibid.*

[12] *Ibid.*

[13] *Ibid.*

[14] Labarre, P., 1994, *op. cit.*

[15] Research Technology Management, 1996, *op. cit.*

[16] Labarre, P., 1994, *op. cit.*

[17] Sellen, A. and Harper, R., *Experience of a "Paperless Office"*, Research Note, Rank Xerox, Cambridge.

[18] Labarre, P., 1994, *op. cit.*

[19] *Ibid.*

[20] *Ibid.*

[21] *Ibid.*

[22] Open the doors, tell the truth, *Management Review*, January 1995, p. 33.

[23] Labarre, P., 1994, *op. cit.*

[24] Excerpts from Kolind, L., The vision – think the unthinkable, in M. Morsing, K. Eiberg (eds.), 1998, *op. cit.* pp. 20–25.

[25] Morsing, M., The history of Otican, in M. Morsing, K. Eiberg (eds), 1998, *op. cit.*, pp. 34–45.

[26] *Ibid.*

[27] Kolind, L., 1998, *op cit.*, p. 21.

[28] Morsing, M., 1998, *op. cit.*

[29] *Ibid.*

[30] *Ibid.*

[31] *Ibid.*

[32] Eskerod, P., Organizing by project – Experiences from Oticon's product development function, in M. Morsing, K. Eiberg (eds), 1998, *op. cit.*, pp. 78–90.

[33] Kolind, L., 1998, *op. cit.*, p. 24.

[34] Labarre, P., 1994, *op. cit.*

[35] Pruzan, P., A friend's view, in M. Morsing, K. Eiberg (eds), 1998, *op. cit.*, pp. 236–238.

[36] Jespersen, K., A minister's view, in M. Morsing, K. Eiberg (eds), 1998, *op. cit.*, pp. 224–225.

[37] *Ibid.*

[38] Holst, S., A subsidiary's view, in M. Morsing, K. Eiberg (eds), 1998, *op. cit.*, pp. 231–233.

[39] *Ibid.*

[40] Morsing, M., 1998, *op. cit.*

[41] Lonberg, A., The flight of the ugly duckling, in M. Morsing, K. Eiberg (eds), 1998, *op. cit.*, pp. 108–112.

[42] Morsing, M., 1998, *op. cit.*

[43] Morsing, M., Transforming identity by transforming image: the media boomerang, in M. Morsing, K. Eiberg (eds), 1998, *op. cit.*, pp. 169–186.

[44] Lanberg, A., 1998, *op. cit.*

Chapter 8

The virtual value chain — Li & Fung

Case description

Li & Fung was established in Canton in 1906. At first dealing in exports from China, it moved its activities to Hong Kong in the mid-1940s and greatly expanded the array of products it sold. It now employs more than 5000 people worldwide. Results from 2000 showed strong internal growth (32 percent). Li & Fung describes itself as a supply chain manager, providing a one-stop shop for customers. Li & Fung offers its clients complete services, from product design, arranging for raw material sourcing, production, product management, shipping, and export documentation[1] (source: www.lifung.com). It sells consumer goods: clothing, luggage, toys, beauty products, and so on.

In an interview given to Barron's, Leah Zell, gives a very illustrative example of Li & Fung services:

Let's say it (The Limited) goes to Li & Fung with a design for a purse. Li & Fung has 39 sourcing offices around the world. It surveys all the possible places they could make this purse and comes back with a quotation as to what it would cost to make the purse. To do that, they will get the leather from Korea, because it's the best quality at the best price. They will get the hardware from Japan. They will get the lining from India and have it made in China. Then they'll ship it to Limited's warehouse in San Francisco.[2]

This description is exactly in line with the one give by Victor Fung. He describes his firm as one that has deconstructed the value chain and dispersed it in various countries, so as to use each country's comparative advantage. The unique value of Li & Fung's service is this ability to manage this virtual value chain efficiently.

History*

When the firm was founded by Fung Pak-Liu and Li To-Ming in China, it was the first Chinese-run company to compete with foreign companies exporting Chinese products. The company opened an office in Hong Kong before Second World War.[3] Originally, a key advantage of the founders was that they mastered both the Chinese and the English languages. The acted as intermediaries.

The company's role changed over time. Originally, it introduced foreign firms to local producers. It then expanded its services to offer quality control and some monitoring. Currently, these traditional roles are not enough to allow the company to survive in the present competitive environment. To keep its clients, Li & Fung has to offer more than simple order transmission from one site to another. The response to these changes was to increase the scope of their role as intermediary, while not transforming the company into a producer of the various goods offered to its clients. Thus, the range of Li & Fung's activities has increased dramatically. Li & Fung starts working with its clients at the design stage of the product, plans all the sourcing aspects, follows the orders, handles the exports activities, takes care of all the haggling associated with quotas and duties, and makes sure the delivery is done on time. Li & Fung literally takes charge of the whole supply side of the business for its clients, while not owning it.

The Fung brothers introduced many of these changes to the company in the 1970s, altering it drastically. Originally it was a typical, patriarchal Chinese family conglomerate. Now, it is a complex, worldwide, trading multinational. Coming back from the U.S. after obtaining a Western education (one is a Ph.D. from Harvard, the other studied Engineering at MIT and earned an MBA at Harvard), they recognized that the company's traditional market was shrinking, as most of the clients were trying to deal directly with their suppliers, bypassing the intermediaries.[4] Their response was to expand their area of expertise into logistics and production management. Doing so, they continued to provide sufficient value to their clients.

---

*Note: The history of the company Li & Fung is mostly based on information from a case published by the Harvard Business School (Young, Fred, McFarlan, Warren, Li & Fund, Harvard Business School Publishing, Boston, MA 9-301-009, 29 November 2000, 18 p.). Unless specified otherwise, the information was drawn from the HBSP case.

Another major change was the acquisition of Inchcape in 1995. This company, Li & Fung's main competitor[5] carried on many complementing activities in distribution. This acquisition enabled Li & Fung to gain access to new markets in Europe and expand its sourcing base.[6] Li & Fung currently dominates the market in the Asian arena. It is five times larger than the size of its two closest competitors.

Li & Fung has to change and remain aggressive. Competition is fierce. The threat of entry from new competitors is high. There are many competitors and each one of them can produce the goods. There are very few barriers to entry in this industry. Any firm or individual with enough money to guarantee an order could become an improvised competitor. In fact, the story of Nike is an example of a new entrant that turned into a giant company. Knight, the founder of Nike, passed himself off as a trader in running shoes while visiting in Asia, and placed an order that started Nike on its way. The key to remaining competitive is providing clients with better and faster service, and lower prices, while maintaining higher margins than competitors.

In fact, the main competitors are the large clients. If a large client decides to source its needs itself, which is possible due to its sizable volume, Li & Fung's business shrinks accordingly. This is what The Gap did in the late 1980s.[7] The only barrier protecting the firm is the array of services offered to its clients (which is more difficult to imitate by new entrants or by clients trying to internalize sourcing) and its extensive knowledge of the supplier market.

To deter clients from seeking other suppliers or trying to bypass intermediaries and handle their sourcing activities in-house, the firm provides more value-added services than its competition. For example, it permits just-in-time changes. A customer can change the color of the products ordered, until the fabric is dyed. Then, the client can change styles, sizes, etc. until the fabric is cut. For its customers, the company provides a virtual in-house, flexible supply chain, without being encumbered with the problems inherent in ownership.[8]

The clients access an Extranet and can follow their orders in real time. Larger clients, using an enterprise resource planning (ERP) internally, can link it directly to the Extranet.[9]

E-tailers were once assessed as potential substitutes for firms such as Li & Fung. They represent a lesser threat than traditional companies, since they do not offer a complete, integrated service. Li & Fung has established a dot.com branch to ensure that the cyber market is covered. This new venture is, moreover, supported by the traditional know-how and the capabilities of the firm, thereby giving it a significant advantage over other E-tailers.[10]

Li & Fung grew and diversified into various businesses including: insurance, real estate, and retail. In 1989, the company was delisted from the Hong Kong stock exchange. In a move aimed at refocusing the company, the Fung brothers, the third generation of Fung heading the firm, took back the control of the company from external investors and other family members. A few years later, in 1992, they had streamlined the operations and re-centered the firm. They then relisted the trading division of the organization.[11]

Now, the company is the node of a global network of factories (most of them not owned by Li & Fung). The client services they offer have expanded enormously. The traditional role of market intermediaries, transmitting orders from clients to suppliers, has changed into handling all the information to organize and coordinate the supply activities for their clients. Li & Fung does a lot more than that to ensure that its services are relevant in 2001. It works with suppliers on production processes, quality control, and optimization.[12]

In the past 2 years, Li & Fung bought Swire and Maclaine Limited and Camberley Enterprises Limited. They also bought Colby Group Holdings Ltd. in 2000.[13] Another recent change in the company is the launch of the Internet venture, www.studiodirect.com.

Business environment

This industry is totally globalized, with players buying and selling all over the world. Tags indicating that a garment was made in Thailand simply mean that the last steps were made there. The fabric may come from China, the zippers from Malaysia, the dyes from India, while the dye process is done in Indonesia. The Thai labels might even have been produced somewhere in North Africa. Production localization is an ever-changing decision.[14]

There are few regulations but some still exist. First, different countries have different work regulations, which affect price. Changes in regulations in one country might require moving some activities to another to ensure lower costs. Certain countries also impose quotas. This puts upper limits on the capacity that can be allocated in such a country.[15]

The market is not a winner-take-all. It is home to many firms of different sizes. The economies of scale are minimal since the company itself outsources all the production. Gains are more apparent in specialization, by using specialized facilities in different countries for each activity, rather than consolidation into one big facility.

The competition is fierce, but "traditional," since no drastic innovation is threatening the players and they have to compete on price, service quality, and so on. There is a very low likelihood of tacit agreement, simply because there are many players on the market.

Innovation is mostly in the process, not in the product. For example, while the dot.com subsidiary opened by Li & Fung does not represent a radical change, it nevertheless enables order pooling to increase economies of scale, thereby supporting the company's dominant position. Barriers to exit are also low. There would be lay-offs, but the company does not have extensive investments, since production is almost all outsourced. The Internet initiative is reported to have cost $200 million (in US$),[16] which would be lost if it became unprofitable. However, it was financed by issuing $250 million in shares. Compared to company sales totaling $2 billion, it cannot be considered life threatening.

Loss of market shares would probably be more damaging to the firm's suppliers, but even that is not certain. Since suppliers have no exclusivity agreement, they might simply turn to the new firms that have secured those market shares.

Li & Fung in the third millennium

Although Li & Fung is constantly changing, it remains under the strict leadership of both Fung brothers, who are able to keep a clear focus on future objectives and command strict discipline. While establishing their 3-year strategic modus operandi, they provide everyone with a clear view of the company's intended achievement. Both were voted among the world's top managers.[17] They are described as Asia's brainiest businessmen.[18]

Victor Fung is the Chairman of the public company and chief executive officer (CEO) of the distribution arm. William heads the trading arm. They really act in tandem and are responsible for all four leadership responsibilities (reimaging, reshaping, realization, and renewal). Victor is often labeled the visionary.[19] In reality, they communicate on an ongoing basis and jointly develop the path to follow.

The Fung brothers are said to have *a highly collaborative and cerebral approach to business.*[20] This indicates a great ability to conceptualize both the company's activities and its direction.

The brothers appear to have a clear understanding of the market, the business environment and the opportunities around it. They convinced their father to take the company public in 1973.[21] They also headed the management buyout in 1988.[22] They refocused the company on its trading business and subsequently took it public once again, after restructuring it. Their leadership must have been successful, considering the results obtained by the firm. Leah Zell, lead portfolio manager at Acorn International, described it as one of the companies with the best potential.[23] It has been outperforming the Hong Kong stock exchange average by a comfortable margin.[24]

Integrated supply chain management

The current mission of the company is to provide integrated supply chain management to its clients. Li & Fung sees itself as a borderless manufacturing environment. The first difference from conventional companies is in the use of the word environment, instead of organization. Li & Fung is not a manufacturing company. It does not generally manufacture the products it sells. Li & Fung sells products to numerous clients, dealing with them through offices worldwide. The company describes itself as a maestro, conducting an orchestra of suppliers and partners who are scattered on every continent.

The company's core competence is undoubtedly its ability to assemble suppliers seamlessly. By orchestrating partners all over the world in a transparent fashion for the clients, it enjoys tremendous flexibility. To do so, it must have a better knowledge of the market than its competitors and clients.

One element that is hard to replicate is the scale of the activities. By aggregating orders, marginal cost is driven very low. This is hard to imitate for any new entrant. The geographical spread of the activities ensures that the firm takes advantage of currency fluctuations, labor costs differences, and so on. Building such a network of business partners is a major investment and cannot be replicated easily by competitors.

Copying the basic elements of the strategy might seem easy. One can think of a supplier trying to use countries' comparative advantages. However, no one can replicate 96 years of knowledge and experience. Li & Fung acts as the node between n suppliers and *m* clients. The number of partners and the level of integration attained are quite difficult for competitors to imitate.

The company explicitly mentioned that it kept an open mind, challenged past successes and kept the culture humble. Bi-annual retreats help to foster communication across groups in the company. At the operational level, constant monitoring of the market and maintaining close links with clients also contribute to foster the firm's competencies.[25]

Objectives are measurable. They include profit margin, number of units per continent, lead time for customers, number of changes allowed per order, etc. This emphasis on measurable objectives is also tangible when observing division managers' compensation. Division managers are all called "little John Waynes," because they are very independent, and are allowed to conduct business as they see fit in their environment. They pay their employees (at lower level) using the scheme that is most appropriate for the group, respecting cultural and country differences. The division managers themselves are evaluated according to performance and given strong salary incentives. Some make more money than the top executives in the company, even more than the Fung brothers.[26]

As described by Slater and Amaha, many of these managers are ready to work anywhere, as long as the deal is right.[27] The company has applied this very simple mode of compensation, relying on incentives and bonuses to encourage managers. They also have very different compensation schemes depending on local cultures. One challenge of any company operating in different regions of the globe is adjusting its management practices successfully to the local environment. The firm has done just that, adapting rules and compensation plans to local customs. The 100 top managers worldwide each have an individual compensation package, tied to performance. They are free to conduct business as they see fit. This gives them considerable latitude. While this strong incentive culture has slowed collaboration with Japanese partners, it has worked well in most other parts of the world.[28]

Operationally, Li & Fung has decentralized and customized the value chain in all geographical areas of the world. It assigns activities to various suppliers, independent of their location, according to their comparative advantages. This leads to a leaner organization, one with shorter response time than its competitors' and one with better service. The objectives of the company are measurable: usually by evaluating lead time between order and delivery, and by measuring the number and timing of changes allowed once the order is in (while maintaining the delivery date). Speed is definitely a critical success factor in the business. Time-to-market has to be short to ensure that trends are followed and clients can adjust to demand. Speed has been a key driver of company actions in the past and continues to be today.

Managing human resources

Strong leadership from the Fung brothers is not synonymous with imposing a single model on their collaborators. As mentioned earlier, division managers are very independent, and allowed to conduct business as they see fit in their environment. However, their evaluation is formal, strict, and directly linked to their compensation package.

The development of human capital is more difficult to assess. The firm provides a culture where competencies and performance are rewarded. Seniority and hierarchy do not seem to be a major driver, resulting in some misunderstandings with potential Japanese trading partners.

With the acquisition of the British group, Inchcape, it seems that the Fung brothers are also able to integrate new approaches and new employees. Although this company had more employees than Li & Fung, it was integrated rather smoothly; its managers were evaluated very positively, and provided with the same great opportunities as Li & Fung's managers.

The two brothers maintain a vast array of contacts and sources of information.[29]

An organization with two strong arms

The organization is a mixture of traditional hierarchy and innovative structure. First, it is an organization with a clear line of command. Authority resides higher up in the organization. The two Fung brothers head the company and the Web venture. The structure appears traditional. A holding company controls Li & Fung Ltd., which is publicly traded. This company encompasses Li & Fung Trading, which controls the sourcing network and LF Capital Management. While the latter is a modest $30 million

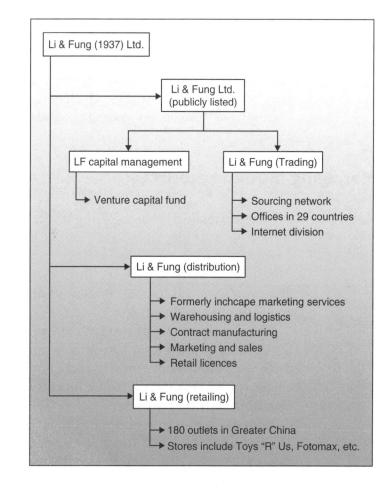

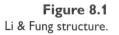

Figure 8.1
Li & Fung structure.

venture capital fund, the former is a 2-billion dollar company, with offices in approximately 30 countries.

The other groups under the holding are the distribution and retailing branches (see Figure 8.1). The first one is formed by what was originally Inchcape, acquired in 1999. The latter has 180 outlets in Greater China.[30]

On the sell side

When one looks into the groups, differences from traditional manufacturing groups appear. For example, Li & Fung Trading is totally decentralized, organized according to its main clients (except for the Internet venture) and scattered geographically. It is a very agile organization in which entire groups can be created, or folded, almost instantly. As Victor Fung mentioned, *We think of our divisions as a portfolio we can create and collapse, almost at will.*[31]

This emphasis on flexibility is at the core of the decision not to own the production facilities. As the company expands, relying on external suppliers frees up capital and enables faster growth. It also prevents irreversible investments, which would be a burden in case of decline. With its present organization, the company can literally eliminate one group without affecting another.

Within the trading group, divisions are made according to clients. For example, the Avon group works solely with Avon. They think, work, breathe, and organize all their activities for this sole client. Each major client has a dedicated group.[32] If the group were to lose its client, the group would be dismantled immediately. Since each group is dedicated to a client and operates like a mini company, it has considerable freedom in organizing its activities. A group works closely with its client, usually generating business totaling between $20 and $50 million. The financial function is centralized.[33]

This ensures that the sales groups do not compete. Since they do not share clients, they are autonomous. Economies of scale are reached through the production side of the business. Within groups, there is no specialization according to traditional functional departments.

There are two groups of customers, presenting different characteristics and served very differently: the first one comprises large companies such as Abercombie and Fitch, The Limited, and Avon. These companies have distinctive needs, order in large quantities and generate large volumes. The other group is made up of numerous small and medium firms. Individually, they do not generate large business volumes; however, Li & Fung consolidates their orders, thereby generating volumes leading to economies of scale for these clients.[34]

Since Li & Fung's customers are firms, not individuals, they are limited in number and can thus be reached easily through trade magazines and trade shows.[35]

The firm offers mass-customization to all clients, at different levels. While the larger clients are given total liberty to customize their products, smaller ones have enough choice to individualize their orders from a series of menus for each product. Moreover, the firm offers clients many opportunities to adjust their orders, even after the orders have been accepted.[36] The company is closely linked with both clients and suppliers. Clients are directly linked to the company through the Extranet and feed its systems with information about their changing needs. Using the web site, the small clients can do the same, even if they are not regular clients.[37]

critical Service

Li & Fung monitors market trends for its clients on a continual basis. They control key areas of the design and production processes in order to ensure that innovations are adopted.[38]

For smaller firms advertising is done through the web. Larger clients are each assigned a dedicated specialist who works with them on a continual basis. This ensures that the company really understands the clients' needs and develops a tight relationship with each one.[39]

The smaller clients are able to access the web site to select products (clothing, small goods, and promotional items) from a catalog. They are also able to customize these products by selecting different fabrics, finishing details, and logos. Li & Fung then consolidates all these small orders and has them executed through its channels. The customization options are varied enough to give clients a satisfying choice and limited enough so that Li & Fung does not generate costly small batch production.

Young and McFalran reported that Li & Fung had determined that this market represented a potential of $54 billion (in US$).[40] The clients in this market would be attracted by the studiodesign.com offer because of better prices (individually they do not have any purchasing power) and increased flexibility for customization (compared to other competitors). Moreover, the authors stress that Li & Fung do not require a minimum order, thereby making the site accessible to any company. The firm also encourages clients to buy small quantities to test the market, then order larger quantities of the most popular items.

On the buy side

While the company headquarters are in Hong Kong, and will remain there, the owners describe the organization as boundaryless. It has 48 offices in 32 countries.[41] On the sourcing side, since suppliers are not part of the company, any of the company's 7500 suppliers can handle orders anywhere, across boundaries, in a very coordinated fashion.[42]

Country managers also serve as division managers. Each country is assigned to a manager responsible for scanning and monitoring the production side of the business in that country while also carrying the responsibility for a division, a group dedicated to a client (which is usually in another country). This ensures that division managers stay in touch with the production side and understand the constraints of supply chain management.[43]

Suppliers often produce similar goods in parallel, ensuring faster delivery to the client. Suppliers are small firms: each produces only a part of the whole. One will provide the fabric, another will dye it, a third will cut it and ship it to a fourth one for sewing. Buttons and zippers will come from still another. Only Li & Fung has the complete view. The information is totally integrated for Li & Fung.[44]

The key to sending necessary information to suppliers is the Extranet. Collaboration with suppliers is essential to ensure flexibility for the clients. This is done by securing capabilities with suppliers, rather than placing orders, and by handling all the links between each activity of the value chain. For example, when an order is processed for a client, Li & Fung secures capacity for certain dates from a supplier responsible for cutting fabric, and capacity for following days from a supplier handling assembling. The first supplier does not know what it will be cutting before the fabric arrives. Thus, the client can change its mind about the patterns until the very last minute. This requires a level of trust from the suppliers. Since they are guaranteed X number of days of work, the patterns itself does not really matter to them. Similarly, the second supplier does not know what it will be assembling before the cut pieces arrive. It simply knows that it will assemble garments for Li & Fung for the next 2 weeks.[45]

Li & Fung likes to use at least 30 percent of each supplier's capacity, thereby ensuring that it is perceived as an important client, and, at the same time, preventing the supplier from becoming totally dependent.[46]

By retaining control over each activity, and by dealing with suppliers in a way very similar to internal capacity, the firm maintains a virtually totally integrated value chain. All the information is integrated, while all the physical activities are totally atomized. *Revolu-tionary*

In this way, Li & Fung also remains the only one company with knowledge about clients' needs and patterns, and does not need to share this information with any other business partner. In fact, the suppliers do not even know for which client(s) they are preparing an order.

Knowledge is acquired in different ways. First, an ongoing process is always in place to gain better knowledge of the market. Dealing with partners, through minority investment, is also an avenue used by the company. Finally, acquisitions, such as Inchcape, are a third way used to gain access to expertise.

Interestingly, while it is very flexible and always changing, the company perceives itself as only moderately innovative. It innovates with caution. For example, the Internet division was launched after thorough marketing analysis, not on some whim generated by the series of investments made in the late 1990s.[47]

Technology

Li & Fung is not an information technology (IT) company, nor does it provide a service relying on IT for complete delivery. It produces physical goods including garments, shoes, and toys. However, in the past several years, technology has taken on a critical role in the management of the virtual value chain, mainly as a support to business strategy. The company aimed at building a more efficient value chain, and deconstructing it as much as possible. The technology innovations appearing during the last decade were integrated to facilitate and accelerate the changes in the company. As mentioned by Victor Fung, the company is more dependent on IT now than it was in earlier years. IT helps stretch the company across the globe.[48]

The technology affects both clients and suppliers: first, large clients can now place, modify, and follow orders. They can still interact with the company through people, since they have a dedicated team working for them. Small and medium enterprises interact solely with the company through the web, using the studiodirect web side (www.studiodirect.com).

Many different systems are used by Li & Fung. The technological environment is extremely varied. Large clients are extremely sophisticated with respect to technology. They used systems such as ERP systems, customer relationship management (CRM), and Extranets. Smaller clients can be at the opposite of the technology continuum, using very little technology, or none at all.

Among the systems used, we can mention:

- Li & Fung has a standardized, fully computerized system to execute and track orders, used by all employees.[49]
- An Intranet links the firm with the manufacturing sites, speeding communication and facilitating coordination. It also enables the company to avoid travel delays and face-to-face interactions. For example, high-resolution pictures

can be sent over the web much more rapidly than actual samples: they are detailed enough to enable problem solving. Some product development, as well as cost and time evaluation, is done on the web sites.[50]

■ An Extranet enables suppliers and customers to connect to the same system, for order tracking, and making changes. Some customers took full advantage of the system and connected their ERP to the Extranet.[51]

It is interesting to note that with the suppliers, the variability in the level of technology used is considerable. As for the firm itself, it relies on IT: its activity coordination, allied to the sheer size its own operations, makes the firm information-intensive. However, operations at the supplier level are on a different, smaller scale. Garments have to be assembled, and this cannot be "virtualized." As a significant portion of the work done by suppliers is labor-intensive, these suppliers might not adopt technology to a great extent.

Technological links are essential to the company. Only by ensuring a constant and immediate data flow can Li & Fung maintain its short lead time and minimal delays for its customers. A key element remains making sure that all orders are processed according to the firm's standards.

The company deals with 350 large clients (many more if web site clients are considered), each ordering a wide variety of products, made by 7500 suppliers, scattered in more than 26 countries, each handling a fraction of the activities required for any given product.[52] There is no way activities presenting such a high level of complexity could be managed without the support of technology.

At the same time, the company is improving coordination drastically, thereby providing information flows to both clients and suppliers. This is essential to support the first and second ranked critical success factors: speed and mass customization.

As for the Internet, the firm carefully studied the implications of electronic retailers, and concluded that they were not an immediate threat. While it is very easy to set up a web site and take orders, organizing back-office operations and orchestrating the production chain is not so simple. Newcomers to the market would have a hard time reproducing the level of customization offered by Li & Fung. It was clear to the Fung brothers that if they were to benefit from the Internet, they would have to leverage their strategic assets, not change the company. After careful analysis, an Internet venture was launched.

Li & Fung invested $200 million in the new Internet venture–seen as a B2B company catering to small retailers – and stand ready to attack a new market.[53] This is not a separate venture from the regular business. As described by Victor Fung, having a separate Internet business arm would be as ridiculous as having a separate "fax" arm, only operating by fax. The online venture is linked with the regular business. It enables small companies, or even one-time customers, to order and customize items, without imposing a minimal order size.[54] The main goal is to attract the small and medium size enterprises which do not generate enough business to justify the formation of a group to attend their business. The very large clients are already well served with the current structure and they would see no advantage to a new web site. With its Internet venture, Li & Fung will be able to offer an alternative solution to these smaller companies.

Is Li & Fung successful?

The company strives for sustained profitability. Its goal is to double profits every 3 years. Expansion is on the strategic agenda.[55] In the past years, they added a new arm to their operations: selling in Asia. They started by buying a distributor and are enhancing its operations.[56]

From the latest Li & Fung web site press release:

Li & Fung reports strong growth in annual net profit to HK$1.08 billion, up 38 percent

Hong Kong, March 24, 2003 – Hong Kong-based global consumer goods exporter, Li & Fung Limited ("Li & Fung" or "the Group"; HKEx: 494) today announced strong results for 2002 despite a slow first half.

Profits attributable to shareholders achieved in the year ended December 31, 2002 was HK$1.08 billion, a significant increase of 38 percent from HK$782 million in 2001. Turnover increased by 13 percent to HK$37.3 billion, compared with HK$33 billion in 2001.

Earnings per share were 37.4 HK cents (2001: 27.3 HK cents). The Board of Directors has recommended a final dividend of 22 HK cents per share (2001: 18.5 HK cents). Together with the interim dividend of 8.5 HK cents per share, total dividend for 2002 would be 30.5 HK cents per share (2001: 26.5 HK cents).

Commenting on the Group's results, Group Managing Director Mr. William K. Fung said, "We are very pleased to report such robust results for 2002 though the first half of the year was slow. The Group's performance in the second half was strong and in line with the growth rate required to achieve our Three-Year Plan targets."

The healthy increase in turnover for 2002 was a reflection of the Group's expanded market share due to strong positioning in the right sourcing markets in a lackluster consumer environment. The Group started to reap benefits from efforts to build more value-added services for customers, leading to an improvement in profit margins. The absence of losses from a discontinued Internet operation also helped boost the Group's results for the year.

"Even on a continuing operation basis disregarding the write down on the Internet investments in 2001, the Group's profit increased by a healthy 13.6 percent" Mr. Fung explained further.

Information management

Li & Fung clearly shows many distinctive characteristics: it is interesting to pinpoint its unique nature, its key element around which all the others are aligned to ensure the company's success and how its non-traditional form serves it well. In this case, the key elements revolve around the control of information. While Li & Fung does not qualify as a company operating in the knowledge-based industries, the unique way in which it conducts its operations, the decentralization and the information-intensive coordination of the whole value chain imply information-age competencies.

When it was founded early in the twentieth century, Li & Fung offered information. Its unique abilities were knowledge of Chinese and English, and its position of intermediary: for this it could charge a commission. What it is doing now is not entirely different, although it is infinitely more sophisticated. Instead of translating the buyers' needs from English to Chinese, it uses a web site to translate the buyers' needs, expressed in the form of a drawing or a pattern into a decentralized, efficient production function, and ultimately into a finished good. All this, as always, by handling the information associated with the transaction, not the exchanged materials themselves.

As the quantity of information processed has increased tremendously, IT is used mainly to support the business strategy by enabling the organization to track all of its activities. It is an enabler. The company's aim was to build a more efficient value chain, and deconstruct it as much as possible. The technology innovations appearing during the last decade were integrated to facilitate and accelerate the changes in the company. Such a decentralized value chain would be impossible to coordinate if it were not for IT. As mentioned by Victor Fung, the company's dependence on IT has increased. IT helps stretch the company across the globe.[57]

The technological links are essential to the company. Only by ensuring a constant and immediate data flow that Li & Fung can maintain their short lead time and minimal delays for its customer. It is also a key element to make sure that all orders are processes up to the firm's standards. There is no way activities presenting such a high level of complexity could be managed without the support of technology. In doing so, the company is both redesigning the manufacturing processes and the way it is dealing with the clients. At the same time, the company is improving coordination drastically. It is providing information flows to both clients and suppliers.

Technology affects both clients and suppliers. First, large clients use their computers to place, modify, and follow up orders. They can still interact with the company through people since they have a dedicated team working for them. Small and medium enterprises interact solely with the company through the web, using the studiodirect web site (www.studiodirect.com).

Information and success

Looking at what makes Li & Fung successful, clearly information is the key element to ensure success. Li & Fung has to know exactly:

- where to get all the components;
- how to have the components assembled;
- how to minimize delays and shipment costs.

Owning and transferring information is essential to performing these activities adequately. They all involve information first, not physical components or assembly procedures.

Speed is definitely a critical success factor in the business. Time-to-market has to be short to ensure that trends are followed, and clients can adjust to demand. Companies need to know instantly how the market is responding in order to minimize stocks and avoid missing sales. Speed has been and remains a key driver of company actions. Information is the enabler for speed.

Information technology and flexibility

To deter clients from seeking other suppliers, the firm provides more value-added services than the competition. For example, it permits just-in-time changes. As mentioned earlier, a customer can change the color of the products ordered until the fabric is dyed. Then, the client can change styles or sizes until the fabric is cut, etc. Li & Fung provide a virtual in-house, flexible supply chain, for the customer, without the trouble of owning one.[58]

Flexibility takes another form. Using the same people, Li & Fung is able to manage the upstream and the downstream sides of its business very differently. Large clients deal with dedicated groups characterized by very large autonomy. Division managers are allowed to conduct business as they see fit in their environment. This makes the downstream side of business very loosely coupled.

At the same time, the upstream (supplier) side is extremely tightly coupled. In order to guarantee correct deliveries, every single detail is fixed with the suppliers. Although based in different countries, the division managers are dedicated to the clients, and, interact with the suppliers while they manage their groups. These managers are a precious source of local information.

Geography and information

A distinctive attribute of Li & Fung is its ability to manage activities in a borderless way. It is able to coordinate activities conducted all over the planet, taking advantage of each location, while not suffering from lags or confusion that often come with excessive decentralization. Being able to do so implies an access to information at all times, and thorough knowledge of each step of the activity. To this end, IT is a precious ally. Through technology, the firm can shorten delays and information flow dramatically. It can also change some of the business rules. For example, Li & Fung modified container-filling procedures. Traditionally, orders were grouped from one supplier and containers were filled before shipping. Li & Fung reversed the approach. Containers are filled according to clients (delivery points). Each supplier puts material that goes to a given client into the container. By doing this, Li & Fung bypasses the aggregators and lowers the overall shipping costs. To do so, one has to control the information.

The firm's control of information is also paired with a deep understanding of the business. Li & Fung knew which activities it could decouple, to lower the information complexity, and which ones they had to keep tightly integrated. This explains the very different approach taken regarding the sales groups – very autonomous, and the supply side – tightly coordinated.

Case analysis

The pieces of the puzzle at Li & Fung

Environment

This organization is a good example of new structure and adaptability to the environment. Li & Fung's operation is in a very competitive industry. Margins are slim, competitors are numerous, barriers to entry are low, and most of the large clients can handle their sourcing operations themselves. In order to remain in business, Li & Fung has to constantly provide value to its clients. To do so, the organization has established an interesting configuration, adapting its strategy and its structure to thrive in a very competitive environment. Technology is used to support these elements (Figure 8.2).

This environment is fierce, the competition constant, and the margins slim. The products sold by the various firms are not differentiated; each has to rely on superior service and unbeatable cost structure to keep its clients.

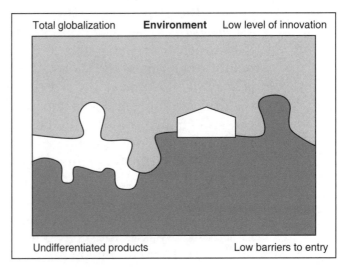

Figure 8.2
Environment.

This environment is unlikely to change. Companies are providing mass-market products to a variety of clients. As there are no "trade secrets" in producing clothing, luggage, or toys, many companies have the required tools and knowledge themselves and do not even need an intermediary such as Li & Fung – the large ones could deal directly with the manufacturers and integrate their sourcing activities.

Strategy

Li & Fung aims at being the most efficient and profitable intermediary between clients and manufacturing firms. In doing so, it will become the universal node between buyers and sellers.[59] Its strategy is formulated every 3 years, very formally. The leaders adopt a triennial plan to guide their actions and do not formally revise it during that period.[60]

One way of providing better operations and lower cost is to take advantage of different suppliers in different countries. Li & Fung does this very efficiently – in fact, this is at the very core of Li & Fung's strategy. The company aims at assembling the best supply chain, without being hampered by geographical considerations. This means that suppliers in different countries are selected for their respective comparative advantage. The different activities are assembled and coordinated across distant sites to provide a single integrated interface for the client. The whole strategy of Li & Fung can be encapsulated into this idea of a virtual supply chain (Figure 8.3).

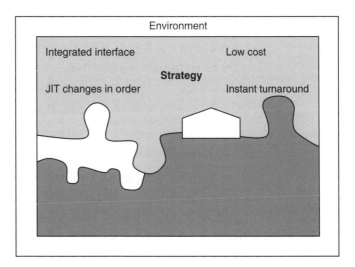

Figure 8.3
Strategy.

The strategy of Li & Fung is an interesting mixture of total integration and total decentralization. At the strategic level, everything appears integrated. At the structural level, everything is dispersed. When first looking at the strategy, it is clear that the firm appears totally centralized to the clients. In fact, a client may get the impression that the company is working solely for its account. By dedicated a group for each large client, the company ensures that the client reaching Li & Fung gets *dyed-in-the-wool* dedicated service. Since the performance of the group is solely dependent on this one client, all members of the group will make sure that they are answering their client's expectations.

Four elements were identified as critical at the strategical level: an integrated interface provided to each client, flexibility of the organization that provides instant turnaround capabilities to respond to any market change, low-cost structure, and finally, flexibility given to the client to modify orders at will during order processing.

Integrated interface

Li & Fung provides its large clients with a dedicated group who organize all their activities around them and give them all the information they need. Thus, clients do not get the feeling of dealing with a very large company, in an anonymous way. On the production side, although production is totally decentralized – not only from one activity to another, but even for one given activity which can be assigned to multiple suppliers – the client gets an integrated view. It does not have to deal with the various suppliers. All deliveries are coordinated. When accessing the information system, the client sees the integrated view and is unaware that its order is being processed in multiple countries at the same time. The client does not have to bother about countries' quotas or regulations. This greatly simplifies client-sourcing activities and increases the value of the service provided.

Instant turnaround

The company has to be able to adjust to any growth in the orders or to any reduction of activities. By using different suppliers and avoiding fixed capacity that would be associated with plant ownership, Li & Fung is able to face increased activities by transferring more orders to suppliers. Similarly, if the volume of order decreases in a given market, it simply awards fewer contracts. Even the sales group can be folded at will, should their client decide to move its business elsewhere.

Low cost

As presented in the case description, low cost is a key element in a very competitive market. Large clients have the size required to justify integrating their sourcing activities. They have the scale to deal directly with their numerous suppliers (just as The Gap did). In order to remain very competitive in terms of price, Li & Fung has to monitor costs constantly at every step of the process. To do so, it has to update its information regularly about every production site. It also has to be able to open new sites in cheaper locations and fold sites that are growing themselves out of the market. By avoiding ownership, they solve this constraint in part. They use suppliers and award contracts at will, keeping competitive pressure on each supplier and preserving the ability to move operations to a different location.

Just-in-time changes in orders

The strategy also emphasizes flexibility for the client. Li & Fung enables the client to change its mind at all stages of the process. By linking all suppliers tightly and providing just-in-time information about the various production activities, Li & Fung retains the possibility to marginally change all steps of the process. For a material dyer, the color is not a problem. If the garment arrives with the color code at the last minute, the color can be changed at that point. This flexibility is valued by clients in a volatile market.

These key strategic orientations are explicitly stated by the Fung brothers. Strategic decisions are supported by both the company structure and its IT infrastructure. Both will be discussed in sequence.

Structure

Li & Fung is definitely a network organization, it acts as the node coordinating all activities for its business partners. This structure supports the strategy in many ways.

As was mentioned in the strategy description, this structure is not visible to the client. The client always deals with Li & Fung

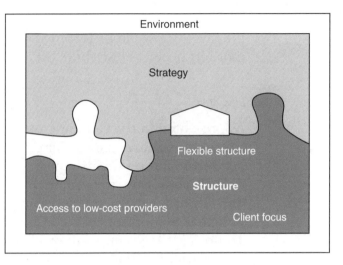

Figure 8.4
Structure.

and receives integrated information. All the complexity linked with the decentralized supply chain is handled by Li & Fung. This structure makes many of the strategic elements possible (Figure 8.4).

Access to low-cost providers

The decentralized structure provides access to a multitude of suppliers and is probably the key to supporting the strategy. Li & Fung is built around this core idea of a decentralized supply chain, in which each piece is kept as long as it is the most competitive one. Using suppliers within market transactions gives the company the flexibility to drop those not performing up to standards. An integrated organization would have the natural reaction to improve, instead of cutting under-performing departments. This would be more time consuming and probably less efficient. The geographical dispersion of the suppliers also helps Li & Fung take advantage of currency differences, lower wages in different countries, and other comparative advantages.

Flexible structure

Again, the network structure makes the organization very flexible and, adaptable, and enables the company to provide just-in-time changes, as well as instant turnaround, to its clients. When a client increases its order volume, Li & Fung automatically adjusts its structure through its supplier network. It increases volume bought at a given supplier, or adds another supplier to handle the additional volume.

When a client wants a new product, new suppliers are found. Due to the large volume of activities, it is unlikely that one client will ask for a product that was never requested by anyone. The various client groups can benefit from the sourcing experience of the other groups and the information collected about the suppliers in all areas.

Client focus

The company has also designed a client-focused structure. Groups on the sell side are dedicated to one client and survive only as long as the client orders product. This dedication ensures employee familiarity with their client without the distractions due to business with other customers. Dedicated teams act like an internal design department for the client, while relying on the backbone of Li & Fung for organizing production. Again, Li & Fung's structure provides dual sides of a strategic orientation: dedicated groups that act like a small entity focus solely on one client and have access to global sourcing practices, in an integrated manner.

Leadership

Li & Fung is under strong leadership by its two leaders: Victor and William Fung. Victor is the chairman of the public company and the CEO of the distribution arm. William is head of the trading arm. All authors agree that they really act as a team and jointly develop the path for the company to follow.

They are highly educated, cerebral, and very collaborative. They provide the strategic direction for the firm, and formally produce the company's triennial strategic plans. They were termed the brainiest businessmen of Asia.[61]

While they provide clear directions, they also create a culture that leaves the managers a great deal of flexibility. They create employee incentive schemes. As long as the managers attain or surpass their objectives, they are compensated generously and remain free to organize work as they please. This enables them to adjust their business practices differently in each country, if necessary. Therefore, the managers can adjust their behavior in each part of the structure (Figure 8.5).

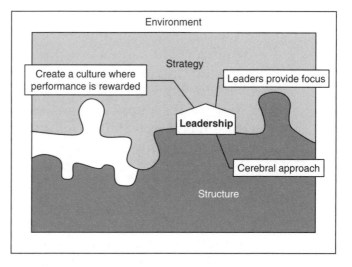

Figure 8.5
Leadership.

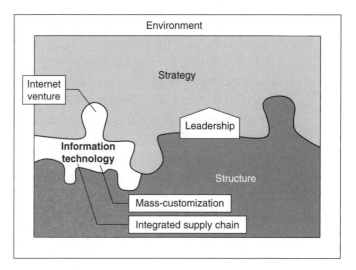

Figure 8.6
Information
technology.

Information technology

Many elements of the strategy are supported by IT initiatives. While the organization is not really high-tech, it uses IT to support strategy. For one thing, coordinating the supply side of the business is very information-intensive. Li & Fung has to track all the activities performed by the various suppliers and each order's position in the supply process (especially since it allows clients to modify orders during processing). Moreover, monitoring containers and their route allocation requires careful real-time planning (Figure 8.6).

Integrated supply chain

IT is a key element in operating such a decentralized supply chain in an integrated way. Many systems have been implemented to keep track of each order, its status, and its movement. Technology is also open to clients who can link into the system to monitor their own orders just as they would do if these orders were processed in-house. This enables many clients to pump information into their ERP systems directly from Li & Fung's Intranet.

Internet venture

The studiodesign.com venture is also an IT initiative that supports strategy, both in terms of low costs and just-in-time changes. By offering customization possibilities to smaller clients, the company is able to secure new markets, made of a large number of smaller orders. Technology enables the clients to auto-select product features. By aggregating these orders, the company is able to reach sufficient volumes to generate economies of scale. Even if clients select numerous features, if enough orders are collected, there will be sufficient items of each possible model to enable efficient production.

While the company cannot create dedicated groups for such small clients, the Internet has made smaller clients profitable for Li & Fung. The clients can self-select their products online without the intervention of a vendor. Li & Fung then combine orders from several clients to create a large order volume. The combined orders create a large enough bundle to be profitable for the firm.

Mass-customization

Technology is also the key to enabling mass-customization. This is tightly associated with the Internet venture. Due to the possibilities offered by Internet technology, clients can personalize all their orders at will (within some pre-defined parameters). The firm evaluated that the number of customizable items was sufficient to offer a real choice to the customer and to provide a level of service that was unbeatable (at the proposed price). Again, this feeds directly into the just-in-time and low-cost strategy components.

Finally IT also has a link with the structure. While IT is not solely at the service of the structure, it makes it possible because it enables coordination among so many components, whether or not they are owned by the firm.

Putting the puzzle together

In this case, strategy is the key element of the puzzle. Li & Fung has a clear vision of its role as a network node, linking buyers, and sellers across the globe. The strategy is explicit, well articulated, original, and leads to tangible results. It is coherent with the company history. In fact, one could say that Li & Fung has kept the same strategic orientation for most of its history. While its content has changed over time, Li & Fung's role as most valuable intermediary has been a constant.

The structure is a network which enables the flexibility and low costs defined in the strategy. By adding nodes at will, the company can respond almost instantly to new client demands. This flexibility allows the company to extend its activities and its volume, while keeping its core small and nimble. Growth is covered by subcontractors. Remaining a virtual supply chain for its clients is much more flexible than trying to establish a fully-owned, traditional one. It is also less risky, since it can be adjusted downward as well as upward.

IT can be seen as the wiring between all the components, enabling their coordination. Dispersing production across the globe and across different suppliers needs tremendous levels of information exchange. Technology is there to serve this purpose. Tracking orders is the key to good customer service. IT also makes it possible to offer clients needed flexibility (just-in-time changes). The Internet venture is another example of a way to extend the company activities, enabling it to become a valuable intermediary for small and medium firms. Again, IT is not the primary driver but is chosen with respect to the strategic orientation of the organization.

Just as the other components were chosen and planned to support strategy, leadership is strong and promotes the strategic vision of the firm very explicitly. The leaders produce a triennial plan and follow it. This leadership links the various elements. The clear image of the strategy clarifies the role of the managers. They know their task, how it will be evaluated, and how it will contribute to the overall success of the firm (Figure 8.7).

In studying Li & Fung, it becomes clear that no single characteristic explains the company's success. Any competitor could copy its web site, products, or idea of geographical dispersion. So, why is it so successful?

The answer lies in its overall configuration. While any of the pieces can be copied individually, their respective arrangement

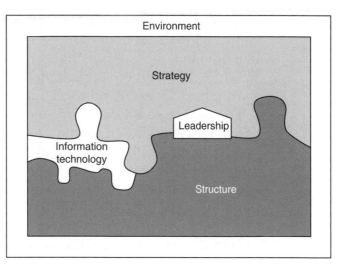

Figure 8.7
The puzzle.

makes for a better company overall. The leaders have a clear vision of their market, their activities, and their conduct. They have a company structure that serves this vision well. This structure is varied, with each part of the company suiting its targeted market or goal. The technology in place is an enabler of the strategy, making the geographical dispersion possible. Flexibility is also a key element. This new type of organization is flexible, ready to morph in response to environmental requirements.

Conclusion

The three cases provide a diversified array of new forms of organization. They are dissimilar but share some common characteristics. First, all three companies operate in competitive, even fierce, environments. They have seen their markets threatened by various rivals and have responded to the challenge by adapting their ways to the new conditions. Their various responses were quite different, however.

In all three cases, strategy is a key component. Oticon and Li & Fung had strategy as a key driver, with IT positioned as a supporting role. Progressive Insurance was different. In this case, IT and strategy are intertwined and defined simultaneously. It becomes difficult to separate them.

All three cases show strong leadership. Leaders articulate the vision and help communicate the respective images, which the firms were striving to achieve. These images were different in many ways. One key difference is in the organizational boundaries. At Progressive, the vertical boundaries within the firm are dissolved.

However, the organizational boundaries are untouched. In Oticon, almost all internal boundaries are broken. Again, the organizational boundaries are not changed. Li & Fung shows a different structure, in which the organization boundaries are porous. Most activities are, in fact, conducted outside the firm frontiers.

The cases also differ significantly with respect to the geographical location chosen to conduct the activities. In Oticon, the location is stable (the head office) and all activities are conducted there. For Progressive, location is variable and depends on the client's needs. The activities are conducted where the client needs them to be conducted – at the accident location. Finally, in the case of Li & Fung, location becomes irrelevant. Activities are conducted all over the globe, the sites vary, and all this is done without even informing the client. Activities are conducted where it is cheaper to do so, at a given moment in time.

While the three configurations are very different, each one has proven adequate as far as responding to the challenges. Oticon was able to foster creativity through the spaghetti organization, facilitating the exchange of ideas and knowledge among its members and grouping them together to maximize interactions. Progressive Insurance was able to increase customer loyalty by sending claim representatives into the field. They are empowered to respond to the clients' needs from beginning to end, and have access to all the required information to do so. Finally, Li & Fung, adjusts to changing market conditions and customer demands by constantly redesigning its network, altering its configuration to maintain costs as low as possible, while maximizing quality.

The three cases show that no single configuration is adequate for every organization. On the contrary, by adapting a unique and innovative arrangement, these three firms were able to succeed. In all cases, the firms accepted drastic changes and, even now, they remain open to further transformation. Organization structure, strategy, technology, or even the type of leadership chosen are not selected permanently. They are appropriate at a given point in time, and they remain candidates for adjustment or even radical transformation if changes in the environment demand it.

The role of IT was critical to the success of each of the firms described here. Yet, it is essential to note that while IT was essential in each case, its contribution is important because it was aligned with the rest of the organizational components. At Progressive, where the information systems and products were quite innovative, IT was not the sole driver of change. Rather, business strategy and IT strategy were codetermined, influenced each other, and fed back into each other. In the case of Li & Fung, IT was described as the wiring among the other pieces of the puzzle, ensuring smooth coordination. This was required by the strategic decision of scattering production activities around the globe and among several suppliers, which created an important need for information exchange. At Oticon, IT played a quite different role. Kolind's strategy and the accompanying structure and work environment required a "paperless office" and much collaboration between employees. IT was used for these very purposes.

All three cases confirm that for IT to actually play its role, it has to be closely intertwined with the organization, rather than being an independent piece. Research has shown that when such an alignment does not exist, the so-called collaborative technologies can even become a means for creating electronic fence boundaries rather than allowing for a boundaryless organization.[62]

Questions

1   How can an organization with a structure like the one Li & Fung has adopted support strategic changes?
2   What are the core competencies of Li & Fung?
3   How should Li & Fung proceed to survive after the Fung brothers will have reached retirement age?
4   Arrow[63] mentioned that history mattered, meaning that, if organizations could be changed, they were still very dependent from past actions and events. Can a company like Li & Fung be reproduced?
5   Can you imagine another traditional industry in which a company could be virtualized like Li & Fung?

Endnotes

[1] www.lifung.com
[2] Barron's, Buying Future Big-Caps, 23 March 1998, p. 44.
[3] Balfour and Fredrick, Stick to knitting, *Far Eastern Economic Review*, 18 June 1992, 80.
[4] Slater, J. and Amaha, E., Master of the trade, *Far Eastern Economic Review*, 22 July 1999, 10–14.
[5] Slater, J., Corporate culture, *Far Eastern Economic Review*, 22 July 1999, 12.

[6]Young, F., McFarlan, W. and Li & Fung, Boston, MA: Harvard Business School Publishing, 9-301-009, 29 November 2000, 18 p.

[7]Slater, J. and Amaha, E., 1999, *op. cit.*

[8]Young, F. and McFarland, W., 2000, *op. cit.*

[9]*Ibid.*

[10]*Ibid.*

[11]Balfour, F., 1992, *op. cit.*

[12]Slater, J. and Amaha, E., 1999, *op. cit.*

[13]www.lifung.com

[14]Magretta, J., Fast, global, and entrepreneurial: supply chain management, Hong Kong style an interview with Victor Fung, *Harvard Business Review*, September–October 1998, 102–111.

[15]*Ibid.*

[16]Young, F. and McFarland, W., 2000, *op. cit.*

[17]Leung, J., New trade era, *Asian Business*, March 1996, 32.

[18]Slater, J. and Amaha, E., 1999, *op. cit.*

[19]*Ibid.*

[20]*Ibid.*

[21]Magretta, J., 1998, *op. cit.*

[22]Roy, B., Third generation takeover, *Asia Finance*, 15 April 1989, 20–22.

[23]Welling, H., Stirring IT up with the experts, *Apparel Industry Magazine*, August 2000, 58–60.

[24]Kraar, L., Hong Kong is buzzing ..., *Fortune*, 15 May 2000, 324.

[25]Young, F. and McFarland, W., 2000, *op. cit.*

[26]Leung, J., 1996, *op. cit.*

[27]Slater, J. and Amaha, E., 1999, *op. cit.*

[28]*Ibid.*

[29]*Ibid.*

[30]Slater, J., 1999, *op. cit.*

[31]Magretta, J., 1998, *op. cit.* p. 110.

[32]Magretta, J., 1998, *op. cit.*

[33]*Ibid.*

[34]Young, F. and McFarland, W., 2000, *op. cit.*

[35]*Ibid.*

[36]*Ibid.*

[37]*Ibid.*

[38]Magretta, J., 1998, *op. cit.*

[39]Young, F. and McFarland, W., 2000, *op. cit.*

[40]*Ibid.*

[41]*Ibid.*

[42]Magretta, J., 1998, *op. cit.*

[43]*Ibid.*

[44]*Ibid.*

[45]*Ibid.*

[46]*Ibid.*

[47] Young, F. and McFarland, W., 2000, *op. cit.*

[48] Magretta, J., 1998, *op. cit.*

[49] *Ibid.*

[50] Young, F. and McFarland, W., 2000, *op. cit.*

[51] *Ibid.*

[52] Magretta, J., 1998, *op. cit.*

[53] Kraar, L., 2000, *op. cit.*

[54] Young, F. and McFarland, W., 2000, *op. cit.*

[55] *Ibid.*

[56] Slater, J. and Amaha, E., 1999, *op. cit.*

[57] Magretta, J., 1998, *op. cit.*

[58] Young, F. and McFarland, W., 2000, *op. cit.*

[59] *Ibid.*

[60] *Ibid.*

[61] Slater, J. and Amaha, E., 1999, *op. cit.*

[62] Newell, S., Pan, S.L., Galliers, R.D. and Huang, J.C., The myth of the boundaryless organization, *Communications of the ACM*, **44**(12), December 2001, 74–76.

[63] Arrow, Kenneth J., *The Limits of Organization*, W.W. Norton and Company, 1974.

PART IV

The management challenges

Organizing a business is similar to putting together a puzzle; it all comes down to execution. The frame may be right, the picture clear, and the pieces carefully selected, but if the puzzle cannot be pieced together or the pieces do not fit properly, then you have nothing but an assortment of pieces. Unlike jigsaw puzzles, however, the management puzzle does not have carefully machined pieces with edges that are designed to interlock closely. Instead, it must be put together with the skills, techniques, and practices that enable each part of the business to connect seamlessly and present a coherent picture to the outside world. It is the execution capabilities of the organization's managers that enable the strategy, structure, information Technology, and leadership pieces to work together smoothly and effectively in a given environment. These capabilities are created in four ways – people management, IT management, knowledge management, and change management (Figure IV.I).

Like everything else in the management puzzle, the manager's job in today's organization has become much more complex and

Figure IV.I
Putting the management puzzle together requires many skills.

challenging. Only a few years ago, the staff of most organizations consisted of full-time, dedicated employees and a few contract staff. While people and work are still essential to execution, today it is a radically-changed world for both workers and their managers. Staffing options such as outsourcing, telecommuting, partnerships, alliances, and a global workforce (to name just a few), are all being used by companies as they grapple with the economic challenges and technology choices confronting them. New organizational structures and interorganizational projects mean that staff may be reporting to not one, but several, different managers. Through information and telecommunications, staff can now work anywhere, anyplace, and anytime. Thus, the very nature of work is changing. The managers of the next decade will be pioneers in creating an environment to obtain maximum value and productivity from all staff, wherever they are located and whatever their employment status.

While people must put the puzzle together, IT provides critical support for the big picture. As we have seen, IT is often the very means of implementing organizational strategy and transforming businesses. The technical architecture of the organization acts as the platform for a wide variety of working arrangements and a strong communications infrastructure is the backbone of any modern organization. As workers become more mobile and enterprises more open to the outside world, they will need increasing access to a wide variety of technologies, applications, and information. Technology must, therefore, be both flexible and aligned with the organization's needs. In order to provide this, the information systems function needs four key capabilities: structures that facilitate responsiveness to business needs, processes that deliver quality, cost-effective IT, skills in designing and deploying IT, and an IT architecture that integrates all organizational technologies, systems, and data seamlessly.

As IT addresses more of the routine tasks of the enterprise, knowledge is increasingly becoming the means whereby organizations differentiate themselves and deliver value to their customers. The development of organized knowledge acquisition and dissemination processes, and structured processes to support individual and group learning is, therefore, critical in this more complex environment. In the modern corporation, poorly-managed knowledge can be a clear source of failure. On the other hand, well-managed knowledge creates a great potential for increased learning and knowledge creation.[1] Ensuring that the right knowledge is in the right place at the right time involves detailed analysis of a firm's knowledge needs, integration with business strategy and processes, and careful implementation. It also requires considerable attention to the culture, learning styles, and capabilities of the individual organization.

Today, there is enormous pressure on organization members to do things differently and change has become a fact of life for almost all enterprises. Organizations of all types are only just beginning to realize the importance of change management in effectively deploying new business ideas. Unfortunately, change management as a discipline is still in its infancy and we have much to learn about how to do it well.[2] Today's managers need to better understand the full implications of change on their organizations and become better equipped to guide them through the process.

These four factors: people management, IT management, knowledge management, and change management all share the term "management," emphasizing the significant role that managers have in providing the means of putting the puzzle pieces together. This part of the book will examine each of these aspects of management individually and explore how they contribute to aligning the pieces of the puzzle. First it looks at managing the workforce – the changing nature of work itself, the need to deal with a wide variety of types of workers, new demands on management, and relationship management both inside and outside the firm. Next it discusses the management of the technology and the knowledge that must be put into place to support organizational strategy and operations. Finally, it explores the concept of change management and how to control and drive organizational transformation forward.

Chapter 9

People management

People are a key element in organizations. While strategies, structures, environments, technologies, and leaders may change, the fundamental management job remains the same – to nurture, develop, and use optimally the key resources of the organization, of which resources organization members are among the most valuable. Traditionally, this has been accomplished by a combination of management practices and human resources (HR) policies. While these are still important in the twenty-first century workplace, a few key differences have to be addressed (Figure 9.1).

Today, the combination of IT and increasing business pressures are driving organizations to experiment with a variety of alternatives to the traditional office environment. For example, some firms are dispensing with the office and becoming either partially or completely virtual. In 1998, approximately 40 million people in the U.S. were either telecommuters (i.e. working part-time from home), or full-time home-based workers and these numbers are growing annually.[3] Many firms are now using a blended workforce – a mix of core and temporary staff combined with personnel

Figure 9.1
People must put the
puzzle together.

from their suppliers and partners. Traditional workplaces are changing too – whether they like it or not – because organizations that are networked through e-mail and other technologies work fundamentally differently from those that are not. Progressive Insurance was a very good example of that trend. The Immediate Response Vehicles, literally offices on wheels, enable the claim representatives to work where the clients need them, instead of working inside an office. These technologies irrevocably alter the nature of managerial authority and work, and inspire a new, informal style of operations that circumvents old-style hierarchies and supercharges social networks. As networked organizations cross functional boundaries, they change the very nature of supervision.[4] As a result of this new workplace malleability, managers and HR departments have to explore how they manage both work and workers.

Managing in a twenty-first century organization requires a turnaround in management style from one based on rigid hierarchical roles and responsibilities to one that adapts to a diversity of working arrangements, depending on the situation. Unfortunately, these changes do not come easily to many managers. Traditional management systems have been set up on the assumption that people cannot be trusted or relied on, and to prevent anyone from doing the wrong thing, even by accident. This has developed into an attitude Handy[5] calls *audit mania* – a paraphernalia of systems, checkers, and checkers checking checkers that is both expensive and deadening. For managers to guide their staff through the challenges and changes of the modern management puzzle effectively, these attitudes and many others will have to be abandoned.

While IT is clearly both a driver and a facilitator of new ways of working, it is a common misconception among many managers that providing the right electronic tools, such as e-mail and data bases, is all they need to do to make them happen. However, nothing could be further from the truth.

> Business is ... a highly personal activity and we don't yet have tools that can fully replace the richness of face-to-face contact. When you lose the synergy that comes from daily informal contact, you risk alienating workers from one another and from the company's goals.[6]

As a result, companies are already discovering that it is the "human factors" associated with modern work that make the difference between success and failure for most initiatives.[7] They are also learning that failure to manage work effectively in a contemporary organization, with its wide variety of working relationships, can lead to disastrous results.[8] Conversely, new ways of working can also be the source of significant business benefits.[9]

This chapter looks at the challenges facing managers in dealing with work and workers in the modern organization. It first examines how both are changing. Then, it explores the key management and staff skills that will be critical to have in place to deal with these new working arrangements. Finally, it discusses the increasing importance of relationship management, both within the organization itself and beyond organizational boundaries.

The changing nature of work

Traditional jobs are now largely considered to be change inhibitors that limit an organization's ability to be flexible and responsive. Thus, long-term jobs in a traditional office are no longer the standard. Functions and departments are increasingly being replaced by processes and narrow jobs with broad roles on multi-functional teams. This was apparent at Progressive Insurance, where formal lines of authority were greatly reduced in favor of process owners. Coordination and responsibility are replacing direct supervision. In the future, instead of a single job with a defined organizational role and responsibilities, most people will juggle a number of jobs (similar to today's "projects"), and play several organizational roles. In other words, instead of a "football team" workforce, where everyone has a position and the plays are charted and orchestrated, companies will develop "volleyball teams" where anyone can hit the ball over the net and everyone has to be ready to help do so. This trend was observed at Oticon, where organization members played multiple roles simultaneously. They were assigned to projects according to their availability and potential contribution. A given individual could be project manager for a given project and simultaneously a simple project member on another one. Status varied for each task and each individual was expected to adjust behavior accordingly, thus ensuring that each contributes to a maximum number of tasks and projects. Table 9.1 outlines some of the changes that are already happening to jobs.[10]

Not only is work changing inside offices, companies are also investigating a variety of different *ways* of working outside of

Table 9.1
The changing nature of work (after Bridges, 1994[11])

Yesterday's job	Tomorrow's job
Value defined by position in the organizational hierarchy	Value defined by contribution to group
Reports to one manager	Reports to everyone in group
Well-defined responsibilities, job description	Must be able to do whatever needs to be done, to shift focus rapidly
Clear career path	Careers are managed individually
Narrow wage ranges, regular increases	Wide range of compensation, more emphasis on shared earnings
Rewards linked to position, seniority	Rewards linked to outcomes delivered
Benefits packages	Benefits are the work itself
Work in corporate offices	Work where the customer is or where needed
Regular working hours	Flexible working hours
Managers are coordinators	Managers are coaches, business process owners
A job for life	Individual skills and capabilities are security
Retirement	No retirement
Limited access to corporate information	Wide access to corporate information
Limited understanding of strategies and costs	Wide understanding of strategies, costs

the traditional office. There are five main alternative working arrangements:[12]

- *Telecommuting*: Workers do occasional work from home. This is by far the most common alternative and requires the least amount of managerial change.
- *Hoteling*: Workers only need to come to an office occasionally; they do not have fixed office space. They work where they are needed and can reserve a space in the office when necessary.
- *Tethering*: While workers come regularly to an office, mobile technology enables them to roam around the office or nearby, as needed.

- *Home work*: Workers function from a home office and only meet with their coworkers on a periodic basis.
- *Mobile work*: Workers are on the road almost constantly and interact largely with customers at their offices.

All three cases discussed in Part III show some alternative work arrangements. These were selected to ensure that the organizations remained able to benefit from valuable HR, while providing them with a context, which maximized their efficiency or creativity. On a different scene, many consulting firms have adopted such work arrangements, since they enable them to minimize office costs while sharing expertise among different locations.

The rules for managing all these new forms of work are still evolving. However, we know that there are no "silver bullets" or one right answer for every company.[13] Isolated efforts such as empowerment, self-directed teams, re-engineering, total quality management, telecommuting, job sharing, networking, and flattening the organization are not going to work in and of themselves. Instead, organizations will have to change more holistically and managers will have to try out and adopt a variety of new attitudes and strategies until they find a combination that is right for them.

The changing nature of workers

Not only is work changing, workers themselves are changing as well. As IT takes over most routine types of processing, firms increasingly need knowledge workers skilled in such foundational competencies as math, writing, communication, and interpersonal skills and able to perform in a variety of capacities. A modern workforce can consist of many different types of workers, including full-time staff in a center of excellence (where employees with specialized skills are assigned to jobs on a project-by-project basis) part-time/contingent staff, mobile staff (employees who work in customer locations), telecommuting staff working some or all of the time from a home or satellite office, global staff, working in locations around the world, contract staff, consultants, outsourced staff, staff from allied organizations working on a joint venture, and matrixed staff (individuals who report to more than one manager for different reasons).

Management's responsibility is obtaining the appropriate people for a particular task and ensuring that the job gets done. It aims to organize these different types of staff to achieve flexibility and innovation, and assemble "just in time" resources to accomplish a specific objective.[14] Oticon was the epitome of such an organization of work. The result is a *virtual workforce* that is present in effect, but not in form.

In order to achieve this goal, managers must address a number of organizational challenges. First, they must change the traditional nature of manager–worker relationships, which are rapidly becoming inappropriate to the new ways of working. Second, they must develop ways to manage work and achieve results in a dramatically changing working environment. And third, they must cope with the huge difficulties of communicating with, and integrating the work of, a widely dispersed and increasingly diverse workforce.

While managers have significant responsibilities in helping staff cope with change and creating an environment in which new forms of work and workers can thrive, workers themselves and organized labor also have important roles to play. Changes can be killed just as effectively from below as above.[15] Traditional staff and organized labor attitudes to work (e.g. "It isn't in my job description.") must also adapt to changing times. Unions have long depended on the stability of the workplace and the compactness of the worksite to underwrite their multi-year contracts. However, if organized labor is to survive the changes that are now taking place, it too must make major changes in its culture and behavior.[16]

To a large extent, how unions respond to alternative workplace initiatives will depend on how they perceive the motivations of management. Where managers seek to build a "win–win" scenario for the firm and its personnel, unions will likely be willing to meet them halfway. In addition, more future-oriented labor leaders are making efforts to develop a vision for a twenty-first century union and to explore the pros and cons of various alternative working arrangements. Furthermore, as managers increase their use of teams, it is expected that increased training in group dynamics and problem solving will lead to a more cooperative and less contentious workplace. While trust and cooperation are expected to play a more important role in most future working arrangements, unions can, nevertheless, be expected to continue to insist on the ongoing shield of due process protections.[17]

New management and staff skills

Most new forms of working arrangements have a significant number of human implications, many of which are extremely complex. "Many people don't have an appreciation of the issues involved," one manager noted.[18] These human factors can be a key limiting factor in organizations. As a result, both managers and staff need to develop new skills in dealing with their work and with each other.

Work management skills

Traditional management practices and HR policies have to be updated for managing new forms of work, although many senior managers and HR departments are only gradually becoming more aware of what will be needed in the future. Many HR and management policies still directly mitigate against the effective use of new ways of working. For example, compensation systems often reward individual success, while companies are trying to encourage and promote teamwork. HR departments will have to reassess their policies in a number of areas to ensure that they are in keeping with corporate goals. This implies revisiting traditional concepts and facets of HR management to adjust them to the new reality. Specifically, they should assess their practices and policies in the following areas:[19]

- *Staffing*: HR will need to evaluate all aspects of how it recruits, evaluates, and terminates different types of staff to achieve the right mix of skills and flexibility.
- *Compensation*: In the future, learning how to pay for value delivered, rather than on an hourly or a salaried basis according to hierarchical position, will be essential. Compensation systems must also be designed to recognize "soft" performance measures for workers.
- *Orientation*: To a large extent, HR policies hold an organization's culture together. With an increasingly diverse workforce operating out of many locations, this role becomes even more important and may need to be expanded. Furthermore, if HR cannot get staff to buy into the changes the organization is trying to make in work, the company is unlikely to achieve its goals.

- *Training*: Companies are finding that staff frequently need training in how to make new ways of working function effectively. Many now offer courses in how to work from home, planning, and maintaining good communications.[20]
- *Infrastructure*: The more mobile and dispersed an organization's workforce, the more HR policies and programs will have to be redesigned to accommodate its needs. Job descriptions, methods of promotion, means of determining who qualifies for a job and benefits should all be reconsidered in light of these changes.
- *Checks and balances*: Not everyone is suited to alternative work. HR practices should be designed to identify how and where it is working and under what conditions these arrangements should be terminated or modified.
- *Human interaction*: Finally, HR policies will need to promote and encourage human interaction in all types of alternative working arrangements. Without some face-to-face interaction, it is impossible to build the relationships and trust on which a twenty-first century organization will thrive.

Unquestionably, new ways of working make management's job more complex. Many managers have concerns about controlling and coordinating what gets accomplished when people work non-standard hours and in a wide variety of locations. They worry about how to structure, control, and evaluate work and managing such things as communications, security, and productivity at a distance or across functional or organizational boundaries.

Managers need to pay particular attention to how they determine success in the modern workplace. Measurement based on performance is fundamental to all types of alternative work. More emphasis should, therefore, be placed on managing people, not the work itself and on clearly defining outcomes. Li & Fung clearly showed an emphasis on outcomes. Managers were compensated according to how well they achieved their goals. These goals were set for each one and they were left free to select the most appropriate way to attain them. Managers must learn how to set clear expectations for work and help people translate general strategies into action plans with specific outcomes, time frames, and accountabilities.[21] Measurements of customer satisfaction are also being used more and more as a success indicator.[22]

It is especially important to define success for external staff carefully. Many contract staff, e.g. consultants, are "successful" because, while they deliver what they have been contracted to do, they do not have to deal with the consequences of their work. Choosing clear deliverables is certainly one key component of measurement. However, as work becomes more complex, such things as evaluation against expectations, general knowledge, and relationship management skills are also important measures for individuals. Thus, success should not be too narrowly measured at any level. When BP exploration initially outsourced IT work it "mistakenly set cost reduction as the most important target for (its) suppliers to achieve. (Later, it) shifted the emphasis from costs to service responsiveness, quality, and customer satisfaction" because it realized that cost reduction was simply one of several things the company wanted these staff to accomplish.[23]

Increasingly, organizations are also separating task and resource management. By establishing centers of excellence headed by resource managers for particular staff skills, they ensure that HR issues such as skills development, career management, and compensation are dealt with effectively and fairly. Resource managers are responsible for obtaining appropriately skilled people – from whatever source – and for their management. Task managers can then focus on getting the work done. While resource and task management cannot be totally divorced from each other because they deal with the same people, there is a clear consensus that separation leads to both better use of resources and more attention to the issues of people management.

Coordination of work and conflict resolution are important skills for task managers to have because many projects can only realize benefits in conjunction with other related and complementary projects.[24] If corporate strategies are to be executed effectively, companies will need improved integration functions. To ensure this happens, integration needs to be made *explicit* in every aspect of work. Formal integration mechanisms should also be established whenever interdepartmental or interorganizational teams are involved.

Other work management skills that will increasingly be needed include:[25]

- *Managing teams*: Managers will need to encourage and train coaches in techniques to build and strengthen team dynamics, no matter where the members are located or what types of staff participate. In addition, when working with virtual teams, a key management skill is knowing when a face-to-face meeting is essential to team performance.[26]

■ *Managing processes*: A wide variety of company processes may need to be adapted to new ways of working. These include: operational processes that deal with customers; supportive processes for workers (e.g. access to company files and research); and administrative and work-flow processes (e.g. message taking, e-mail, forms, and approvals).

■ *Managing facilities*: Technologies, technology support, and general office facilities (e.g. meeting space, telephones, and furniture), which are relatively easy to provide in a limited number of locations, become problematic when staff work outside the office or when non-company staff work in a company location. Managers will have to identify the facilities needed for the type of work being done and develop processes for accommodating the various needs that can arise.

Technology or cost saving should never be the sole justifications for implementing new ways of working. Changes must be made for the right reasons and people must be able to put them in the context of their company's purpose, mission, and values.[27] Today, most organizations are trying to develop an appropriate mix of traditional and alternative working arrangements.[28] Successful and effective use of new ways of working will require careful analysis of how and where traditional jobs, as well as management policies and practices, need to be adapted and modified.

Individual skills

An increasingly important challenge for organizations is the problem of how to develop individual skills so that they will be effective in the new virtual workplace.[29] Modern workers will need new and different kinds of skills at all levels. Managers will need to be more empowering and less controlling, and workers will need to be learning continually and able to take on more responsibilities. The development of the intangible skills that help workers cope in new work environments (whether or not they are alternative) will be critical to organizational success in the future.[30] Some of the skills that *all* individuals in the twenty-first century organization will need include:

■ *Communication*: The ability to communicate quickly and effectively on a number of levels (e.g. team-building, work, contact, and social). This has been shown to be a key difference between high-performing and low-performing teams.[31]

■ *Results orientation*: The ability to work with short, fast project cycles and to handle several activities at once.

■ *Proactive thinking*: The ability to work with incomplete information and to seek out and nurture creativity, both individually and as a team; the ability to identify and respond to potentially disruptive situations.

■ *Team work*: The ability to rapidly form teams and build the trust necessary to make them work; the ability to respond positively to effective and committed leadership; the ability to follow a leader without feeling like a slave.

■ *Stress management*: The ability to deal with the stress that is endemic to change (e.g. loss of familiar things, time pressures, and continual accessibility); the ability to help others cope with their stresses.

■ *Meeting commitments*: The ability to manage time appropriately and to self-supervise, no matter where work is done (e.g. at home, on the road, etc.); the ability to plan and schedule work effectively and to meet multistage commitments.

Increasingly, companies are expecting staff at all levels to manage their own careers and to develop the skills and attributes that will enhance their employability. Furthermore, companies are removing many of the career management and development structures that employees have been brought up to expect (e.g. promotion). Nevertheless, managers will continue to have an important role to play in developing employee skills and competencies. With human skills becoming increasingly valuable to organizations, companies cannot afford to neglect their human assets. For in the end, a company's intangible assets, whether research, brands, know-how, or networks of experience, all amount to one thing: people.

At Progressive Insurance, the representatives are on their own, making the required decisions and taking responsibilities. They start processing the information as events happen, directly on the accident site. Once there, they can complete the whole compensation process, from damage evaluation to emitting the check to the claimant. When they leave a site, the case is often closed. In order to do that, they have to be empowered to make all the decisions. These responsibilities imply most of the skills presented earlier. At Oticon, time management is key. Since employees divide their time among several projects and assignments, they have to manage their time efficiently, while remaining accountable for their responsibilities on each project.

Management skills

As companies grow increasingly dependent on their human assets, the management of these assets is becoming more and more critical. And managers have a responsibility to understand the challenges their workers face so they can find ways to help their staff cope with them. Skills needed by managers in particular include:

- *Making connections*: A key fear of workers who operate outside of company boundaries is the loss of visibility. Remote workers often feel they are missing out on critical business advances. Effective managers, therefore, work actively to counteract this feeling. They provide frequent updates about what's happening in the company; they give all individuals a chance to participate in planning processes; and they communicate what individuals are doing to the rest of the group. As one manager commented on how his people management style has changed as a result, "I have to do things differently now. I can't just walk around to supervise people and call a meeting whenever I think one is needed ... This would favor team members working in my office and alienate those who work at other sites."[32] People still working in the office also need to be trained how to work with and include those working outside of the office,[33] and efforts need to be made to include enough face-to-face contact between dispersed workers to build relationships and trust.[34]

■ *Facilitating personal productivity*: Even with committed and skilled workers, there are two key reasons why personal productivity can decline in contemporary workplaces: poor relationships and poor workspaces. Managers have a responsibility to ensure that workers have a workspace that promotes productivity and that their relationships with others are positive. New forms of work require considerable individual self-discipline in dealing with the work-life balance. While many people are initially concerned that they might give the company short shrift if they are not in an office, research shows that the opposite is more often true. Many home-based and mobile workers feel considerable stress at never being able to leave their jobs behind.[35] Thus, they have to learn how to cope with this *mobility paradox* and decide when and where they should disconnect electronically.[36]

■ *Leading and modeling*: While the responsibilities of leaders are not significantly different than in the past, new ways of work bring the importance of leadership into the spotlight more than ever before. Leaders need to make increasing use of their personal resources to guide, support, and influence staff in environments that function without rigid rules and hierarchies. Leadership also becomes more broadly distributed under these circumstances, with different people taking leading roles at different times. For example, some teams have two leaders: a manager and a facilitator to monitor the way in which the team works. And at times, almost every member of a team will have to be a leader when others have to rely on that person's knowledge. Leaders need to make a clear personal commitment to making alternative working arrangements successful. An essential element of leadership is the ability to communicate and integrate personal, team, and business goals. Good leaders articulate a specific goal clearly and then lead by both exhortation and personal example. They also give people time to consider the experience of change and to understand its implications. Finally, leaders recognize that not everyone is able to adapt to changes in working conditions; they give individuals an accurate picture of the opportunities, implications, and expectations involved.

- *Communicating*: As working arrangements become more varied, it becomes easy for managers to slip into task-oriented communication and to omit relationship-building communication. Managers need to design ways to improve all forms of communication and information flows when not all staff members are working the same hours or in the same locations. Staff need to be trained how to access and use electronic tools, share information virtually, and to become more effective providers and consumers of information. Managers must also recognize that the new and more numerous communications pathways of networked organizations may bypass them and the traditional corporate hierarchy. They need to let staff know that this type of communication is valid and that they have the right to seek out whatever information they need to do their job effectively. Conversely, managers also need to deal with "infoglut," whereby they receive so much information that they cannot deal with it all. Finally, it is interesting to note that, as workplaces become more flexible, there is a corresponding need to *increase* traditional forms of communication (e.g. newsletters and visits). Many companies have found that the managerial skills that become most important in new forms of working are those that revolve around old-fashioned human contact.[37]

- *Building trust*: Trust forms the basis for almost all new ways of working. The foundation of effective teamwork is the ability of people to develop personal trust in each other. In order for an organization to truly exploit the potential of workplace flexibility, therefore, it must trust its employees and they must trust each other.[38] Trust has at least two dimensions: *personal trust* – the understanding that people must establish with each other to deal with the issues and challenges that inevitably arise during work; and *competence* – the trust that comes from performance.[39] Managers must facilitate both kinds of trust. They must find ways to ensure that all staff members have both the opportunities they need to interact and develop personal trust relationships, and the abilities to do what they are expected to do. Managers also have a responsibility to define their goals and then trust people to get on with their jobs. And when trust is misplaced, managers must deal with the problem quickly and firmly.

Relationship management

Relationships have always been important in business. Old-boy networks and personal connections have always helped people to do their jobs effectively. What is new in contemporary organizations is the technological networks that broaden the number of relationships possible, and make them more superficial and task-oriented. As a result, companies are learning that "high-tech business" must be balanced by "high-touch relationships" in order to be successful. Whether these are relationships inside the firm or with external partners or service providers, personal contact is the key.

Internal relationships

No matter how remotely people work, managers must find ways to develop good relationships between team members. The most important means of doing this is through face-to-face contact. At Verifone, a completely virtual company, e.g. senior managers meet personally every 6–8 weeks. Meeting locations are varied, so other people in the organization also get an opportunity to meet with senior management. Some firms, such as Price-Waterhouse, have people work together for a few weeks before moving into a virtual situation. Others arrange regular times for dispersed team members to get together. Indeed, many practitioners do not believe that a virtual team can be successful without personal contact.

In addition to formal contact, informal socializing can be extremely important to building trust in all forms of teams. Social get-togethers, informal meetings, and fun, help team members size each other up. Socializing is not a waste of money because it creates a sense of belonging and develops the necessary relationships to make remote and cross-functional work successful. With virtual teams, more time for socializing than would be normal for a co-located team should be scheduled. At Oticon, the managers built coffee bars to facilitate informal gatherings and foster the exchange of ideas.

When necessary, managers should also find other ways to compensate for the loss of daily face-to-face contact. Videoconferencing and telephone calls are common means of doing this. Other tactics include developing an online chat area for informal employee schmoozing and allowing the creation of personal home pages. Furthermore, teams also need norms and facilitation about how to disagree virtually, when the inevitable conflicts arise.

Communication is another key to relationship building. Virtual meetings do not suffice; face-to-face meetings are also often required. No matter how the workforce is organized, managers should ensure that communication is their number one priority. "How (team members) communicate and what they voluntarily communicate are as important as the advanced knowledge (they) may have."[40] As noted above, widely dispersed teams need more formal mechanisms of communication than co-located teams. However, in all cases, managers should create a range of informal opportunities to force communication to take place. Tactics such as making people overlap on different teams, keeping hierarchical roles purposely ill-defined, using the compensation system to encourage information sharing, and having team evaluations are recommended for motivating ongoing communication among team members.

External relationships

With company boundaries becoming more permeable (e.g. through such things as partnerships, outsourcing, and joint ventures), there is an increased need to better manage external relationships as well. Such external relationships have become much more complex in recent years and more critical to an organization's success. Many companies now have so many different types of external relationships in place, they are rapidly growing out of control. For example, one IT organization discovered that it was currently managing 147 different external relationships with various independent service providers including hardware vendors, body shops, service bureaus, skills trainers, consultants, and boutique firms … not to mention a multitude of software product vendors.[41]

Managers need to recognize external relationships formally as part of their overall work and people management strategy. This will help to ensure that adequate resources are committed to organizing and managing this activity. When establishing external relationships, organizations should be extremely clear about their objectives and assign a manager to co-ordinate all relationship management activities, even if they do not necessarily perform them all. Internally, the broader functional unit should be informed about the nature and details of the external relationships that affect them, so that everyone understands the boundaries of the work being handled externally and its relationship to the work that is handled in-house. The proliferation of external relationships is, therefore, giving rise to a new managerial competency – managing staff and relationships outside the firm. Those organizations that are successful at this task will undoubtedly gain advantage over those who fail to meet the challenge.

Conclusion

The most important means of connecting the management puzzle is people. The significant amount of change occurring in modern organizations is leading to new working arrangements, new types of jobs, and new ways of managing them. New forms of work also have the potential to empower workers in ways that have never been possible before and to make work both more satisfying and more productive. However, changing expectations and traditional management–staff relationships can also put people under a considerable amount of stress. How organizations choose to implement their people and work management policies and practices, therefore, provides an essential foundation to how work will be executed. If care is taken to design work and relationships appropriately, companies will find themselves able to achieve their goals successfully.

Questions

1 What are the key challenges of managing workers who are geographically dispersed and remote from face-to-face supervision?
2 While several people work from there home, either on a full-time or a part-time basis, we are far from the pictures drawn a few years ago of almost empty office buildings, with most of the workforce working from their home. What do you think were the main factors that contributed to keeping people in their office rather than telecommuting?
3 What is the role of trust in virtual teamwork?

4   If you were to manage a virtual team, how would you proceed to assess the performance of the team members, as well as their contribution to the team's output?

5   What do you think are the key skills managers must have to successfully manage external relationships?

Endnotes

[1] Fritz, M.B. and Manheim, M., Managing virtual work: a framework for managerial action, in P. Sieber and J. Griese (eds.), *Organizational Virtualness*, Bern, Switzerland: Simona Verlag Bern, 1998, pp. 123–132.

[2] Markus, M.L., Benjamin, R.I., IT-enabled organizational change: new developments for IT specialists, in C. Sauer, P. Yetton and L. Alexander (eds.), *Steps to the Future: Fresh Thinking on the Management of IT-based Organizational Transformation* (Jossey-Bass Business & Management Series), San Francisco, CA: Jossey-Bass Publishers, 1997, pp. 115–142.

[3] Apgar, M., The alternative workplace: changing where and how people work, *Harvard Business Review*, May–June 1998, pp. 121–136.

[4] Stewart, T.A., Managing in a wired company, *Fortune*, 11 July 1994, pp. 44–56.

[5] Handy, C., Trust and the virtual organization, *Harvard Business Review*, May–June, 1995.

[6] Pape, W., Remote control, *INC – The Magazine for Growing Companies*, September, 1996.

[7] Geber, B., Virtual teams, *Training*, April, 1995.

[8] Pape, 1996, *op. cit.*; Fritz, M.B. and Manheim, M., 1998, *op. cit.*

[9] *Ibid.*

[10] Bridges, W., *Job Shift*, Reading, MA: Addison-Wesley Publishing, 1994.

[11] Bridges, W., 1994, *op. cit.*

[12] Davenport, T.H. and Pearlson, K., Two cheers for the virtual office, *Sloan Management Review*, **39**(4), Summer 1998, 51–65.

[13] Bridges, W., 1994, *op. cit.*

[14] Chesbrough, H.W. and Teece, D.J., When is virtual virtuous? *Harvard Business Review*, January–February 1996, 65–73.

[15] Shostak, A.B., Virtual corporations and American labor unions: so many unknowns, so many potential, in M. Igbaria and M. Tan (eds.), *The Virtual Workplace*, Hershey, PA: Idea Group Publishing, 1998, pp. 360–367.

[16] *Ibid.*

[17] *Ibid.*

[18] Alford, R.J., Going virtual, getting real, *Training & Development*, January 1999, 34–44.

[19] Greengard, S., Making the virtual office a reality, *Personnel Journal*, **73**(9), September 1994, 66–79.

[20] Davenport, T.H. and Pearlson, K., 1998, *op. cit.*

[21] Alford, R.J., 1999, *op. cit.*

[22] Stewart, T.A., 1994, *op. cit.*

[23] Cross, J., IT outsourcing: British petroleum's competitive approach, *Harvard Business Review*, May–June 1995, 95–102.

[24] Chesbrough, H.W. and Teece, D.J., 1996, *op. cit.*

[25] Davenport, T.H. and Pearlson, K., 1998, *op. cit.*

[26] Dubé, L. and Paré, G., Global virtual teams, *Communications of the ACM*, (44) 12, December 2001, pp. 71–73.

[27] Alford, R.J., 1999, *op. cit.*

[28] Davenport, T.H. and Pearlson, K., 1998, *op. cit.*

[29] Norton, B. and Smith, C., *Understanding the Virtual Organization*, Barron's Educational Series, 1997.

[30] Fritz, M.B. and Manheim, M., 1996, *op. cit.*; Grenier, R. and Metes, G., *Going Virtual*, NJ: Prentice Hall, 1995.

[31] Iacono, C.Z. and Weisband, S., Developing trust in virtual teams, *Proceeding of the HICSS'96*, 1996.

[32] Geber, B., 1995, *op. cit.*

[33] Davenport, T.H. and Pearlson, K., 1998, *op. cit.*

[34] Greengard, S., 1994, *op. cit.*

[35] Davenport, T.H. and Pearlson, K., 1998, *op. cit.*

[36] Apgar, M., 1998, *op. cit.*

[37] Stewart, T.A., 1994, *op. cit.*

[38] *Ibid.*

[39] Geber, B., 1995, *op. cit.*

[40] Quinn, J.B., Baruch, J.J. and Zien, K.A., *Innovation Explosion: Using Intellect and Software to Revolutionize Growth Strategies*, New York, NY: The Free Press, 1997, 20–42.

[41] McKeen, J.D. and Smith H.A., Managing external relationships in IS, *Proceedings of the 34th Hawaii Conference on System Sciences*, Maui, Hawaii, 5–8 January 2001.

Chapter 10

IT management

The information technology (IT) department is charged with delivering technical solutions to business problems. Whereas until recently, organizational change facilitated by IT has focused largely around processes, we are now beginning to see the radical transformation of organizations themselves as a result of technology. The advent of the Internet and other recent technologies in the mid-90s has opened up new possibilities for doing business across organizational boundaries. As businesses come to recognize and exploit these opportunities, they are also realizing that technology can be used to create and enhance inter-enterprise effectiveness and efficiency.[1] As companies have come to realize that technology can not only be used to make its processes more effective and efficient, but can also fundamentally transform the way business operates, there has been a significant broadening of IT's strategic, tactical, and operational responsibilities. Table 10.1 illustrates how these have changed over the last two decades.

One of the most important characteristic features of the changes affecting the IT department over the last 20 years is how many responsibilities have been added-on to this function. This also explains why IT has become increasingly more difficult and complex to manage. As Table 10.1 shows, IT's influence now encompasses not only much of the traditional organization, but is also expanding to include the new forms of organization towards which the world is evolving.

There are two characteristics of IT departments that directly contribute to how well it performs. First, IT must be *aligned* with the business. In other words, the work it does should be designed to realize business strategy directly, support business structures, enable environmental assessment or facilitate new styles of leadership.[3] Second, IT must be *flexible* enough to adapt to the

Table 10.1

IT's growing list of responsibilities[2]

1980s Responsibilities	1990s Responsibilities	2000s Responsibilities
Systems development	Systems development	Systems development
Operations management	Operations management	Operations management
Vendor relationships	Vendor relationships	External relationship management
	Data management	Knowledge management
	End-user computing	Infrastructure management
	Education and training	Change management
	Managing emerging technologies	Environmental scanning
	Corporate architecture	Corporate architecture
	Strategic systems	Strategic leadership
	Systems planning	Strategy implementation
		Network management
		E-commerce
		Business integration (CRM, ERP, etc.)
		Resource management
		Risk management

changing conditions of business and technology environments and to enable the business to respond to them.[4] Alignment and flexibility, in turn, are dependent on four key features of the IT function's design: structure, processes, skills, and architecture. Together, these provide comprehensive support for the pieces of the management puzzle, enabling it to be put together in whatever way makes sense for the organization. In this chapter, we explore the ways in which these elements of the IT function help an organization to deliver value. First, the concepts of alignment and flexibility are examined and how these can best be achieved. Then, best practices for achieving effective IT structure, processes, skills, and architecture are discussed.

Aligning IT internally and externally

"Alignment" describes the fit between an organization's strategy and the administrative structure that supports its execution.[5] Just as it is becoming increasingly difficult to distinguish between business and IT strategy in practice, it is also practically impossible to separate business processes and technology in strategy execution. What is clear, however, is that a firm's economic performance is strongly related to how well it can actually carry out its strategic intent, and this is strongly related to the degree of alignment between business and IT at a number of levels.[6]

In the recent past, business and technical infrastructures (i.e. processes and service delivery mechanisms) were two different components that simply needed to be coordinated. Today, they are much more likely to be combined into one overarching structure designed to accomplish and support the goals and objectives of the enterprise.[7] This is not always easy to do, given the multiple (and often conflicting) demands on both business and the IT function to: support the existing business, transform how it operates, and change how it grows and competes.[8] To achieve success, however, a strong alignment of human and software systems is necessary. This is most likely developed as a result of an ongoing process of mutual adaptation of people and technology, rather than a one-time, one-way event.[9] It has been showed that shared domain knowledge, between business and IT executives is closely related to the degree of alignment. Shared domain knowledge is defined here as "the ability of IT and business executives, at a deep level, to understand and be able to participate in the others' key processes and to respect each others' unique contribution and challenges".[10]

While the need for alignment in strategy execution would seem to be intuitively obvious, many organizations and most IT practitioners believe that changing technology is enough to change how an organization works. While the evidence piles up that this is not the case, many companies continue to underestimate and underfund the effort needed to actually implement their strategies, with the result that these strategies are often unsuccessful or only partially successful.[11]

There are four areas where IT must be aligned with business.

Cultural alignment

Culture is pervasive throughout an organization and colors the meaning that individuals ascribe to all organizational acts. It is the pattern of basic assumptions, which are taught as the "correct" way to perceive, think, and feel by members of an organization. Culture is, therefore, a stabilizing influence in the organization, and once in place, an inherently conservative force, which can inhibit change.[12] IT can have profound effects on organization strategies and structure, but only if the organizational culture can accept change. Three cultural visions have grown up around the way technology should be implemented in organizations.[13]

The first vision is automation, whereby IT is used to enable routine kinds of work (e.g. document preparation) to be done largely by machines with little human intervention. The second one, labeled "informate," proposes using IT to create information about organizations and activities that never existed previously or could not be accessed easily. Informate's primary purpose is to support and enhance decision-making, not to replace human intervention. Finally, transformation is the last vision, in which IT is used to integrate human and technical capabilities, thus achieving radical transformations in work.

Culture can be influenced and designed. In the Oticon case, the four-page document drafted by Kolind on January 1st was an instrument to reshape the company culture. IT was later used to support the transformation of the organization and the reorganization of the work. In Progressive Insurance, IT is intertwined with the strategy and supports the whole business. Its culture was receptive to IT from the beginning. The approach at Progressive is both to informate and to transform. They are chan-ging the way service is delivered to the customers, by synchronizing events (accidents), interaction between clients and company representatives (on the site), and processing of information. By making the information accessible everywhere to its representatives, the company was able to modify the way it conducts business.

Strategic alignment

At a strategic level, business and IT strategy must complement and support each other relative to the external business environment. As we have noted earlier, given IT's potential, strategy development should be a two-way process between business and IT management. In practice, however, this will not be achieved unless the formal decision-making processes of the firm are connected at various levels. Furthermore, if the IT and business strategy formulation processes are not compatible (e.g. if they take place at different times or involve different business units), it is unlikely that the end result will be aligned.[14] There are three key processes that will promote strategic alignment:

- *Connection at the top*: Research shows that in organizations where top business managers see themselves as responsible for making technology decisions and where the chief information officers (CIOs) (or chief IT executives) report directly to the chief executive officer (CEO), there will be a much stronger link between technology and business goals. The attention paid to integration at this level also filters down through the rest of the organization and makes integration of systems and processes at lower levels easier.[15] CIOs have been entrusted with more responsibilities in recent years. A very good example of the increased role of the CIO is observed in the case of Progressive Insurance, where the CIO, Glen Renwick, was named CEO after the retirement of Peter Lewis.

- *Planning systems*: These should incorporate both technology plans and business plans. Frequent formal planning meetings appear to be the most effective means of ensuring that business and technology strategies are synchronized. These meetings should include both business and IT heads and contain directives about how and where their plans are linked. Li & Fung showed formal planning systems. Every 3 years, the company strategy is laid out and adjusted. IT is later adjusted to sustain company strategy.

- *Timing*: Although business plans have traditionally been developed first, and technology plans expected to follow, in today's organizations there is a wide variation of sequencing. Frequently, it is no longer desirable or appropriate for planning to take place in such a sequential fashion, but rather in a more iterative fashion. Managers should, therefore, examine their planning cycles to ensure that they are appropriate for how the company wants to use technology. If IT is to be used as a competitive weapon, more integrated and dynamic planning cycles will be especially desirable.[16,17]

Once strategic plans are in place, alignment can be enhanced by articulating a clear, common vision throughout the organization, thereby ensuring that every part of the firm (including IT) understands and is working toward that vision in some way.[18] In addition, with IT an integral part of most business strategies, an "us and them" mentality blaming IT for ineffective technology and systems is clearly inappropriate. While IT has the mandate to deliver technology to the organization, it is the business' responsibility to ensure it gets what it needs. It can only do so by taking overall responsibility for all aspects of strategy, including the technological ones.[19]

In all three cases presented earlier, Oticon, Progressive Insurance, and Li & Fung, deliberate efforts were made to share the vision, to enhance everyone's understanding of what the company was striving to do. Leaders kept promoting their ideas, using simple messages and powerful images to convey their vision of the organization's future.

Business process alignment

Equally critical is a good fit between an organization's processes and infrastructure and those of the IT department. It is essential that there be internal coherence between these two, if the firm is going to have the capability to deliver on its strategies. Frohman explains, "A company's decision to rely more heavily on technology should be coupled with a commitment to satisfy the conditions necessary to implement it."[20] Some of these conditions include establishing standards for the meaning and format of information and good relationships with business managers at all levels[21] designing interfaces that will help systems work together and enable ease of access, and finally, designing reward mechanisms to encourage the appropriate use of technology.[22]

This type of alignment becomes even more significant when the business processes of several organizations must be closely coupled, as in a business-web (b-web) or value network. Inter-enterprise integration is based on sophisticated data exchange between partners' processes.[23] Tightly coupled integration was a key success factor for Li & Fung. The difficulty of achieving integration across business units and organizations is one reason for the popularity of enterprise resource planning (ERP) and customer relationship management (CRM) systems, which literally impose alignment of standards and integration across one or more organizations. Regardless of how alignment is achieved, managers must recognize that fit between IT and business processes is essential to the success of any IT strategy, whether internally or externally.

IT marketplace alignment

A frequently overlooked aspect of alignment is the fit of an organization's IT strategy with the external IT marketplace, which can be important for maximizing the performance of a business.[24]

The particular external IT marketplace with which an IT department should align itself is shaped by the scope of the IT activities, the portfolio of the organization's competencies, and the systemic character of these activities the extent to which the activities are interconnected with other activities of the organization, and finally the governance structure(s) adopted by the organization.

How IT delivers technology to the organization will also affect the alignment chosen with the marketplace. This includes:

- *IT architecture*: a firm's portfolio of applications, data architecture and hardware, software and communication infrastructure;
- *Information system (IS) processes*: processes central to the operations of the IT organization, e.g. systems development and maintenance;
- *IS skills*: the capabilities of the individuals needed to manage and operate the IT infrastructure.

As technology today plays such an important role in the development of business strategy, available resources in these areas in the IT marketplace actually help to both shape and support a firm's business strategy. Research suggests that an inadequate fit between these domains of IT is "a major reason for failure to derive benefits from investments."[25]

Another aspect of the need for fit with the IT marketplace is determining the right time in the "hype" cycle to invest seriously in a particular technology. If a firm invests too early, it faces the pain and expense of deploying an immature technology. For this reason, the early adoption of technology should only be driven by a strong business need. On the other hand, if a firm delays too long, competitors may succeed in getting a technology to work to their advantage. Companies that choose to wait should pay close attention to the external IT marketplace, so that they can deploy a new technology when it is better understood and its benefits outweigh the risks.

Creating a flexible IT organization

While we refer most often to technology as an array of tools, a strategic enabler, or a piece in the organizational puzzle, it is important to keep in mind that IT is generally an organization function or department. In the not too distant past, the role of the IT function was to create and manage an infrastructure that would meet the needs of a stable, static organization. Cycles of change averaged 5–7 years and could be responded to *after* the change had occurred. More recently, the IT function has been asked to partner with senior executives to capture business changes *as they occur* and to match the IT strategy to them. Today, changes in business are practically continual and the IT function is now being asked to understand the *future* business environment and to *predict* the infrastructures that will support it.[26]

It is clear that traditional ways of delivering technology to an organization will not meet the present and future conditions of business change. Yet, some structures and principles must be in place to direct the choices a company makes. IT managers are thus wrestling with two seemingly conflicting concepts: the need for concrete structure and direction, and the need to be flexible and constantly changing. The challenge IT executives face is, therefore, to develop an organization (i.e. the structures, processes, capabilities, and architecture) that will guide but not limit IT choices, anticipate likely IT needs but not restrict the future, and accelerate the implementation of new technology without taking unacceptable risks.[27] They need to create an IT organization that is neither too rigid nor too lax, but moderately flexible. The Appendix (page 298) discusses the structuring of the IT department in more detail.

Flexibility in IT is something business executives have been demanding for years, but it is now becoming imperative in the current business and technology environments. Flexibility generally refers to the ability or the potential of an organization to adapt or change. But how managers interpret this ability varies widely. Upton notes that, at minimum, it involves three key abilities: respond quickly to customers (users), introduce new products or services without delays, and provide a broad range of existing products and services.[28]

The increasing need for flexibility is being particularly driven by shrinking product cycles. In the past 10 years, cycle times have shrunk from around 5–7 years to between 12 and 24 months. Thus, business processes are having to change more rapidly too. In fact, according to Prager,[29] in a world of continuous change, flexibility is becoming equivalent to stability:

> In a rapidly changing market, stability really means long-term, healthy survival … Flexible employees also create a sense of stability because they feel more secure knowing their organization can readily adapt to change.

But why are product cycles shrinking? Baldwin and Clark explain that complex products and processes are being increasingly developed in a modular fashion.[30] That is, they are being built from smaller components that are designed independently but which function as a whole because their interfaces are clearly specified. The adoption of modularity in product/service development is driving a number of important changes in organizations: *innovation* is increasing, the *rate of change* is increasing, *complexity* is increasing, as is the organization's ability to deal with complex products/services; *relationships between companies* are changing as individual companies become responsible for designing products or producing individual modules, and finally *flexibility* is increasing.

These changes are ever-present in the three cases presented earlier. Oticon showed how an organization could respond to increased pressure to innovate. The products Oticon sells are always improving. The rate of change is increasing as new competitors force the company to surpass itself constantly and to introduce new and better products. This market thrives on innovation. By reorganizing work differently, the firm could respond to the faster pace of innovation required by the market. Progressive Insurance also innovates at a fast pace. The market is becoming more complex and the company has responded by innovating in the way it handles the relationship with its clients. Finally, Li & Fung may be the best example of modularity. By deconstructing the value chain, it is able to adjust production in a just-in-time manner, doing so across partnering companies. This is an extreme response to the challenge of flexibility.

The key to being flexible in any part of an organization is, therefore, to develop strategies based on *modularity*.[31] Modularity emphasizes loose linkages or intentional independence between individual components. Changes in one component, therefore, do not affect other components. This increases adaptability. At a design level, modularity emphasizes standard interfaces between components, enabling individual components to be substituted without completely redesigning the overall product. This enables mixing and matching of components to create a large number of variations, again increasing flexibility and adaptability.[32]

IT departments are trying to support this flexibility in a number of ways. First, they are aligning their strategy development processes more closely with the business' strategic priorities so they can become more sensitive to business needs and respond to them more quickly. Second, they are looking for ways to balance the centralized guidance of IT and the benefits of shared economies of scale with the "uninhibited and rapid use of IT" often desired by local business units to ensure some standardization.[33] The desirable equilibrium is often implemented through different IT organization structures (see below). Third, they are developing ways to balance investments in technology that support the business with those that transform it to help the business grow and compete in new ways. Fourth, IT is managing its resources to achieve modularity. Increasingly, IT departments are using packaged software and outside resources (e.g. contractors) to create a just-in-time capability to deal with the wide variety of demands for IT from the business. IT's skills as a resource broker will, therefore, significantly enhance its abilities to respond to business needs in a flexible fashion. Fifth, IT organizations are looking inward to their own processes to ensure that they are enabling optimal responsiveness and flexibility of IT services.[34] Finally, flexibility is being designed into technology infrastructures and application architectures (see below). Technology based on open standards is being used to facilitate "plug and play" solutions and applications are being designed so that many aspects of support can be managed by the users themselves.

IT skills management

While most managers think of IT skills as being technical in nature, in fact, a broad range of technical, managerial, and political skills are needed in IT to plan, acquire, develop, implement, operate, and control IT. Studies show that there is a clear association between a firm's IT management competencies and its success in deploying IT in support of its business strategies and work processes.[35] These skills also contribute to a firm's ability to apply IT in an effective, efficient, and timely manner. In short, IT skills convert the "raw materials" of data, technology, business knowledge, and knowledge of how to apply IT, into new products and services, transformed business processes, enriched organizational intelligence, and flexible organization structures.

Today, IT departments are modifying their resourcing strategies to make increasing use of external contractors for technological components and business staff to work on business requirements and interface issues. IT personnel, with their strategic perspective and business technologist skills, are most useful for their "big picture" view. More and more, they are maintaining the linkages between the various parts of a cross-functional team through relationships, coordination, and intelligent integration. Internal IT staff is, therefore, being utilized more to pull a variety of disparate people and platforms together to achieve a desired result, and to identify and resolve the problems and issues that threaten the delivery of a service, rather than for actual service or product delivery. Thus, internal IT staff is taking on a new role, much like that of a general contractor in the construction industry. These people may or may not do some of the actual building work. However, they always assume responsibility for deadlines, relationship management, project management, and risk management.

There are seven core IT competencies that are relatively stable, regardless of technology and other environmental changes. Their presence or absence represents the extent to which a company is positioned to mobilize its IT assets and investments.[36]

1   *Business deployment*: These capabilities enable IT staff to explore the potential business value of new technologies, develop effective working relationships with business, create useful IT measurement systems, and make appropriate sourcing decisions.

2   *External networking*: These are competencies in developing value-adding partnerships with a variety of external IT partners, including customers, suppliers, vendors, and competitors.

3   *Line technology leadership*: These competencies represent IT's ability to cultivate a willingness among business managers to own and champion IT-based business initiatives.

4   *Process adaptiveness*: These are capabilities in developing the organization's ability to restructure its business processes and understand the potential of IT to transform them.

5   *IT planning*: These capabilities provide a clear vision about the contributions of IT investments to business values and enable the integration of business and IT plans.

6   *IT infrastructure*: These competencies enable a firm to devise, implement and maintain a strong technology resource base.

7   *Data centre utility:* These are the capabilities involved in building, maintaining, and securing a firm's information processing facilities.

These capabilities can be seen as resources. A company will have to develop and nurture these strategic capabilities to ensure that it benefits from adequate IT services. It is by leveraging these capabilities that the company will get the required IT services. Developing a platform of these capabilities within an IT organization is recognized as an important step towards developing competitive agility.

To make sure that these capabilities are at hand, IT managers will have to acquire several key management skills so as to obtain, manage, and retain the earlier mentioned capabilities. These skills are not necessarily new but the extent to which they will be necessary in the IT organization is unprecedented.

The first skill is change management. Many IT specialists have only a limited understanding of what it takes to facilitate organizational change. They frequently assume that technology itself does all the work of change, instead of focusing on the broader social and organizational success factors that are necessary to facilitate change. To promote organizational transformation, IT personnel must have the skills to facilitate and create organizational change.[37]

The second skill is staff recruitment and retention. In the current competitive market for IT staff, companies cannot acquire the skills they need to implement IT effectively, unless they develop competitive competencies in recruiting and retaining technical staff. Some of these include: innovative benefits and compensation; a well-defined recruitment process; a commitment to training; hiring networks; skills management; and professional challenges and advancement.[38]

Finally, resource brokering will become more important since internal staff will perform a more limited array of activities in the future. IT managers, therefore, need to develop resource brokering skills. Increasingly, technology strategy is being implemented through a combination of in-house staff, consultants, outsourcers, vendors, and long-term partners. Therefore, organizations need strong skills in learning how and when to use each type of resource effectively, which resources need to be retained in-house, and which can best be managed by others. These decisions play a key role in building IT's capabilities and flexibility, thus having a direct impact on an organization's ability to use IT.[39]

IT architecture

The term IT architecture is often thought of as referring to technology design only and, therefore, not being of much interest or benefit outside IT. In fact, an architecture for IT must reflect both the needs of business and the current potential of technology. Thus, there is a growing trend to reframe IT architecture into *enterprise* architecture to ensure that the joint influences of *both* business and technology are represented in it.

An IT architecture can be defined as a blueprint for a company's IT. It follows a set of principles, standards, guidelines, and technologies that describe and direct an organization's technology design for the future. It also describes to executives, business managers, IT managers, technical specialists, and vendors, in increasing levels of detail, what needs to be built. The type of business, its geographic layout, its management style, and the nature of its products and services will all affect the type of architecture a business needs, just as the type of function and location of a building dictates the architecture needed in construction. Furthermore, financial considerations, the business' stability, and its relationship to its customers and suppliers will influence the breadth and depth of technology needed. Each of these factors needs to be made explicit so that IT will be able to properly design an appropriate technical architecture to support the business.

In addition to a technical view, there are four further perspectives on architecture that IT must consider in order to generate desired business results.[40] A business view provides a model of the future enterprise showing it as a series of logical services linking internal and external clients. A work view shows who will do what, where, when, and with what tools. An information view describes the information requirements of the future organization. Finally, an application view identifies what applications will support the work of the organization.

Designing an IT architecture is, therefore, not a formula, but the development of a series of principles and strategies which provide the foundation for building the organization's infrastructure and applications.[41]

Several overarching convictions must guide any architectural initiative:

- *Flexibility must be the primary goal*: To achieve organizational flexibility, an architecture must, first and foremost, be adaptable. Other considerations, such as cost, performance, user friendliness, risk, and response time, while important, must be secondary. Companies have to be prepared to accept these tradeoffs to achieve competitive advantage when short cycle times are the driving force behind organizational success.[42]

- *Each enterprise architecture is unique*: Each organization must develop its own architecture and make the tough underlying decisions required to make it work in their business. Architectural development is not something that can be done for a company. There is no such thing as a standard IT architecture (although generic architectures may be a good starting point for some companies). Each is unique because each company functions differently.[43]

- *An enterprise architecture is never finished*: DeBoever and Buchanan[44] note that "architecture efforts are so agonizing that no one wants to undergo them twice." Nevertheless, it is a fundamental principle that architecture must be approached in an ongoing and iterative fashion. Without this evolutionary dimension, it will become a static, concrete entity that will either lose its relevance or become a barrier to change. Many organizations have an ongoing architectural advisory board that regularly feeds new requirements, criticism, and breakthrough ideas to those responsible for the architecture. In addition, one individual must be accountable to maintaining the ongoing integrity of the architecture.

- *Knowledge is critical to an effective architecture*: An effective architecture requires a high level of knowledge about how its components function and interact.[45] Ideally, knowledge should be complete before decisions are made, but in practice, companies usually have to work with only partial information. Baldwin and Clark recommend undertaking deliberate activities to promote learning, especially in those areas, which will have significant economic implications for a company.[46] These, in turn, will have a direct impact on improved organizational knowledge and thus make for better architectural decisions.

■ *Standards are essential:* Standardized interfaces are the most important way to achieve both increased flexibility and inter-organizational connectivity.[47] Selecting hardware and software that follows industry standards is the ideal because these enable complete connectivity and vendor independence, both of which are essential to flexibility. While architecture is more than standards, standards are essential both to portability (i.e. the ability to transfer hardware or software from one environment to another) and to interoperability (i.e. the ability to exchange information with other hardware and software).

The lack of a process whereby organizations can develop an architecture has been a fundamental barrier to its adoption in organizations. Ideally, an architecture's development should follow a process covering five basic steps. First, the direction must be clearly identified. Once the goal is set, the current situation must be assessed to pinpoint current constraints. Following that step, the gap between the ideal situation and the current one can be measured. This gap leads to the establishment of the migration plan, enabling the organization to move to the desired architecture. Finally the evolution of the architecture should be managed actively. Once the desired state is achieved, it cannot be viewed as a stable state – it is only the current state, which has to be compared to the new desired one.

Questions

1 What is the value of strategic planning in an environment where change is constant?

2 How can we balance flexibility with the need for efficiency when selecting different technologies?

3 How will our technological choices will limit or enable strategic choices?

4 How can we change our relationships with our business partners (clients, suppliers, or competitors) using IT?

Endnotes

[1] Tapscott, D. and Ticoll, A., Lowi, A., Boston, MA: Harvard Business School Press, *Digital Capital: Harnessing the power of business webs*, 2000, 272 p.

[2] Smith, H.A. and McKeen, J.D., Whither IT: a look at IT in the year 2005, *I/T Management Forum*, Vol. 10, No. 1, School of Business, Queen's University, Kingston, Canada, K7L 3N6, 2000.

[3] Chan, Y., Huff, S., Barclay, D.W. and Copeland, D.G., Business strategic orientation, information systems strategic orientation, and strategic alignment. *Information Systems Research*, **8**(2), 1997, 125–150.

[4] Prager, K., Managing for flexibility, *Information Systems Management*, **4**(13), 1996, 41–47.

[5] Henderson, J.C. and Venkatraman, N., Strategic alignment: leveraging information technology for transforming organizations, *IBM Systems Journal*, **38**(2–3), 1999, 472–484.

[6] Chan et al., 1997, *op. cit.*

[7] Andrews, Philip, P. and Hahn, J., Transforming supply chains into value webs, *Strategy & Leadership*, July–August 1998, **26** (3), 6–11.

[8] McNee, B., Percy, A., Fenn, J., Cassell, J., Hunter, R., Cohen, L., Keller, E., Goodhue, C., Scott, D., Morello, D., Magee, F., Whitten, D., Schlier, F., Baylock, J., West, M. and Berg, T., The industry trends scenario: delivering business value through IT, *Gartner Group Strategic Analysis Report*, 30 April 1998, 83.

[9] Applegate, L.M., *Managing in an Information Age: IT Challenges and Opportunities*, Harvard Business School Press, #9-196-004, 1995, 19 p.

[10] Reich, B.H. and Benbasat, I., Measuring the information system-business strategy relationship, in R.D. Galliers and D.E. Leidner (eds.), *Strategic Information Management*, Oxford: Butterworth-Heineman, 2003, pp. 265–310.

[11] Markus, M.L. and Benjamin, R., Change agentry: the next IS frontier, *MIS Quarterly*, December 1996, 385–407.

[12] McKeen, J. and Smith, H., *Managing Information Systems: Strategies for Action*, John Wiley & Sons, 1996, 374 p.

[13] Schein, E., *Organizational Culture and Leadership: A Dynamic View*, Jossey-Bass, 1985, 358 p.

[14] Frohman, A.L., Technology as a competitive weapon, *Harvard Business Review*, January–February 1982, 97–105.

[15] *Ibid.*

[16] Henderson, J.C. and Venkatraman, N., 1999, *op. cit.*

[17] Frohman, A.L., 1982, *op. cit.*

[18] McKeen, J. and Smith, H., 1996, *op. cit.*

[19] *Ibid.*

[20] Frohman, A.L., 1982, *op. cit.*

[21] McNee, B., *et al.*, 1998, *op. cit.*

[22] Davenport, T.H. and Pearlson, K., Two cheers for the virtual office, *Sloan Management Review*, **39**(4), Summer 1998, 51–65.

[23] Magretta, J., The power of virtual integration: an interview with Dell Computer's Michael Dell, *Harvard Business Review*, March–April 1998, 73–84.

[24] Henderson, J.C. and Venkatraman, N., 1999, *op. cit.*

[25] *Ibid.*

[26] Prager, K., 1996, *op. cit.*

[27] McKeen, J. and Smith, H., 1996, *op. cit.*

[28] Upton, D., What really makes factories flexible? *Harvard Business Review*, July–August 1995.

[29] Prager, K., 1996, *op. cit.*

[30] Baldwin, C. and Clark, K., Managing in an age of modularity, *Harvard Business Review*, September 1997.

[31] *Ibid.*

[32] Sanchez, R. and Mahoney, J., Modularity, flexibility, and knowledge management in product and organization design, *Strategic Management Journal*, 17, Winter 1996, 63–76.

[33] McNee, B., *et al.*, 1998, *op. cit.*

[34] *Ibid.*

[35] Sambamurthy, V. and Zmud, R., At the hearth of success: Organizationwide Management Competencies, in C. Sauer, P.W. Yetton and Associates (eds.), *Steps to the Future: Fresh Thinking on the Management of IT-Based Organizational Transformation*, CA, San Francisco, CA: Jossey-Bass Publishers, 1997, pp. 143–163.

[36] *Ibid.*

[37] Markus, L., and Benjamin, R., 1996, *op. cit.*

[38] McNee, B., *et al.*, 1998, *op. cit.*

[39] McKeen, J. and Smith, H., 1996, *op. cit.*

[40] Tapscott, D. and Caston, A., *Paradigm Shift: The New Promise of Information Technology*, McGraw-Hill, 1992.

[41] Schlier, F. *et al.*, Enterprise 2003: The technology-enabled enterprise, *Gartner Group Strategic Analysis Report*, 29 January 1998, 66.

[42] DeBoever, L. and Buchanan, R., Three architectural sins, *CIO*, May 1997, **14**(10), 124–126.

[43] Strassman, P., *The Squandered Computer: Evaluating the Business Alignment of Information Technologies*, The Information Economics Press, 1997, 426 p.

[44] DeBoever, L. and Buchanan, R., 1997, *op. cit.*

[45] Sanchez, R. and Mahoney, J., 1996, *op. cit.*

[46] Baldwin C. and Clark, K., 1997, *op. cit.*

[47] Sanchez, R. and Mahoney, J., 1996, *op. cit.*

Chapter 11

Knowledge management

Organizational knowledge is constituted by the insights, understandings, and practical know-how of the employees.[1] Knowledge management (KM) refers to the set of processes, practices, and technologies that aim to leverage the intellectual capital of an organization and enable it to make more effective use of its assets. To date, KM has not yet evolved into a firm discipline. Some companies have had considerable success in using KM, but many others are still struggling to find ways to do it effectively.[2] No one denies, however, that it will be increasingly important to how companies will operate.

> In a post-industrial era, the success of a corporation lies more in its intellectual and systems capabilities than in its physical assets. The capacity to manage human intellect and to convert it into useful products and services is fast becoming the critical executive skill of the age.[3]

While the importance of intellectual capital and its management to organizations is not really a new phenomenon, our awareness of its value has grown substantially in recent years. Over the last decade, there has been a growing recognition that these types of intangible corporate assets have become the most valuable and fastest growing part of our economy. Whereas in 1982, tangible assets represented 62 percent of a company's market value, by 1992 this figure had dropped to 38 percent.[4] Surveys of top U.S. and Canadian firms support this statistic. One showed that between 50 and 90 percent of the value a firm creates comes not from management of traditional assets, but from the management of intellectual capital.[5] Today, intellectual assets and their effective management may, in fact, be the only form of sustainable competitive advantage. This is a major reason why a wide range of companies have launched KM initiatives.[6]

There are many other drivers behind the new interest in KM. There is an increasing recognition of the power of knowledge.[7] While we have mountains of information available, thanks to technology, many managers today suffer from "infoglut." Knowledge (i.e. meaningful information in context) is often lacking.[8] Globalization, virtualization, deregulation, privatization, and increased customer sophistication have raised organizations' competence standards and expectations *vis-à-vis* their knowledge needs. The growing market value of highly capable people, rising job complexity and the universal availability of information are driving the need to do more with knowledge. Finally, network computing and the resulting evolution of new organizational models are making speed a competitive necessity. Therefore, knowledge is needed to deliver high quality, high value products and services in ever-diminishing time frames.

Executives at Oticon, Progressive Insurance, and Li & Fung have long understood that successful companies do not only compete on the basis of their products, services, and operational excellence, but also on their ability to leverage their intellectual capital through such things as product innovation, customer relationship management, and global service delivery, to name just a few. The ability to capture and share knowledge, to reuse it, and to innovate with it, is today widely seen as being both a key determinant and a predictor of value. The combination of accelerating knowledge accumulation with rapid knowledge depreciation rates means that organizations must become more skilled at acquiring and transferring knowledge and at modifying their behavior to reflect new knowledge and insights.[9] Access to knowledge is already a fundamental and pervasive concern of highly competitive industries. And it is becoming ever more important as the knowledge base becomes more complex (e.g. as in the pharmaceutical industry) and when uncertainty is high. As a result, collaboration is becoming a key dimension of competition.

Last and foremost, in an economy where the only certainty is uncertainty, the one sure source of lasting competitive advantage is knowledge. When markets shift, technologies proliferate, competitors multiply, and products become obsolete overnight, successful companies are those that consistently create new knowledge, disseminate it widely throughout the organization, and quickly embody it in new technologies, products and/or services.[10] For all these reasons, knowledge is, therefore, an important part of the management puzzle these days.

While many companies understand the importance of KM, very few are skilled at actually doing it effectively.[11] They are struggling to understand just what KM means for them and their future. They are asking themselves such questions as: *What is the value of knowledge? How can we best tap into company knowledge?* and *What is the right form of KM for our organization?* There are no clear-cut answers to these and other questions about the rapidly evolving field of KM. Practitioners are therefore having to fly by the seats of their pants in deciding how much money to spend on KM, where to spend it, and how to promote and encourage KM in their companies. KM is still a somewhat ambiguous function in organizations. This chapter looks at what businesses are doing to try to leverage their knowledge more effectively. It examines some approaches companies are using to implement KM in their organizations and discusses some successful practices for introducing KM.

Approaches to knowledge management

Reorganizations and transformations are the results of constant dialogue between members of the management team, between managers and employees, and between everyone and customers.[12] At Oticon, where networks of experts replaced traditional hierarchical systems, several measures were taken to encourage contact and informal communication between employees. Among others, elevators were made inoperable, bars were installed on all floors where meetings could be organized, and rooms with circular sofas were provided to encourage discussion. At Li & Fung, bi-annual retreats foster communication across company groups. At the operational level, constant monitoring of the market and close links maintained with clients also contribute substantially to fostering firm competencies.

KM is most appropriately conceived of as a multi-disciplinary approach to the creation, capture, access, and use of an organization's information assets. It is a formal and integrated effort to manage an enterprise's knowledge capital. However, companies implement KM in highly variable ways. For example, some firms are trying to codify corporate knowledge in a data base, while others are trying to promote informal knowledge-sharing between individuals.[13] Approaches to KM, therefore, range from the highly technical to the highly personal. This variety makes it difficult for managers to discern how best to shape an effective KM approach for their organization. Knowledge managers frequently struggle with the fact that "managing knowledge" means a variety of different things to different people. Thus, implementing KM in an organization can often have people working at cross purposes with each other, simply because they are focusing on different facets of an issue. At Oticon, for instance, employees set up for work according to the project they are working on that day and everyone rubs elbows with everyone else: marketing with software engineers, finance with human resources, and so on. Such a work environment not only gives employees knowledge of everything going on in the company, it also creates an atmosphere of mutual respect.

While some KM initiatives are effective, many others miss the boat. A common mistake is to approach KM as a pure technology initiative. While technology is important to KM, research has found that in and of itself, it will achieve very little, unless it is supplemented with significant amounts of human infrastructure.[14] Another common problem is to conceive of KM as an end in itself. Many companies devise extensive data bases and other knowledge collection procedures without a great deal of consideration as to how these will contribute to business value. Effective KM programs must derive from a company's value framework and link knowledge strategy to business strategy and results. Finally, corporate cultures can either act to promote or discourage KM efforts. Companies with cultures that limit or inhibit knowledge sharing, autonomy, and personal responsibility, or experimentation and risk-taking, will find that their investment in KM yields minimal results. At Oticon, Kolind and various work groups spent hundreds of hours setting out the basic values that would guide the reorganization. These discussions led them to conclude that employees should be treated as responsible adults, but also as unique individuals. As mentioned earlier in this book, this was the point of departure for creating the new Oticon.

To date, most effective KM programs in organizations have tended to focus on one particular element of KM and evolve from this point. A recent focus group of senior knowledge managers from a wide variety of organizations identified the following five primary approaches to KM.[15]

Developing client-centered knowledge management

One of the major ways companies are using KM today is to develop more knowledge about products and services for their customers. The experience of Li & Fung, whose primary mission is to provide integrated supply chain management to its clients, is a good case in point. Statistics show that customer satisfaction is strongly related to a firm's ability to keep existing customers and improve sales. The *Mercer Management Journal* points out that "between 1994 and 1996 the stock market valued companies with revenue-related profit growth two times higher than their counterparts with the same profit growth resulting from cost cutting." When viewed from this perspective, client-centered KM is a wise investment in the core business of a company, rather than an overhead expense because:

- existing customers provide more sales at lower costs;
- loyal customers are hard to lose and generate additional sales through word of mouth;
- blended service and selling can provide incremental revenue;
- great customer support builds more aggressive channel partners, further lowering sales costs.

Increasingly, customers are demanding this level of knowledge – globally. As one customer said when a consultant came knocking on his door, "Don't come here to sell me KM products when you don't even know about the last four visits I've had from your company." Consistency of service across companies is also a motivator. Organizations want to provide repeatable, high quality services at all points of contact and KM is the obvious way to do this. Clarica, a Canadian insurance company, e.g. has developed a customer service workbench that integrates both the tools and knowledge a customer service representative needs. It also provides them with a complete list of all business a customer has had with the company and a full history of all contacts between the customer and the company. This makes Clarica look more professional and smarter, and saves time and money for both the company and the customer.[16]

One of the biggest challenges in using client-centered KM in less structured processes is encouraging people to participate in sharing customer information. In some companies, participation is optional and as a result, KM practices are not always widely used. Therefore, the compensation system and the work processes involved are key. KM appears to work better where company processes have been structured to *require* people to use and update a knowledge base. For example, one company uses a pair of sales people for each customer – one external and one internal. It is the job of the internal sales agent to update company information collected from the external agent. The external agent is motivated to do this because the internal agent sets his schedule and deals with the same customers over the phone. Both are compensated in the same way for increased sales.

Improving processes with knowledge

A somewhat broader perspective on KM is using knowledge to improve all types of company processes continuously. A distinctive attribute of Li & Fung is its ability to manage activities in a borderless way. Therefore, innovation is in its process of coordinating supply chain activities for its clients. To do so, the company must have a better knowledge of the market than its competitors and clients.

Knowledge can be integrated into almost any organizational process to improve such things as efficiency, effectiveness, productivity, and quality. Many companies are trying to tap into the tacit knowledge in people's heads in order to document or codify it and use it to improve how work is done. Improving processes with knowledge is clearly specific to a particular process. However, there are a number of standard ways in which knowledge can be used.[17] First, it can be used to document experiences, providing a historical perspective from which to understand and view new situations and events. For example, many consulting firms are trying to collect experiences from seasoned consultants to help others learn what to do in similar circumstances. A second means of using knowledge in processes is to document what actually happens in a real life situation and to use this information to modify how work is done in the future. Collecting technicians' tips in a database is one way Xerox has used to improve its photocopier services, for example. Third, knowledge can be used to assist judgments, e.g. with human resources data bases that help improve the management and retention of staff. Finally, knowledge can also be used to improve more structured workflows.

Companies are taking a wide variety of approaches to process improvement with knowledge. The more standardized and repeatable a process is, the more knowledge can be systematized using automated tools and techniques. These types of processes are clearly easier to work with. Where knowledge becomes more *ad hoc* and idiosyncratic, companies are finding it more difficult to use. The U.S. Center for Army Lessons Learned is clearly the high water mark in this area. Through its "after-action review" program, experiences are quickly incorporated into formal army procedures and training programs. None of the companies in the focus group were in this league, although some were trying to get there. Many companies are trying to capture and improve their best practices through KM, although most are experiencing the dual challenge of trying to encourage staff to take the time to document what they learned and persuade others to use this knowledge. As one knowledge manager noted, "Our biggest challenge is turning knowledge into action." Continuous improvement is one way companies are trying to do this.

Developing communities of practice

Companies are having considerable success in building knowledge communities. A knowledge community is a network of people who create, disseminate, and retain knowledge in particular area, e.g. competitive intelligence. People in a knowledge community can take different roles in the community – information collector, user, analyst, or decision maker – depending on the situation. The major benefit of these communities is that they shorten a company's "time to intelligence" considerably. As one manager pointed out, knowledge communities exist in every company already, but usually informally. Typically, knowledge communities emerge in response to a particular need within the organization. While they cannot be organized by management, they can be encouraged and facilitated.

Companies are applying different organizing logic to these communities. Some require a formal invitation to join and regular contributions to the knowledge base. Others are open to anyone who is interested. Most communities are designed around the core competencies or disciplines of the organization. Management plays a role in identifying or sanctioning the groups it wants to support or promote. Especially important are areas in which a company wants to extend its knowledge or to push what it knows out to the organization. A key role in most communities is that of *knowledge broker.* This is an individual who is able to establish knowledge relationships between people with knowledge and those who need it. Typically, these people are leaders in their disciplines who are well respected and who have a strong personal commitment to their field of knowledge. They are often assisted by a staff person and/or librarian who supports and enhances the leader's work.

To be effective, knowledge communities must serve two key strategic objectives for the organization. First, they must facilitate *knowledge development* (i.e. the identification, creation, harvesting, and organizing of knowledge). Second, they must be a mechanism for *knowledge application* (i.e. the sharing, adaptation, and execution of knowledge to deliver business results). They must also work to develop the linkages between the two and to continually strengthen and clarify them. How knowledge development and application lead to business results are the key challenges that practitioners are facing in this area.

Developing knowledge management processes

Probably the most common KM activity at present is implementing processes to collect and disseminate knowledge. As one manager commented, "The gathering around the coffee pot method of knowledge sharing just doesn't scale up." Therefore, a large company needs KM processes to:

- *collect knowledge* from internal and external sources;
- *identify* what the company needs to know;
- *create new knowledge* from innovations and new ways of looking at information;
- *use knowledge* to make decisions and benefit customers;
- *recycle experiences and lessons learned*, including mistakes;
- *leverage* what is known to grow and build the business.

While effective KM is a combination of people, processes, and tools, it is the processes that provide the framework for KM. There are two meta-processes associated with KM.

Collaboration

This includes all the activities involved in promoting, encouraging, and facilitating knowledge sharing. Developing communities of practice is one such process for doing this. Others include: creating and maintaining global directories; promoting networking; creating incentives for collaboration; establishing mechanisms for working together and providing leadership to make them work; and designing work and methodologies to promote collaboration and to leverage what people know. As an example, by having employees going from project to project, Kolind put into place the conditions for a smooth and efficient transmission and dissemination of knowledge at Oticon.

Content management

The knowledge to collect and its form is only one aspect of content management. Navigation and taxonomies to ensure that knowledge can be found easily and even intuitively are critical to this process. People also need to be made aware of what knowledge is available and encouraged to contribute to it and use it. Processes are needed to identify what the company knows, what the company needs to know, and how to capture these. Finally, there must be a means of determining when knowledge is no longer needed or useful.

Developing the processes associated with KM is a major responsibility of a knowledge manager. As knowledge is specific to a business or a function, and because organization culture is so variable, KM processes are quite idiosyncratic at present. They are likely to remain this way for some time, as we learn more about how to design KM processes and how best to integrate them into organizations.

Developing knowledge products

One of the most exciting "*eureka*" moments in KM has to be when it becomes apparent that a company's knowledge can be packaged and sold, thereby creating a new, virtual source of value for a business. These moments are not typically planned but are the result of serendipity, when the hard-working knowledge manager laboring in the data mines realizes that he or she has found a mother lode of value.

Two of the organizations in the focus group found knowledge products while analyzing their own needs for knowledge. The first, a pharmaceutical company, began by mapping what is known about individual diseases and their outcomes. The result has been a new way to get at the massive amounts of evidence available on any disease and provides a common platform for understanding outcomes and interventions in a disease. This platform has been linked to a series of healthcare decision points and integrated into company strategy. It shows where company knowledge at each of these decision points can provide added value to its customers and ultimately, help the company to maintain its leadership position in the industry. The second organization developed a series of KM tools, which it uses for its own internal management. These have proven to be so effective internally that the company is now beginning to market them to other organizations as a means of integrating all of the daily, weekly, and monthly information an active manager needs to have at his or her fingertips. The tool integrates everything from sales information, to contacts and traffic and weather reports and can be customized to an individual's preferences.

Knowledge products can take a company in a completely different direction from its current business and, as a result, are not always easy to sell internally. Nevertheless, they represent an important opportunity for a company to realize value from what it knows in a very traditional forum – the marketplace. As such, they *may* ultimately be an easier way to justify KM within the organization.

Best practices for successful knowledge management

Knowledge managers are the first to admit that they are still learning how to implement KM successfully. However, an analysis of best practices among knowledge managers shows that effective strategies can be grouped into two main areas: cultural and procedural.[18]

Organizational and cultural best practices

Create an iterative vision

As mentioned earlier, the knowledge-creating company is as much about ideals as it is about ideas. The essence of innovation is to recreate the world according to a particular vision or ideal. In 1990, Kolind called his new vision a "spaghetti organization" because the multiple roles people were to play were so intertwined. Again, Kolind wanted to go from "products based primarily on technology" to "products based primarily on knowledge." For their part, the Fung brothers are said to have a highly collaborative and cerebral approach to business, indicating at once a great ability to conceptualize the company activities and its direction.

Use images and symbols to mobilize people

One of the keys to the process is personnel commitment: the employee's sense of identity with the enterprise and its mission. Mobilizing that type of commitment and embodying tacit knowledge in actual technologies and products requires managers who are comfortable with images and symbols.[19] At Oticon, there are many symbols in the head-office building, from the inscription at the entry "think the unthinkable" to the enormous transparent plastic tube that cuts through the cafeteria from the symbolic paper room. While Progressive must not be considered as much a knowledge-creating company as Oticon or Li & Fung, the CEO's motto "think about the world differently" has contributed to mobilizing all of Progressive's employees towards *delivering the unexpected* to customers.

Use incentives and rewards to motivate people

People need encouragement to share knowledge. Find ways to enhance an individual's reputation or professional skills through knowledge exchange. Also, give something back, such as recognition or a reward for creativity. Include KM activities on performance reviews and give bonuses for KM success. At Oticon, incentive and rewards are based on achievements, on learning new skills or using previously untapped skills to help one's team or project. Employees are also given shares in the company each year. As mentioned earlier, the development of human capital at Li & Fung is more difficult to assess. The company provides a culture where competencies and performance are rewarded but there are still signs of traditional hierarchical systems and structures.

Do not impose KM from the top

While senior management sponsorship is important, local content owners must be involved in and committed to the process for it to work. The process followed at Oticon was participative. It was not restricted to a few managers or led by an external consultant. Everyone was informed and involved, one way or another, in implementing the change and most of it was worked out by the employees themselves. At Progressive, the corporate attitude is to let employees try almost everything that makes sense. It is ingrained in the culture to experiment, but to do so responsibly.

Have fun

Hold contests, give things away, or use a game. The more fun people have while contributing to the knowledge asset, the more they will want to be involved. One chief knowledge officer (CKO) invented a knowledge game and had everyone in the company playing it to demonstrate how knowledge can make everyone more effective in their jobs.

Procedural best practices

Capture success stories

Even if it is difficult to link KM to the bottom line, stories of where KM has been effective are extremely valuable. One organization has an annual contest to collect these. In 3 weeks, it collected 18 stories with demonstrated savings of $20 million.

Monitor e-mail

Questions to experts and their answers can be a most important source of information. One company monitors these types of transactions and tries to organize and structure them meaningfully in their knowledge data base as FAQs.

Follow a change management process

Implementing KM is a major corporate change and should be treated as such. Make sure people know how, why, and what you are doing before you start, and at any point in time.

Work iteratively on KM architecture, infrastructure and culture

As different pieces are built, explain their value. Knowledge managers should never assume they know what users need. The

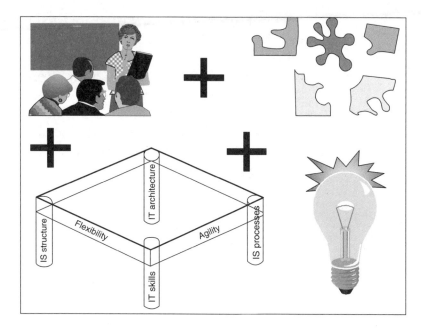

Figure 11.1
Knowledge provides
breakthrough thinking.

way to move up the value chain is to listen to users continuously. The number one principle of KM is, "there is no one right answer."

Adopt knowledge retention standards

Different industries will want to retain knowledge for shorter or longer periods of time. Some companies delete e-mail after 30 days and retain knowledge base contributions for only 6 months. However, in some industries, e.g. pharmaceuticals, years will be a more appropriate time frame (Figure 11.1).

Conclusion

Knowledge is at the heart of any business reinvention or transformation. KM is just "coming of age" in most organizations. As a result, its development is somewhat erratic and variable from company to company. Like any other adolescent, it is experiencing growing pains in determining its role and function. There is thus a great deal of experimentation occurring, resulting in both successes and failures. Wise companies, like wise parents, will encourage such exploration within reason and not try to overly limit or control its development. Nevertheless, they must also provide guidance about priorities and values to make sure KM does not stray too far, too fast, from what has been effective in the past or from the company's business strategy.[20] Similarly, they must carefully assess "peer pressure" to ensure that they are not being unduly influenced by fads and trends in the industry. Over the next few years, we can expect to see KM settling down, becoming more manageable and having an increasing influence on organizational strategy. As this happens, we will see its true character and value emerge more clearly.

Questions

1 Suppose that Oticon mandates you to be their CKO (Chief Knowledge Officer). How would you proceed? What would be your first decisions/activities?

2 How different would be your knowledge management approach if you were to be CKO at Li & Fung?

3 Newell *et al.*[21] describe the case of a large bank, Ebank, which implemented an Intranet as a means of facilitating information sharing across countries and departments. The decision was made following the loss of a major account because Ebank was unable to provide common customer service across the several countries where it was doing business. After many fruitless efforts from individual countries and departments to develop their own Intranets, top management decided to have a common effort. Managers from the major sites were invited to attend a two-day workshop to come with a common solution. Since the line managers were not available for the workshop, IT representatives convened together and came up with the idea of a corporate portal from which users could navigate in the various country Intranets. Finally, six or seven different portals were developed. The authors conclude that the Intranet had failed to facilitate closer collaboration, countries and department boundaries remaining intact, if not reinforced. How would you diagnose this failure?

4 What would be the key features of a knowledge management plan for a large multinational firm involved in consulting?

5 Sir J. Brown, CEO of British Petroleum once mentioned that in some instances, it is more appropriate to know

who detains a certain type of knowledge rather than trying to actually codify it.[22] Give examples of such situations.

Endnotes

[1] Leidner, D.E., The information technology – organizational culture relationship, in R.D. Galliers, and D.E. Leidner (eds.), *Strategic Information Management*, Oxford: Butterworth-Heineman, 2003, pp. 496–525.

[2] Harris, K., Austin, T., Fenn, J., Hayward, S. and Cushman, A., The impact of knowledge management on enterprise architecture, *Gartner Group Strategic Analysis Report*, 25 October 1999, 22.

[3] Quinn, J.B., Anderson, P. and Finkelstein, S., Managing professional intellect: making the most of the best, *Harvard Business Review*, March–April 1996, 71–80.

[4] Dzinkowski, R., Assessing the risk of ideas, *Canadian Banker*, 2nd Quarter, 2000, 28.

[5] Hope, T. and Hope, J., Chain reaction, *People Management*, 25 September 1997, 26–30.

[6] March, A., A note on knowledge management, Harvard Business School, Document #9-398-031, 1997, 20 p.;
Prokesch, S.E., Unleashing the power of learning: an interview with BP's John Brown, *Harvard Business Review*, September–October 1997, 6–19.

[7] Bair, J., Fenn, J., Hunter, R. and Bosik, D., Foundations for enterprise knowledge management, *Gartner Group Strategic Analysis Report*, 7 April 1997, 50.

[8] Harreld, B., Building smarter, faster organizations, in D. Tapscott, A. Lowy and D. Ticoll (eds.), *Blueprint to the Digital Economy*, New York, NY: McGraw-Hill, 1998, pp. 60–76.

[9] Garvin, D.A., Building a learning organization, *Harvard Business Review on Knowledge Management*, Harvard Business School Press, 1998, pp. 47–80.

[10] Nonaka, I., The knowledge creating company, *Harvard Business Review on Knowledge Management*, Harvard Business School Press, 1998, pp. 21–45.

[11] Harreld, B.,1998, *op. cit.*

[12] Ashkenas, D.U., Jick, T. and Kerr, S., *The Boundaryless Organization: Breaking the Chains of Organizational Structure*, Jossey-Bass Publishers, 1998.

[13] Hansen, M.T., Nohria, N. and Tierney, T., What's your strategy for managing knowledge? *Harvard Business Review*, March–April 1999, 106–116.

[14] Newell, S., Pan, S.L., Galliers, R.D. and Huang, J.C., The myth of the boundaryless organization, *Communications of the ACM*, **44**(12), December 2001, 74–76.

[15] Smith, H.A. and McKeen, J.D., Knowledge management in organizations: the state of the practice, in Clyde Holsapple (ed.), *Handbook on Knowledge Management*, Berlin: Springer-Verlag, 2003; Smith, H.A. and McKeen, J.D., Creating and facilitation communities of practice, in Clyde Holsapple (ed.), *Handbook on Knowledge Management*, Berlin: Springer-Verlag, 2003; Smith, H.A. and McKeen, J.D., "Valuing the knowledge management function, in Clyde Holsapple (ed.), *Handbook on Knowledge Management*, Berlin: Springer-Verlag, 2003; Smith, H.A. and McKeen, J.D., Instilling a knowledge sharing culture, *KM Forum*, **2**(3), School of Business, Queen's University, Kingston, Canada K7L 3N6, 2000.

[16] Smith, H.A., Revolutionizing customer service delivery at Clarica, mimeo, October 2000.

[17] Davenport, T.H. and Prusak, L., Technologies for knowledge management, in *Working Knowledge*, Boston, MA: Harvard Business School Press, 1998, pp. 123–143.

[18] See for instance: Smith, H.A. and McKeen, J.D., 2000, *op. cit.*; Ashkenas, D.U. *et al.*, 1998, *op.cit.*; Nonaka, I., 1998, *op.cit.*

[19] Nonaka, I., 1998, *op.cit.*

[20] Newell, S. *et al.*, 2001, *op.cit.*

[21] *Ibid.*

[22] Prokesch, S.E., 1997, *op.cit.*

Chapter 12

Change management

Just when you think the management puzzle is nicely put together and looking pretty good, along comes something to mess it all up again! Change is now a constant for organizations – whether they like it or not – and all businesses these days face some amount of it. Unfortunately, companies do not deal well with change.[1] It is unsettling at best, and frequently frustrating, demoralizing, and confusing. As a result, it is often viewed as being a negative influence in corporations. Is it any wonder that as soon as managers stop paying attention to it, the old, comfortable, satisfying ways slowly creep back in? Documented success rates of change initiatives in organizations are between 20 and 50 percent.[2]

While change has been with us for a long time – in 500 B.C., Heraclitus noted "nothing endures but change" – there is a general consensus that change these days is bigger, faster and different from what it used to be. Since the 1980s, nearly half of all U.S. companies have been restructured and several hundred thousand have been acquired, merged, or downsized.[3] Moreover, the velocity of change is increasing. As the chief executive officer (CEO) of a large company commented, "It used to be a lot of fun to work 10 years ago. You could almost cope. Today, it is almost impossible because things happen at such a rapid rate."[4] There are many reasons for this: intensifying competition, business process re-engineering, IT-enabled transformation, and a host of environmental influences, to name just a few.[5] Together, they all add up to the inescapable conclusion that companies must become much better at dealing with change (Figure 12.1).

While organizations face relentless pressure to change from beyond their boundaries, how they respond to it can make an enormous difference in the effectiveness of their strategies and, ultimately, to their long-term survival. Today, executives are only

Figure 12.1
Change comes from
every direction.

just beginning to realize the need to manage the changes that result from the choices they make in business strategy, IT strategy, and structure. Therefore, this chapter looks at the final dimension of support for the management puzzle: coping well with change. It first examines our understanding of what change is and how it occurs in organizations. Then, it describes what it takes to lead a change initiative. Finally, it looks at some of the change challenges facing organizations in extending beyond traditional corporate boundaries.

Change in organizations

Traditionally, change has been seen as a relatively static entity in organizations. Change usually starts with a high level task force that determines what changes need to be made. The task force then announces what will be done and appoints project teams to implement the different elements involved. From here, each team follows a series of sequential steps for envisioning, planning, implementing, consolidating, and institutionalizing their particular change component.[6] In other words, change has been managed in a mechanistic fashion – broken down into its component items, plotted out over the expected time it will take, and managed in pieces.

However, not all change can be anticipated and planned in this fashion. In fact, many of the difficulties of managing change arise when companies only plan for and manage *anticipated* change. This increases the complexity of change because they do not recognize the *unanticipated* changes that always occur and are, thus,

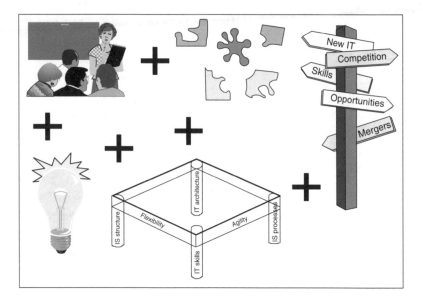

Figure 12.2
Change is *always* a factor in putting the puzzle together.

unprepared to deal effectively with them.[7] A more realistic approach to change recognizes that it operates on at least two levels – superficial and fundamental. For example, a new technology could initially lead to a superficial (i.e. anticipated) change in staffing levels. That it can also lead to more fundamental changes in the psychological or social dimensions of the jobs that are left is often not seen or anticipated.[8] While surface changes are usually obvious, fundamental changes can remain hidden or take time to become visible. Thus, a company's planning for a change may be limited to its immediately obvious and superficial impacts, while its more powerful impacts remain hidden, leading managers to overlook key aspects of the change that can cause problems. The discrepancy between the anticipated impact of a change and how it actually affects organizations contributes significantly to the difficulties businesses face as they attempt to introduce change effectively (Figure 12.2).

Today, managers are beginning to realize that, because of the difficulty of predicting the organizational impacts of change, a mechanistic model may not be the most effective change management approach to use. In addition to changes they can predict, managers should also be prepared to deal with two types of unanticipated change:[9]

- *Emergent change*: They arise spontaneously in response to planned change. Their impacts can be either positive or negative for an organization. For example, the introduction of a new technology can eventually lead to the need for new roles and skills and may also affect organization structures and management processes.

■ *Opportunity-based change*: These are introduced intentionally during the change process in response to unexpected impacts that arise. For example, a new technology can create new strategic options that were not previously envisioned when the change was initially introduced.

An *improvisational model* of change management may, therefore, be a better way of viewing business reinvention or transformation because it takes into consideration the fact that change is an ongoing process, rather than a discrete event. This model recognizes that only anticipated change can be planned. Emergent and opportunity-based changes *require a response*. Thus, the model sees change not as a predefined program charted by management ahead of time, but as an iterative sequence of plans and responses. Through it, "rather than predefining each step and then controlling events to fit the plan, management creates an environment that facilitates improvisation … and supports and nurtures the expectations, norms, and resources that guide the ongoing change process."[10] Figure 12.3 illustrates how change is actually a dynamic process consisting of a series of planned changes, interspersed with controlled organizational responses to emergent and opportunity-based changes as they arise. The ability to view change dynamically provides an organization with

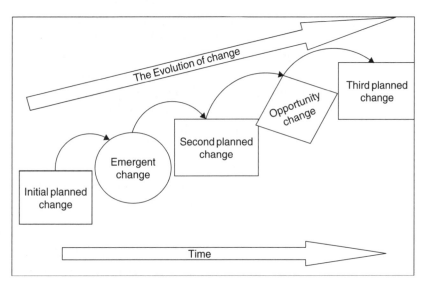

Figure 12.3
Change is a dynamic entity.

an approach to understand and better manage its realities in the modern organization.[11]

Due to the dynamic nature of change, it is extremely important that the individual components of change – structure, strategy, technology, and leadership – be managed together. If one component, e.g. vertical boundaries, gets out of step with the others, then the whole change effort is in peril. Each change component needs to move in concert with the others in order for a change to be effective. As illustrated in Part III, the key to successful change management is, therefore, not to manage each piece of the management puzzle as an isolated project but to deal with all the pieces in a more integrated fashion. Thus, at any point in time, change management can best be conceived of as the act of balancing a delicate mobile. Change leaders need to understand how modifications in one piece can affect the sequencing and pace of changes in the rest of the puzzle and make ongoing corrections to keep the change mobile in balance.[12]

Leading change

While change is necessary, it can involve significant challenges for both individuals and organizations. As we have seen in the Progressive, Oticon, and Li & Fung cases, leadership is therefore a critical element of effective change. Underestimating the scope of the challenges involved, as frequently happens, will greatly increase the likelihood of failure. Change leaders have several important responsibilities. They must begin by articulating and communicating a *vision* of the future. Then, they need to determine how best to drive the change forward. Leaders also have the responsibility for putting the right structure and resources in place to make the change happen as smoothly as possible. Finally, they must inspire commitment to the change and monitor performance.

Envisioning change

By definition, change means doing something differently. The first step towards change is articulating *what* needs to be done differently. As illustrated in the Oticon case, a vision for change involves more than a simple "vision statement." If leaders perceive change to be a single silver bullet and try to get staff to buy into it, the result will be "thousands of cynical employees."[13] A vision for change must put the proposed transformation in the context of the business' competitive situation and provide a rationale for what is being proposed so that individuals and teams will better understand how to align their activities with the company's new direction and also be able to bring to light concerns and insights that might potentially derail or enhance the change.[14] Unless executives learn how to properly communicate a vision for change, staff will always be working at cross-purposes with them.[15]

A compelling picture of 'what could be' reduces the amount of difficulty involved in change because it makes the change more attractive to the people involved. This is particularly true if the picture can immediately be perceived as being the right thing to do. Change visions should communicate across the internal cultures within the organization and appeal to the actual recipients and implementers of change. Thus, for certain individuals and groups, a vision should emphasize such things as practicality for getting the job done, rather than financial survival, shareholder returns, or strategic potential (even though such things may also be part of the vision).

Undercommunicating about the vision and how it will be implemented is a major cause of why transformation efforts fail. "Without credible communication, and a lot of it, the hearts and minds of the troops are never captured."[16] Unfortunately, most change leaders undercommunicate by a factor of 10. Generally, people need to hear a message over and over before they understand and believe it. Personal and hands-on attention to communication from every manager must be a priority during any change. As a general rule, "when you are so sick of talking about something that you can hardly stand it, your message is finally starting to get through."[17]

Driving change forward

Leaders must subjectively assess how much change to impose on their organizations at any one time. At one end of the spectrum, change can be evolutionary, such as when the organization adapts to growth or to its environment. Here, change occurs in small steps and is, therefore, less dramatic, e.g. continuous improvement. The other extreme type is revolutionary change. Here, change is designed to transform one or more fundamental aspects of an organization quickly and radically, e.g. power structures, management, or business assets. On this continuum, the reinventions that took place at Oticon and Progressive are situated on the revolutionary side, while the continuing transformation of Li & Fung would be best characterized by an evolutionary model of change.

Leaders must choose how best to position change in their organizations on this spectrum, in order to achieve the results they want. Many believe that evolutionary change is too slow and cumbersome and that organizational cultures are too entrenched to accept it. Revolution and chaos are the only way to make change because a crisis is the only thing that will shake an organization out of its self-balancing complacency.[18] The challenge involved must be judged carefully. While senior managers may see one type of change in a certain way (e.g. an opportunity to strengthen the business or take on new opportunities), employees at the middle to lower levels may see it in another because it is highly disruptive and intrusive. Unfortunately, senior managers consistently misjudge this gap in perception and this is another reason why change is more difficult than they expect.[19]

A second choice leaders must make is how to present the rationale for change. Many experts feel that true change can only come about as the result of a crisis – even if one has to be created.[20] Without it, they say, there is not enough motivation for people to move out of their present comfort zones. Ideally, a crisis promotes change because it galvanizes staff, and shakes them out of their complacency, encouraging them to align behind common organizational goals. However, a crisis can also overwhelm staff into helplessness and inertia. Using a crisis to promote change can, therefore, be a dangerous balancing act for an organization's leadership.

Can an organization be galvanized into change without a crisis? Many believe this is not only possible, but desirable, since change should be a continual way of life in the modern organization. They suggest that change can also be stimulated, if there is a dynamic change leader in the organization with a strong record of credibility, who can convince users to follow him or her and to put up with the ups and downs of the change process.[21]

Implementing change

Most companies identify a specific person or group of people to be responsible for achieving change. For large-scale changes, a transition management team is recommended.[22] The role of the team is to oversee the corporate change effort and make sure that all parts of the change fit together. It acts as a change catalyst and works cross-functionally to manage and guide the change process. Reporting to the CEO, the team should be on the job until the change process has stabilized, at which point it disbands. As described in Part III, such teams of collaborators (both internal and external) have been implemented in the transformation of both Oticon and Progressive. For large transformation efforts, the CEO should act as the *change champion*. This person creates the strategy for change and articulates the context and rationale for the new corporate direction. He or she provides the necessary resources to implement the change, and also offers ongoing guidance and support.

Change leaders who actually design and implement the change need certain key skills to enable them to do their job effectively. First and foremost, they must have strong personal credibility and be accepted by the power structure of the organization. Attributes such as self-confidence, a willingness to learn, a willingness to take risks, and ability to inspire and motivate others are all crucial to being able to lead change well.[23] Second, change leaders need good analytic and negotiating skills to develop and manage effective change plans, build relationships and gain people's support for change. During the change process, the change team will be required to undertake several different types of analysis, such as:

- *Stakeholder analysis*: This is used to learn who will be affected by a particular change and who will be expected to be involved in making it a success. As one manager commented, "It is often surprising to find out who the real stakeholders in a change are."[24]

- *Risk assessment and management*: Formal risk assessment and management procedures must be in place to address the downsides of change. Organizations that have implemented these practices have found themselves significantly better able to identify and mitigate the potential negative impacts of change.[25]

- *Root cause analysis*: When problems with change arise, as they inevitably will, the change management team must be prepared to cope with them. This involves looking for and addressing the underlying causes of problems, not simply their symptoms.[26]
- *Inconsistency analysis*: Throughout the transition, change leaders should watch for and address inconsistencies in such practices as management policies, success measures, and rewards that undermine the credibility of the change effort. They must ensure that messages, measures, management behavior, and rewards all match the overall thrust of the change initiative.[27]

Finally, change leadership requires a willingness to listen. It does not always mean providing the solutions to change problems. Studies of organizations that have transformed themselves suggest that successful change requires "leading from a different place." This means leaders must resist the temptation to always provide the answer. These companies have found that in order to develop the learning behaviors that promote true change in an organization, "the solutions and the commitment to deliver on them must come from the ranks."[28]

Obtaining results

Conventional wisdom about how change works can be summed up as follows:

> You start by getting people to buy into a new corporate vision, thereby changing their attitudes. They will then automatically change their behavior, which will result in improved corporate performance. After seeing this improvement, they will confirm their commitment to the corporate change program, and the success spiral will continue.[29]

Unfortunately, this approach rarely works. One reason is that people have been through so many botched changes, they are highly skeptical of any new initiatives, viewing whatever change is being promoted as simply another management fad. A more realistic approach to change addresses this reality. It suggests that top management should start by *requiring* a change in behavior, and when that leads to improved performance, commitment and enthusiasm will follow. This approach recognizes that while companies have no control over how their employees feel about change, they can at least direct their behavior. When the results begin to come, they will then begin to believe that the change is working.[30]

Successful change breeds more success when people begin to see its benefits. However, because change can be uncomfortable, it is essential that results come quickly and be highly visible. Thus, large changes should be broken down into smaller deliverables. Not systematically planning for, and creating short-term wins is a key reason why transformation efforts fail.[31] Actively looking for ways to obtain clear short-term improvements and recognizing the people involved boosts the credibility of the change effort. It can also keep urgency levels up and force the detailed analytical thinking needed to clarify or revise visions. Consequently, specific, measurable results achieved within a few months of a change can lead to a subtle but profound shift in mindset that promotes other learning and change initiatives throughout the company.[32]

Technology and change

For better or worse, IT is frequently the means through which change is implemented in a company. The key drivers of change – increasing information flow, technological discontinuity, new business practices, and increasing customer expectations – are each significantly facilitated by IT.[33] Even though the actual changes may have much more to do with workflow, culture, and management than technology, IT is often seen as a miraculous remedy which can magically transform an organization into a lean, trim version of its former self with a minimum of effort. Information system staff members are therefore "agents of change" because they initiate, design, and build this powerful technology.[34] Unfortunately, IT is no panacea for organizational change. All three successful organizational transformations described in Part III reveal that IT is only one element of the organization's management puzzle, which must be balanced and aligned with the other pieces in order to achieve productive and permanent change.

While it is occasionally a driver of change, technology is not usually considered the most important resource of change implementation by change experts.[35] Nevertheless, technology does have a part to play in helping organizations to change. Like all resources, technology can be used to promote or hamper change, depending on the role IT plays in the change process. If an

Figure 12.4
The right skills and the right pieces lead to success.

organization has its technology fundamentals right, e.g. infrastructure, architecture, and technology leadership, IT can facilitate change (Figure 12.4). Conversely, the wrong technology can slow down how much change can be accomplished.

In some companies, however, IT is viewed as the *only* resource necessary for change. This perception can actually hinder change.[36] For example, if executives package new ideas as a mere technology implementation, it helps them to distance themselves from the more difficult "people aspects" of change. Business people too, can find it easier to criticize technology rather than criticize the ideas embedded in it (e.g. "We'd use the technology to cut costs if we could but this software is a real dog"). Thus, sometimes IT can be a scapegoat in organizational change and an excuse for not confronting the real issues involved.

Conclusion

Changing expectations about change is the first step in effective change management. Successful change is not likely to follow a systematic step-by-step process and have clearly-defined impacts. This chapter has shown that a change initiative is better conceived of as an iterative and ongoing series of opportunities and challenges, which are not always predictable at the start. Effective leadership requires balancing the many elements involved in a change initiative and managing change as a dynamic process, not a set of discrete projects. Setbacks *will* occur in any change project. No matter how perfect a plan is in place, the people and processes involved in change are inherently unpredictable. This is why effective change leaders must see setbacks as windows to learning.[37] At the very least, setbacks must force the change team to deal with whatever issues are causing them. True change will only result when *all* issues and concerns are declared and dealt with.

As companies begin to collaborate externally with other organizations, they will face a new set of change challenges.[38] Inter-organizational cooperation requires an entirely new mindset, and the development of a common set of approaches to such things as strategic and operational planning, information sharing, sales and marketing, and sharing of resources. Administrative and operational procedures will need to be reconfigured and a new model of collaboration developed. This will be a massive change management effort for all the companies involved. Success will depend much more heavily on relationships than it does within company boundaries, since companies will have very few other levers to induce commitment to change.

There are a number of potential obstacles to inter-organizational partnering and managers must work together to overcome them. With the exception of legal and regulatory barriers, most other obstacles will fall within the purview of a corporate change initiative. Managers and staff will need to learn new skills, be able to let go of certain areas of control, and deal with competitive confusion. The complexity of the changes involved and a lack of trust in the other companies involved will act as key-limiting factors to how much can be accomplished. To overcome all of these challenges, partnering organizations will have to establish a joint transformation effort to focus on building relationships and solving problems.

Most importantly, leaders must keep in mind that effective transformations, whether they occur within or across organizations, are possible only when they cross their own invisible, self-limiting walls and believe that nothing is impossible, that motivated people can achieve the highest heights, and that organizations in the twenty-first century will have no constraints other than those they impose on themselves. Technology alone will not make the reinvention happen. Strategy will not be enough. Luck will come and go. But leaders such as Peter Lewis, Lars Kolind, and the Fung brothers who push, inspire, motivate, demand, and bring out the creativity in their people, can move mountains.

Questions

- Provide and explain five common reasons why business transformation efforts often fail.
- Explain why a mechanistic model of change may not be the most effective change management approach to use in the particular context of radical business transformation.
- How is the improvisional model of change management proposed by Orlikowski and Hofman different from the most common mechanistic model? Explain the business transformations at Oticon and Progressive Insurance using the improvisional model of change management.
- Explain the differences between the three most common types of changes: anticipated, emergent, and opportunity based. Illustrate.
- What does "a vision for change" mean in the context of business reinvention? Illustrate this concept using the cases presented in Part III of this book. Why is "vision" a necessary condition for successful business transformation efforts?
- Explain the role of a transition management team. In your opinion, what would be the "ideal" profile of the people to be involved in such teams?
- Comment on the following assertion: "IT is no panacea for organizational change." Defend and illustrate your own position with regard to this assertion.

Endnotes

[1] Pritchett, P. and Pound, R., A culture of change, *Executive Excellence*, **10**(2), February 1993, 11–12.

[2] Strebel, P., Why do employees resist change, *Harvard Busines Review*, **74**(3), May–June 1996, 86–92.

[3] Pritchett, P., *Firing Up Commitment During Organizational Change: A Handbook for Managers* (2nd edn), Pritchett Pub Co., 1994.

[4] McKeen, J.D. and Smith, H.A., *Making IT Happen*, Chichester, England: John Wiley & Sons, 2003.

[5] Markus, M.L. and Benjamin, R.I., The magic bullet theory in IT-enabled transformation, *Sloan Management Review*, **38**(2), Winter 1997, 55–68.

[6] Kotter, J.P., Leading change: why transformation efforts fail, *Harvard Business Review*, **73**(2), March 1995, 59–68;

Benjamin, R.I. and Levinson, E., A framework for managing IT-enabled change, *Sloan Management Review*, **34**(4), Summer 1993, 23–33.

[7] Orlikowski, W.J. and Hofman, J.D., An improvisional model for change management: the case of groupware technologies, *Sloan Management Review*, **38**(2), 1997, 11–21.

[8] Benjamin, R.I. and Levinson, E., 1993, *op. cit.*; Strebel, P., 1996, *op. cit.*

[9] Yetton, P.W., Johnston, K.D. and Craig, J.F., Computer-aided architects: a case study of IT and strategic change, *Sloan Management Review*, **35**(4), Summer 1994, 57–67.

[10] Orlikowski, W.J. and Hofman, J.D., 1997, *op. cit.*

[11] *Ibid.*

[12] Duck, J.D., Managing change: the art of balancing, *Harvard Business Review*, **71**(6), November–December 1993, 109–118.

[13] Brill, P.L. and Worth, R., *The Four Levers of Corporate Change*, New York, NY: AMACOM, 1997.

[14] Duck, J.D., 1993, *op. cit.*

[15] Schein, E.H., Three cultures of management: the key to organizational learning, *Sloan Management Review*, **38**(1), Fall 1996, 9–20.

[16] Kotter, J.P., 1995, *op. cit.*

[17] Duck, J.D., 1993, *op. cit.*

[18] Prokesch, S.E., Unleashing the power of learning: an interview with British petroleum's John Browne, *Harvard Business Review*, **75**(5), September–October 1997, 146–168.

[19] Strebel, P., 1996, *op. cit.*

[20] Brill, P.L. and Worth, R., 1997.

[21] McKeen, J.D. and Smith, H.A., 2003, *op. cit.*

[22] Duck, J.D., 1993, *op. cit.*

[23] *Ibid.*

[24] McKeen, J.D. and Smith, H.A., 2003, *op. cit.*

[25] Aubert, B.A., Patry, M. and Rivard, S., Assessing the risk of IT outsourcing, *Proceedings of the 31st Hawaii International Conference on System Sciences*, Vol. VI, Organizational Systems and Technology Track, January 1998, pp. 685–693.

[26] Goldratt, E.M. and Cox, J., *The Goal: A Process of Ongoing Improvement*, New York, NY: North River Press, 1992.

[27] Duck, J.D., 1993, *op. cit.*

[28] Pascale, R., Millemann, M. and Gioja, L., Changing the way we change, *Harvard Business Review*, **75**(6), November–December 1997, 126–139.

[29] Duck, J.D., 1993, *op. cit.*

[30] *Ibid.*

[31] Kotter, J.P., 1995, *op. cit.*

[32] Schaffer, R.H. and Thompson, H.A., Successful change programs begin with results, *Harvard Business Review*, **70**(1), January–February 1992, 80–89.

ensure that agreement can be reached on enterprise-wide business or technical issues. Therefore, many companies are choosing to adopt a hybrid, or federal, structure for IT that combines elements of both centralization and decentralization.

Within IT, isolating different skills into different structural groups (e.g. development, maintenance, and support), so that business units must deal with different groups, can lead to unclear lines of responsibility and accountability. And such isolation of IT groups can also lead to internal misalignments by discouraging interaction between them, in turn discouraging the development of informal relationships and knowledge, which can overcome some types of structural misalignments.

As noted above, structure is a key way that organizations try to build flexibility into their IT functions. Although almost all IT departments are now designed using a federal model as a base structure, IT managers are finding many distinctive ways within this generic design to deliver value to their organizations.[5] There are three aspects to a good organization design for IT:

1 *Modular design*: Managers should first determine how IT will organize to deliver the key capabilities (i.e. skills and knowledge) they believe are essential to the effective use of IT (see also "IS skills", page 113). These include both technical and business skills and the mechanisms for obtaining them (e.g. internal groups, outsourcing, and joint ventures). They must then design how IT will deliver value to the organization in such areas as value innovation, solutions delivery, services provisioning, i.e. data centers and help desks (see also "IS processes", page 116).

2 *Integration structures*: When the design for each individual capability and service has been completed, managers then need to develop ways of integrating them together into a seamless structure. To do this, firms make considerable use of coordinating mechanisms. These are used not only inside IT (e.g. project management offices to coordinate all solutions delivery) but also outside it with the rest of the organization and with external partners and service providers. Three formal generic mechanisms are used to coordinate IT work.[6] These are:

- *integrators*: people with formal responsibilities for linking across units, either internally or externally;

- *groups*: formal teams with specific responsibilities for linking;
- *processes*: routines to provide decisional guidance.

In addition, informal relationships play a key, but frequently unidentified, role in providing integration and coordination.

3 *Modification*: Finally, IT managers must be sensitive to the need for structural change. No IT organization structure can remain static. As the management puzzle evolves, IT structure will need to change as well. Therefore, research shows that a frequent "patching" of IT structures is necessary to enable them to deal with different contingencies as they arise.[7]

Endnotes

[1]Klenke, K., Information technologies as drivers of emergent organizational forms: a leadership perspective, in R. Baskerville, S. Smithson, O. Ngwenyama and J.I. DeGross (eds.), *Transforming Organisations with Information Technologies*, North Holland, 1994, pp. 15–94.

[2]Brown, C.V. and Magill, S.L., Alignment of the IS functions with the enterprise: toward a model of antecedents, *MIS Quarterly*, **18** (4), December 1994, 371–404.

[3]McKeen, J.D. and Smith, H.A., *Making IT Happen*, Chichester, England: John Wiley & Sons, 2003.

[4]*Ibid.*

[5]Agarwal, R. and Sambamurthy, V., Principles and models for organizing the IT function, *MIS Quarterly Executive*, **1**(1), 1–16.

[6]Brown, C.V. and Sambamurthy, V., Linking intra-organizational stakeholders: CIO perspectives on the use of coordination mechanisms, *Working paper #304*, Center for Information Systems Research, Sloan School of Management, MIT, November 1998.

[7]Agarwal, R. and Sambamurthy, V., 2001, *op. cit.*

Bibliography

Chapter 1 – The puzzle frames

Andersen Consulting, survey conducted by Gallup Canada and Goldfarb Consultants, reported in the *Globe and Mail*, 23 July 1996.

Applegate, L., DeSanctis, G. and Jackson, B., Technology, teams and organizations: implementing groupware at Texaco, *Texaco*, 1996.

Avgerou, C., Ciborra, C.U. and Land, F.F. (eds) *The Social Study of IT*, Oxford University Press, 2004 (in press).

Baird, M., The virtual office: real deal for design, *Electronic Engineering Times*, December 1997, 39.

Barner, R., The new millennium workplace: seven changes that will challenge managers – and workers, *The Futurist*, March–April 1996, **30**, 14–18.

Benhamou, E. and Saal, H., Smart Valley Telecommuting Guide, *www.svi.org/projects/tcommute/tcguide/htmlvers/tcg.1.html*

Bleecker, S., The virtual organization, *The Futurist*, March–April 1994, 9–14.

Bozman, J. and Booker, E., Looking forward to Office 2001, *Computerworld*, January 1993, 28.

Brown, S.L. and Eisenhardt, K.M., *Competing on the Edge*, Boston: Harvard Business School Press, 1998.

Brown, T., Think in reverse, *Industry Week*, 19 July 1993, 14–22.

Browne, J. and Prokesch, S.E., Unleashing the power of learning, *Harvard Business Review*, September –October 1997, 146–162.

Byrne, J., The virtual corporation, *Business Week*, February 1993, 98–102.

Chatterji, D., Accessing external sources of technology, *Research Technology Management*, March–April 1996, 48–56.

Chesbrough, H.W. and Teece, D.J., When is virtual virtuous? *Harvard Business Review*, January–February 1996, 65–72.

Coates, J., 83 Assumptions about the year 2025, *The Highly Probable Future*, 1994, 1–7.

Cravens, D., Shipp, S. and Cravens, K., Reforming the traditional organization: the mandate for developing networks, *Business Horizons*, July–August 1994, 19–28.

Davidow, H.D. and Malone, M.S., *The Virtual Corporation: Structuring and Revitalizing the Corporation of the 21st Century*, New York, NY: Harper Business, 1993.

Donoghue, J., Back offices, far afield and frugal, *Air Transport World*, 1993, 51–53.

Drucker, P.F., The coming of the new organization, *Harvard Business Review*, January–February 1988, 45–53.

Drucker, P. and Peter, F., Management and the world's work, *Harvard Business Review*, September–October 1988, 2–9, 65–76.

Flynn, G., An ad agency pitches for the virtual office, *Workforce*, November 1997, 56–61.

Goldman, E., Execs believe telecommuting benefits employers, *Spector & Associates*, 1995, 1–2.

Gomes-Casseres, B., *Managing International Alliances Conceptual Framework*, Harvard Business School 9-793-133, May 1993, 1–19.

Gray, P., The virtual workplace, *OR/MS Today*, 22(4), August 1995, 24.

Greengard, S., How technology will change the workplace, *Workforce*, January 1998, 74–78.

Hamilton, J., Baker, S. and Vlasie, B. The new workplace, *Business Week*, April 1996, 106–108.

Hardwrick, M. and Bolton, R., The industrial virtual enterprise, *Communications of ACM*, **40**, September 1997, 59–60.

Holland, C., The importance of trust and business relationships in the formation of virtual organizations, in P. Sieber and J. Griese (eds.), *Organizational Virtualness*, Bern, Switzerland: Simona Verlag Bern, 1998, pp. 53–64.

Horwitt, E. and Condon, R., Right here, right now, *Computerworld*, 9 September 1996, 20–24.

Jagers, H., Jansen, W. and Steenbakkers, W., Characteristics of virtual organizations, in P. Sieber and J. Griese (eds.), *Organizational Virtualness*, Bern, Switzerland: Simona Verlag Bern, 1998, pp. 65–76.

Jarvenpaa, S. and Ives, B., The global network organization of the future: information management opportunities and challenges, *Journal of Management Information Systems*, **10**, 1994, 25–57.

Jarvenpaa, S. and Todd, P., Consumer reactions to electronic shopping on the world wide web, *Working Paper #96-18*, School of Business, Queen's University, Kingston, Ont., Canada K7L 3N6.

Kalakota, R. and Whinston, A., *Frontiers of Electronic Commerce*, Addison-Wesley, 1996.

Kennedy, C., Future shock – or future success? *Director*, July 1995, 42–46.

Klein, M., The virtue of being a virtual corporation, *Best's Review*, **95**, October 1994, 88–94.

Maccoby, M., Knowledge workers need new structures, *Research-Technology Management*, **39**(1), 1996, 56–58.

Malone, M. and Davidow, W., Virtual corporation, *Forbes ASAP*, 1992.

Malone, T.W. and Laubacher, R.J., The dawn of the E-lance economy, *Harvard Business Review*, September–October 1998, 144–152.

McKeen, J. and Smith, H., Electronic commerce, *IT Management Forum*, **6**(1), February 1996.

McKeen, J.D. and Smith, H., *Management Challenges in IS: Successful Strategies and Appropriate Action*, Chichester: Wiley, 1996.

McKeen, J., Todd, P.A., Parent, M., Smith, H., Chan, Y., Gallupe, R.B. and Wagar, L., The impact of information technology on employees and the organization, *IT Management Research Programme*, HEC Montreal and Queen's University School of Business, Phase II, **3**, July 1996.

Norton, B. and Smith, C., Understanding the virtual organization, *Barron's*, 1997.

Pape, W., Beyond data, *Inc. Technology*, 1995, **17**(13), 31–32.

Pape, W., Divide and conquer, *Inc. Technology*, 1996, **28**(9), 713–721.

Pape, W., Remote control, *INC – The Magazine for Growing Companies*, September 1996, **18**(13), 25–26.

Pine II, B.J., Peppers, D., Rogers, M., Do you want to keep your customer forever? *Harvard Business Review*, March–April 1995, 103–114.

Pollock, J., ING to spend $50 million on launch of virtual bank, *Marketing Magazine*, 2 December 1996, **101**(46), 3.

Rasmussen, J., Safe and secure business transactions now a reality, *Computing Canada*, 11 April 1996, 33.

Rowan, G., The end of the travel agent, *Globe and Mail*, 24 July 1996.

Rodin, R., Marshall Industries & L. Eliot and Eliot & Associates, Virtual distribution: the new business enterprise model, *SIM Executive Brief*, **7**, April 1997.

Sheridan, J., The agile web, *Industry Week*, March 1996, **245**, 31–35.

Skyrme, D., The realities of virtuality, in P. Sieber and J. Griese (eds.), *Organizational Virtualness*, Bern, Switzerland: Simona Verlag Bern, 1998, pp. 25–34.

Solomon, C., Sharing information across borders and time zones, *Workforce*, March 1998, 12–16.

Snow, C., Miles, R. and Coleman, H., Managing 21st century network organizations, *Organizational Dynamics*, **20**(3), 1992, 5–20.

Stephens, G. and Szajna, B., Perceptions and expectations: why people choose a telecommuting work style, *Proceedings of the HICSS'98 Conference*, HICSS, 1998, 112–120.

Stewart, T., *Intellectual Capital: The New Wealth of Organizations*, New York, NY: Bantam Doubleday Dell Publishing Group Inc., 1999.

Tapscott, D. and Caston, A., *Paradigm Shift: The New Promise of Information Technology*, New York, NY: McGraw-Hill, 1993.

Tapscott, D., Ticoll, D. and Lowy, A., *Digital Capital: Harnessing the Power of Business Webs*, Harvard Business School Press, 2000.

Thomas, G., Strategic alliances key to the future, *Executive Journal*, July–August 1998.

Townsend, A., DeMarie, S. and Hendrickson, A., Are you ready for virtual teams? *HRMagazine*, **41**, September 1996, 122–126.

Townsend, A., DeMarie, S. and Hendrickson, A., Virtual teams: technology and the workplace of the future, *Academy of Management Executive*, **12**(3), 1998, 17–29.

Tully, S., The modular corporation, *Fortune*, **127**(3), February 1993, 106–111.

Upton, D. and McAfee, A., The real virtual factory, *Harvard Business Review*, **47**, July–August 1996, 123–133.

Venkatraman, N. and Henderson, J.C., Real strategies for virtual organizing, *Sloan Management Review*, Fall, 1998, 33–48.

Vogt, E., The nature of work in 2010, *Telecommunications*, International Edition, **29**(9), September 1995, 21–28.

Voss, H., Virtual organizations: the future is now, *Strategy & Leadership*, July–August 1996, **24**, 12–16.

Webber, A.W., What's so new about the new economy, *Harvard Business Review*, January–February 1993, 4–11.

Chapter 2 – The strategy piece

Applegate, L.M., *Managing in an Information Age: Organizational Challenges and Opportunities*, Harvard Business School Press, 1995.

Brandenburger, A.M. and Nalebuff, B.J., *Co-Opetition*, Harvard University Press, 1996.

Brown, S.L. and Eisenhardt, K.M., *Competing on the Edge*, Harvard Business School Press, 1998.

Carlin, B.A. *et al.*, Sleeping with the enemy: doing business with a competitor, *Business Horizons*, September–October 1994, 9–15.

Coase, R., The nature of the firm, *Economica*, 1937, 386–405.

Cummings, S. and Wilson, D. (eds.), *Images of Strategy*, Blackwell Publishers, 2003.

Davidow, H.D. and Malone, M.S., *The Virtual Corporation: Structuring and Revitalizing the Corporation of the 21st Century*, New York, NY: Harper Business, 1993.

Davis, S. and Botkin, J., The coming of knowledge-based business, *Harvard Business Review*, September–October 1994; Evans, P.B. and Wurster, T.S., Strategy and the new economics of information, *Harvard Business Review*, September–October 1997, 70–82.

Garvin, D.A., Building a learning organization, in *Harvard Business Review on Knowledge Management*, Boston: Harvard Business School Press, 1998, pp. 47–80.

Gilmore, J.H. and Pine II, B.J., The four faces of mass customization, *Harvard Business Review*, January–February 1997, 91–101.

Hagel III, J. and Rayport, J.F., The coming battle for customer information, *Harvard Business Review*, January–February 1997, 53–60.

Harris, K., Austin, T., Fenn, J., Hayward, S. and Cushman, A., The impact of knowledge management on enterprise architecture, *Gartner Group Strategic Analysis Report*, 25 October 1999.

Hitt, M.A., Keats, B.W. and DeMarie, S.M., Navigating in the new competitive landscape: building strategic flexibility and competitive advantage in the 21st century, *Academy of Management Executive*, **12**(4), 1998, 22–42.

Mohrman, S.A., Galbraith, J.R. and Lawler III, E.E., *Tomorrow's Organization: Crafting Winning Capabilities in a Dynamic World*, San Francisco, CA: Jossey-Bass Publishers, 1998.

Moon, Y., Interactive Technologies and Relationship Marketing Strategies, *Harvard Business Note #9-599-191*, 19 January 2000.

Peppers, D., Rogers, M. and Dorf, B., Is your company ready for one-to-one marketing? *Harvard Business Review*, January–Febuary 1999, 3–12.

Peppers, D. and Rogers, M., *Enterprise One to One: Tools for Competing in the Interactive Age*, Doubleday, 1999.

Porter, M.E., *Competitive Strategy*, Free Press, 1980.

Porter, M.E., What is strategy? *Harvard Business Review*, November–December 1996, 61–78.

Prahalad, C.K. and Hamel, G., *Competing for the Future*, Harvard Business School Press, 1996.

Rockart, J. and Short, J., The networked organization and the management of interpedence, in Scott Morton (ed.), *The Corporation of the 1990s*, New York, NY: Oxford Press, 1991.

Sauer, C., Yetton, P.W. and Associates (eds.), *Steps to the Future: Fresh Thinking on the Management of IT-Based Organizational Transformation*, San Francisco, CA: Jossey-Bass Publishers, 1997.

Shapiro, C. and Varian, H.R., *Information Rules: A Strategic Guide to the Network Economy*, Boston, MA: Harvard Business School Press, 1999.

Tapscott, D., Ticoll, D. and Lowy, A., *Digital Capital: Harnessing the Power of Business Webs*, Harvard Business School Press, 2000.

Tapscott, D., *The Digital Economy: Promise and Peril in the Age of Networked Intelligence*, New York, NY: McGraw-Hill, 1996.

Chapter 3 – The structure piece

Apgar, M., The alternative workplace: changing where and how people work, *Harvard Business Review*, May–June 1998, 121–136.

Aldrich, H.E., *Organizations and Evolving*, Thousand Oaks: Sage, 1999.

Applegate, L.M., Managing in an information age: transforming the organization for the 1990s, in R. Baskerville, S. Smithson, O. Ngwenyama and J.I. DeGross (eds.), *Transforming Organisations with Information Technologies*, North Holland, 1994.

Ashkenas, D.U., Jick, T. and Kerr, S. (eds.), *The Boundaryless Organization: Breaking the Chains of Organizational Structure*, San Francisco, CA: Jossey-Bass Publishers, 1998.

Brown, D., Telework not meeting expectations – but expectations were nonsense, *Canadian HR Reporter*, **16**(4), 3, 11.

Davenport, T.H. and Pearlson, K., Two cheers for the virtual office, *Sloan Management Review*, Summer 1998, 51–65.

Davis, T. and Darling, B., How virtual corporations manage the performance of contractors: the super bakery case, *Organizational Dynamics*, **24**, Summer 1995, 70–75.

Davis, T. and Darling, B., Update on Super Bakery, Inc., *Organizational Dynamics*, **25**, Fall 1996, 86–87.

Day, G.S., Managing market relationships, *Academy of Marketing Science Journal*, **28**(1), Winter 2000, 24–30.

Drucker, P., The coming of the new organization, *Harvard Business Review*, January–February 1988, 45–53.

Dubé, L. and Paré, G., Global virtual teams, *Communications of the ACM*, **44**(12), December 2001, 71–73.

Dubé, L. and Paré, G., The multifaceted nature of virtual teams (Chapter 1), in D.J. Pauleen (ed.), *Virtual Teams: Projects, Protocols and Processes*, Idea Group Inc., 2004, pp. 1–39.

El Sawy, O.A., Malhotra, A., Gosain, S. and Young, K.M., IT intensive value innovation in the electronic economy: insights from marshall industries, *MIS Quarterly*, **23**(3), September 1999, 305–335.

Flynn, G., An ad agency pitches for the virtual office, *Workforce*, **76**(11), November 1997, 56–63.

Galal, H., *Verifone: The Transaction Automation Company (A)*, Harvard Business School, Case #9-195-088, 12 July 1995.

Galbraith, J.R., *Designing Organizations: An Executive Briefing on Strategy, Structure, and Process*, San Francisco, CA: Jossey-Bass Publishers, 1995.

Geber, B., Virtual teams, *Training*, **32**(4), 36–42.

Hammer, M. and Champy, J., *Reengineering the Corporation, A Manifesto for Business Revolution*, New York, NY: Harper Business, 1993.

Hammer, M. and Stanton, S., How process enterprises really work, *Harvard Business Review*, **77**(6), 1999, 108–118.

Hitt, M.A., Keats, B.W. and DeMarie, S.M., Navigating in the new competitive landscape: building strategic flexibility and competitive advantage in the 21st century, *Academy of Management Executive*, **12**(4), 1998, 22–42.

Magretta, J., The power of virtual integration: an interview with Dell Computer's Michael Dell, *Harvard Business Review*, March–April 1998, 73–84.

Mathews, J., Holonic organizational architectures, *Human Systems Management*, **15**(1), 1996, 1–29.

Miles, R. and Snow, C., Organizations: new concepts for new forms, *California Management Review*, **28**, 1986, 62–73.

Miles, R.E. and Snow, C.C., Causes of failure in network organizations, *California Management Review*, **34**(4), Summer 1992, 57.

Mohrman, S.A., Galbraith, J.R. and Lawler III, E.E., *Tomorrow's Organization: Crafting Winning Capabilities in a Dynamic World*, San Francisco, CA: Jossey-Bass Publishers, 1998.

Niles, J.M., *Managing Telework: Strategies for Managing the Virtual Workforce*, New York, NY: John Wiley & Sons, Inc., 1998.

Ostrofsky, K. and Cash, J.I., *Mrs. Fields' Cookies*, Harvard Business School, 1989.

Pape, W.R., Becoming a virtual company, *INC Journal*, **17**(17), 1995, 29–31.

Quinn, J.B., Baruch, J.J. and Zien, K.A. (eds.), *Innovation Explosion: Using Intellect and Software to Revolutionize Growth Strategies*, New York, NY: The Free Press, 1997.

Rockart, J. and Short, J., The networked organization and the management of interpedence, in Scott Morton (ed.), *The Corporation of the 1990s*, New York, NY: Oxford Press, 1991.

Smithson, S., Ngwenyama, O. and Baskerville, R., Perspectives on information technology and new emergent forms of organizations, in R. Baskerville, S. Smithson, O. Ngwenyama and J.I. DeGross (eds.), *Transforming Organisations with Information Technologies*, North Holland, 1994.

Tapscott, D., *Digital Capital: Harnessing the Power of Business Webs*, Boston, MA: Harvard Business School Press, 2000.

Tapscott, D., *The Digital Economy: Promise and Peril in the Age of Networked Intelligence*, New York, NY: McGraw-Hill, 1996.

Townsend, A.M., DeMarie, S.M. and Hendrickson, A.R., Virtual teams: technology and the workplace of the future, *The Academy of Management Executive*, **12**(3), August 1998, 17–29.

Venkatraman, N. and Henderson, J.C., Real strategies for virtual organizing, *Sloan Manangement Review*, **39**(5), Fall 1998, 33–48.

Volberda, H.W., Toward the flexible form: how to remain vital in hypercompetitive environments, *Organization Science*, **7**(4), 1996, 359–374.

Whithouse, G., Diamond, C. and Lafferty, G., Assessing the benefits of telework: australian case study evidence, *New Zealand Journal of Industrial Relations*, **27**(3), October 2002, 257–268.

Chapter 4 – The IT piece

Bank of Montreal's Chicago FX Exchange, Bank of Montreal's Chicago foreign exchange operation first to use voice recognition for live FX trading, *www.bmo.com/news/voice.htm*, May, 1997.

Caldwell, B., Computer Services – The new outsourcing partnership – vendors want to provide more than just services. They'll help you create a virtual corporation, *Techsearch Results*, (585), June, 1996.

Ching, C., Holsapple, C. and Whinston, A., Toward IT support for coordination in network organizations, *Information & Management*, **30**, July 1996, 179–199.

Feitzinger, E. and Lee, H.L., Mass customization at Hewlett-Packard: the power of postponement, *Harvard Business Review*, January–February 1997, 116–121.

Henry, J. and Hartzler, M., *Tools for Virtual Teams*, ASQ Quality Press, Wisconsin, 1998.

Godin, S., Permission marketing: the way to make advertising work again, *Direct Marketing*, **62**(1), May 1999, 40–43.

Haeckel, H. and Nolan, R.L., Managing by wire, *Harvard Business Review*, September–October 1993, 123–132.

Heasley, P.G. and Gross, P.W., Getting the most out of customer information, *Chief Executive*, **130**, December 1997, 36–39.

Jarvenpaa, S.K. and Ives, B., The global network organization of the future: information management opportunities and challenges, *Journal of MIS*, **10**(4), Spring 1994, 25–57.

Kling, J., Seven great ways to use your company's web site, *Harvard Management Update*, January 1999, 3–4.

Lackner, D., One-to-one marketing: maximising database marketing with customer intelligence, *Call Center Solutions*, **16**(8), February 1998, 68–71.

Moon, Y., *Interactive Technologies and Relationship Marketing Strategies*, Harvard Business Note #9-599-191, 19 January 2000.

Nolan, R.L., *Drugstore.com*, Harvard Business School Teaching Case #9-300-036, 29 September 1999.

Peppers, D. and Rogers, M., *Enterprise One to One: Tools for Competing in the Interactive Age*, Doubleday, 1999.

Pine II, B.J., Peppers, D. and Rogers, M., Do you want to keep your customer forever? *Harvard Business Review*, March–April 1995, 103–114.

Treacy, M. and Wiersema, F., Customer intimacy and other value disciplines, *Harvard Business Review*, January–February 1993, 84–93.

Chapter 5 – The leadership piece

Armstrong, C.P. and Sambamurthy, V., Information technology assimilation in firms: the influence of senior leadership and IT infrastructures, *Information Systems Research*, **10**(4), 1999, 304–327.

Ashkenas, R., Ulrich, D., Todd, J. and Kerr, S., *The Boudaryless Organization, Breaking the Chains of Organizational Structure*, San Francisco, CA: Jossey-Bass Publishers, 1995.

Boeker, W., Strategic change: the influence of managerial characteristics and organizational growth, *Academy of Management Journal*, **40**(1), 1997, 152–170.

Brown, S.L. and Eisenhardt, K.M., *Competing on the Edge*, Harvard Business School Press, 1998.

Cross, J., Earl, M.J. and Sampler, J.L., Transformation of the IT function at British petroleum, *MIS Quarterly*, December 1997, 401–423.

Frohman, A.L., Technology as a competitive weapon, *Harvard Business Review*, January–February 1982, 97–105.

Hill, L. and Wetlaufer, S., Leadership when there is no one to ask: an interview with Eni's Franco Bernabè, *Harvard Business Review*, July–August 1998, 80–94.

Kostner, J., *Virtual Leadership*, Warner Books, 1994.

Kotter, J.P., Leading change: why transformation efforts fail, *Harvard Business Review*, March–April 1995, 59–67.

Magretta, J., The power of virtual integration: an interview with Dell Computer's Michael Dell, *Harvard Business Review*, March–April 1998, 73–84.

Mohrman, S.A., Galbraith, J.R. and Lawler III, E.E., *Tomorrow's Organization: Crafting Winning Capabilities in a Dynamic World*, San Francisco, CA: Jossey-Bass Publishers, 1998.

Porter, M.E., What is strategy? *Harvard Business Review*, **74**(6), 1996, 61–79.

Schrage, M., The real problem with computers, *Harvard Business Review*, September–October 1997, 3–7.

Tapscott, D., *Paradigm Shift: The New Promise of Information Technology*, New York, NY: McGraw-Hill, 1993, 283.

Warner, M. and Witzel, M., The virtual general manager, *Journal of General Management*, **24**(4), Summer 1999, 71–92.

Chapter 6 – Progressive delivers the unexpected – Progressive Insurance

Hammer, M., *Beyond Reengineering*, HarperCollins, 1996.

Loomis, C.J., Sex. Reefer? And auto insurance! *Fortune*, **123**(3) 8 July 1995, 76–83.

MacSweeney, G., Progressive inside and out, *Insurance and Technology*, **24**(10), September 1999, 13–14.

MacSweeney, G., Progressive goes wireless with WAP technology, *Insurance and Technology*, **25**(13), December 2000, 14–15.

Progressive's press releases consulted at www.progressive.com

Progressive Insurance Receives CIO-100 Award for Innovative Business Practices and Services, 15 August 2001.

Progressive Insurance named by Ziff Davis SMART BUSINESS As One of the Top 50 Companies to Successfully Use the Internet to Grow Their Business, 7 August 2001.

Progressive.com's Superiority Proven by Being Named No.1 Online Insurance Carrier by Gomez™ for the Fourth Consecutive Quarter, 8 May 2001.

Financial Release: 2000 4th Quarter Results, 24 January 2001.

Salter, C., Progressive makes big claims, *Fast Company*, **19**, November 1998, consulted at *www.fastcompany.com/online/19/progressive.html* in June 2001.

Scott Morton, M.S. (ed.), *The Corporation of the 1990s: Information Technology and Organizational Transformation*, New York, NY: Oxford University Press, 1991.

Siggelkow, N. and Porter, M.E., *Progressive Corporation*, Harvard Business School, Case Study #9-797-109, 14 May 1998.

Stepanek, M., Q&A with Progressive's Peter Lewis, *Businessweek Online*, 12 September 2000.

Whitney, S., Think small, *Best's Review*, September 2000, 6.

Yeh, R., Pearlson, K. and Kozmetsky, G. (eds.), Progressive Insurance: an instant execution company in *Zero Time*, New York, NY: John Wiley & Sons, Inc. 2000, pp. 195–210.

Yetton, P.W., Johnston, K.D. and Craig, J.F., Computer-aided architects: a case study of IT and strategic change, *Sloan Management Review*, **35**(4), Summer 1994, 57–67.

Chapter 7 – The organization without an organizational chart – Oticon

Ashkenas, D.U., Jick, T. and Kerr, S. (eds.), *The Boundaryless Organization: Breaking the Chains of Organizational Structure*, San Francisco, CA: Jossey-Bass Publishers, 1998, pp. 191–220.

Bjorn-Andersen, N. and Turner, J.A., Creating the twenty-first century organization: the metamorphosis of Oticon, in R. Baskerville, S. Smithson, O. Ngwenyama and J.I. DeGross (eds.), *Transforming Organisations with Information Technologies*, North Holland, 1994, pp. 379–394.

Browne, J. and Prokesch, S.E., Unleashing the power of learning, *Harvard Business Review*, 9/1/97; No de commande 97507.

Fully digital sound processing revolutionizes the ability individual needs of hearing impaired, *PR Newswire*, 30 September 1996.

Furniture sale starts culture change, *Personnel Management*, May 1993, 13.

Harari, O., Open the doors, tell the truth, *Management Review*, January 1995, 33–35.

Hearing health products expected to grow, study says, *The Maturing Marketplace*, 1 January 1998.

Hagström, P., *Oticon A/S: Cogitate Incognito*, Harvard Business School Case #9-195-140, 1995.

Labarre, P., The dis-organization of Oticon, *Industry Week*, July 1994, 22–26.

Morsing, M. and Eiberg, K. (eds.), *Managing the Unmanageable for a Decade*, Oticon S/A, 1999.

Ostroff, F. and Smith, D., The horizontal organization, *McKinsey Quarterly*, **1**, 1992, 148–168.

Oticon realises 30% productivity boost with client–server system, *IMC Journal*, 1995, 14–15.

Quinn, J.B., Baruch, J.J. and Zien, K.A. (eds.), *Innovation Explosion: Using Intellect and Software to Revolutionize Growth Strategies*, New York, NY: The Free Press, 1997.

Quinn, J.B. and Paquette, P.C., Technology in services: creating organizational revolutions, *Sloan Management Review*, Winter 1990, 67–78.

Sellen, A. and Harper, R., *Experience of a Paperless Office*, Research Note, Rank Xerox, Cambridge.

The revolution at Oticon: creating a Spaghetti Organization, *Research Technology Management*, September–October 1996, 54.

Chapter 8 – Li & Fung: the virtual value chain

Andrews, P.P. and Hahn, J., Transforming supply chains into value webs, *Strategy & Leadership*, **26**(3), July–August 1998, 6–11.

Ashkenas, R., Ulrich, D., Todd, J. and Kerr, S., Toward partnership with customers and suppliers, in D.U. Ashkenas, T. Jick and S. Kerr (eds.), *The Boundaryless Organization: Breaking the Chains of Organizational Structure*, San Francisco, CA: Jossey-Bass Publishers, 1998, pp. 191–220.

Balfour, F., Stick to knitting, *Far Eastern Economic Review*, 18 June 1992, 80.

Barron's, Buying Future Big-Caps, 23 March 1998, 42–44.

Kraar, L., Hong Kong is buzzing…, *Fortune*, 15 May 2000, 324.

Leung, J., New trade era, *Asian Business*, March 1996, 32.

Magretta, J., The power of virtual integration: an interview with Dell Computer's Michael Dell, *Harvard Business Review*, March–April 1998, 73–84.

Magretta, J., Fast, global, and entrepreneurial: supply chain management, Hong Kong style: an interview with Victor Fung, *Harvard Business Review*, September–October 1998, 102–111.

Rayport, J.F. and Sviokla, J.J., Exploiting the virtual value chain, *Harvard Business Review*, November–December 1995, 75–85.

Venkatraman, N. and Henderson, J.C., Real strategies for virtual organizing, *Sloan Management Review*, **39**(5), Fall 1998, 33–48.

Slater, J., Corporate culture, *Far Eastern Economic Review*, 22 July 1999, 12.

Slater, J. and Amaha, E., Master of the trade, *Far Eastern Economic Review*, 22 July 1999, 10–14.

The economist, business: link in the global chain, *The Economist*, **359**(8224), 2 June 2001, 62–63.

Willing, H., Stirring IT up with the experts, *Apparel Industry Magazine*, August 2000, 58–60.

Young, F. and McFarlan, W., *Li & Fung*, Boston, MA: Harvard Business School Publishing, #9-301-009, 29 November 2000, 18.

Chapter 9 – People management

Bridges, W., *Job Shift*, Reading, MA: Addison-Wesley Publishing, 1994.

Coutu, D., Organization: trust in virtual teams, *Harvard Business Review*, June 1998, 20–21.

Davis, S., Rumble, Rumble, *Training & Development*, **50**, November 1996, 44–45.

Fritz, M.B. and Manheim, M., Managing virtual work: a framework for managerial action, in P. Sieber and J. Griese (eds.), *Organizational Virtualness*, Bern, Switzerland: Simona Verlag Bern, 1998, pp. 123–132.

Gebauer, J., Virtual organizations from an economic perspective, *Communications of the ACM*, **40**, September 1997, 91–103.

Geber, B., Virtual teams, *Training*, April 1995, 36–40.

Grenier, R. and Metes, G., *Going Virtual*, New Jersey: Prentice Hall, 1995.

Iacono, C.Z. and Weisband, S., Developing trust in virtual teams, *Proceeding of the HICSS'96*, 1996.

Jarvenpaa, S. and Shaw, T., Global virtual teams: integrating models of trust, in P. Sieber and J. Griese (eds.), *Organizational Virtualness*, Bern, Switzerland: Simona Verlag Bern, 1998, pp. 35–52.

Lipnack, J. and Stamps, J., *Virtual Teams*, New York, NY: John Wiley & Sons, Inc., 1997.

Melymuka, K., Tips for teams, *Computerworld*, April, 1997, 72.

Musthaler, L., Effective teamwork virtually guaranteed, *Network World*, October 1995.

Warner, M., Working at home – the right way to be a star in your bunny slippers, *Fortune*, **135**(4), 1997, 165–166.

Chapter 10 – IT management

Applegate, L.M., Managing in an information age: transforming the organization for the 1990s, in R. Baskerville, S. Smithson, O. Ngwenyama and J.I. DeGross (eds.), *Transforming Organisations with Information Technologies*, North Holland, 1994.

Baskerville, R., Smithsen, S., Ngwenyama, O. and Degross, J.I. (eds.), *Transforming Organization with Information Technology*, North Holland, 1994.

Bergeron, F. and Raymond, L., The contribution of IT to the bottom line: a contingency perspective of strategic dimensions, *Proceedings of the 16th International Conference on Information Systems*, Amsterdam, 1995, pp. 167–181.

El Sawy, O., Malhotra, A., Gosain, S. and Young, K.M., IT-intensive value innovation in the electronic economy: insights from Marshall industries, *MIS Quarterly*, **23**(3), September 1999, 310, 305–335.

Galliers, R.D. and Leidner, D.E. (eds.), *Strategic Information Management*, Oxford: Butterworth-Heineman, 2003.

Henderson, J.C. and Venkatraman, N., Strategic alignment: leveraging information technology for transforming organizations, *IBM Systems Journal*, **38**(2–3), 1999, 472–484.

Walsham, G. and Waema, T., Information systems strategy and implementation: a case study of a building society, *ACM Transactions on Information Systems*, **12**(2), 150–173.

Ward, J., Griffiths, P. and Whitmore, P., *Strategic Planning of Information Systems*, Chichester: Wiley, 1990.

Wells, J.D., Fuerst, W.L. and Choobineh, J., Managing IT for one-to-one customer interaction, *Information & Management*, **35**(1), January 1999, 53–62.

Chapter 11 – Knowledge management

Bair, J., Fenn, J., Hunter, R. and Bosik, D., Foundations for enterprise knowledge management, *Gartner Group Strategic Analysis Report*, 7 April 1997, 50 (lire p. 1–24 seulement).

Brethenoux, E. and Block, J., Intelligent agents: a day in the life of a software agent, *Gartner Group Strategic Analysis Report*, 28 September 1995, 23.

Brethenoux, E., Dresner, H., Strange, K. and Block, J., Data warehouse, data mining, and business intelligence: the hype stops here, *Gartner Group Strategic Analysis Report*, 28 October 1996, 39.

March, A., *A Note on Knowledge Management*, Harvard Business School, #9-398-031, 20.

Davenport, T.H. and Prusak, L., Technologies for knowledge management, in *Working Knowledge*, Boston, MA: Harvard Business School Press, 1998, pp. 123–143.

Davis, S. and Botkin, J., The coming of knowledge-based business, in D. Tapscott (ed.), *Creating Value in the Network Economy*, Harvard Business Review Book, 1999, pp. 3–12.

Duck, J.D., Managing change: the art of balancing, *Harvard Business Review*, **71**(6), November–December 1993, 109–118.

Garvin, D.A., Building a learning organization, *Harvard Business Review on Knowledge Management*, Harvard Business School Press, 1998, 47–80.

Haeckel, H. and Nolan, R.L., Managing by wire, *Harvard Business Review*, September–October 1993, 123–132.

Hansen, M.T., Nohria, N. and Tierney, T., What's your strategy for managing knowledge? *Harvard Business Review*, March–April 1999, 106–116.

Harreld, B., Building smarter, faster organizations, in D. Tapscott, A. Lowy and D. Ticoll (eds.), *Blueprint to the Digital Economy*, New York, NY: McGraw-Hill, 1998, 60–76.

Harris, K. and Dresner, H., Business intelligence meets knowledge management, *Gartner Group Research Note*, 1 March 1999, 4.

Harris, K., Austin, T., Fenn, J., Hayward, S. and Cushman, A., The impact of knowledge management on enterprise architecture, *Gartner Group Strategic Analysis Report*, 25 October 1999, 22.

Harris, K., Fleming, M., Hunter, R., Rosser, B. and Cushman, A., The knowledge management scenario: trends and directions for 1998–2003, *Gartner Group Strategic Analysis Report*, 11999, 38.

Jacobs, P., Data mining: what general managers need to know, *Harvard Management Update*, October 1999, 2.

Julien, P.A., Raymond, L., Jacob, R. and Ramangalahy, C., Types of technological scanning in manufacturing SMEs: an empirical analysis of patterns and determinants, *Enterpreneuship & Regional Development*, **11**, 1999, 281–300.

Lei, D., Slocum, J.W. and Pitts, R.A., Designing organizations for competitive advantage: the power of unlearning and learning, *Organizational Dynamics*, Winter 1999, 24–38.

Leidner, D.E., The information technology – organizational culture relationship, in R.D. Galliers and D.E. Leidner (eds.), *Strategic Information Management*, Oxford: Butterworth-Heineman, 2003, 496–525.

Leonard, D. and Strauss, S., Putting your company's whole brain to work, *Harvard Business Review*, July–August 1997, 111–122.

March, A., *A Note on Knowledge Management*, Harvard Business School, #9-398-031, 20.

Miles, R.E., Snow, C.C., Mathiews, J.A. and Coleman Jr., H.J., Organizing in the knowledge age: anticipating the cellular form, *The Academy of Management Executive*, **11**(4), November 1997, 7–20.

Newell, S., Pan, S.L., Galliers, R.D. and Huang, J.C., The myth of the boundaryless organization, *Communications of the ACM*, **44**(12), December 2001, 74–76.

Newell, S., Scarbrough, H., Swan, J. and Robertson, M., *Managing Knowledge Work*, Palgrave Macmillan, 2002.

Nonaka, I., The knowledge creating company, *Harvard Business Review on Knowledge Management*, Harvard Business School Press, 1998, 21–45.

Nurmi, R., Knowledge-intensive firms, *Business Horizons*, May–June 1998, 26–32.

Prokesch, S.E., Unleashing the power of learning: an interview with BP's John Brown, *Harvard Business Review*, September–October 1997, 6–19.

Quinn, J., *The Intelligent Enterprise*, New York, NY: Free Press, 1992.

Quinn, J.B., Anderson, P. and Finkelstein, S., Managing professional intellect: making the most of the best, *Harvard Business Review*, March–April 1996, 71–80.

Sarvary, M., Knowledge management and competition in the consulting industry, *California Management Review*, **41**(2), Winter 1999, 95–107.

Slocum, J.W., McGill, M. and Lei, D.T., The new learning strategy: anytime, anything, anywhere, *Organizational Dynamics*, **23**(2), Fall 1994, 33–48.

Stear, E., Wecksell, J. and Bosik, D., The evolving role of information resource centers, *Gartner Group Strategic Analysis Report*, 26 September 1996, 19.

Strange, K., Twenty assorted data warehouse strategy questions and answers, *Gartner Group Strategic Analysis Report*, 25 October 1996, 20.

Vedder, R.G., Vanecek, M.T., Guynes, C.S. and Cappel, J.J., CEO and CIO perspectives on competitive intelligence, *Communications of the ACM*, August 1999, **48**(2), 109–116.

Weinger, E.C. and Snyder, W.M., Communities of practice: the organizational frontier, *Harvard Business Review*, January–February 2000, 139–145.

Chapter 12 – Change management

Ashkenas, D.U., Jick, T. and Kerr, S. (eds.), *The Boundaryless Organization: Breaking the Chains of Organizational Structure*, San Francisco, CA: Jossey-Bass Publishers, 1998.

Aubert, B.A., Patry, M. and Rivard, S., Assessing the risk of IT outsourcing, *Proceedings of the 31st Hawaii International Conference on System Sciences*, Vol. VI, Organizational Systems and Technology Track, January 1998, 685–693.

Benjamin, R.I. and Levinson, E., A framework for managing IT-enabled change, *Sloan Management Review*, **34**(4), Summer 1993, 23–33.

Brill, P.L. and Worth, R., *The Four Levers of Corporate Change*, New York, NY: AMACOM, 1997.

Kotter, J.P., Leading change: why transformation efforts fail, *Harvard Business Review*, **73**(2), March 1995, 59–68.

Markus, M.L. and Benjamin, R.I., The magic bullet theory in IT-enabled transformation, *Sloan Management Review*, **38**(2), Winter 1997, 55–68.

McKeen, J.D. and Smith, H.A., *Making IT Happen*, Chichester, England: John Wiley & Sons, 2003.

Orlikowski, W.J. and Hofman, J.D., An improvisional model for change management: the case of groupware technologies, *Sloan Management Review*, **38**(2), 1997, 11–21.

Pritchett, P. and Pound, R., A culture of change, *Executive Excellence*, **10**(2), February 1993, 11–12.

Pritchett, P., *Firing Up Commitment During Organizational Change: A Handbook for Managers* (2nd edn), Pritchett Pub Co., 1994.

Prokesch, S.E., Unleashing the power of learning: an interview with British petroleum's John Browne, *Harvard Business Review*, **75**(5), September–October 1997, 146–168.

Pascale, R., Millemann, M. and Gioja, L., Changing the way we change, *Harvard Business Review*, **75**(6), November–December 1997, 126–139.

Schaffer, R.H. and Thompson, H.A., Successful change programs begin with results, *Harvard Business Review*, **70**(1), January–February 1992, 80–89.

Schein, E.H., Three cultures of management: the key to organizational learning, *Sloan Management Review*, **38**(1), Fall 1996, 9–20.

Strebel, P., Why do employees resist change, *Harvard Business Review*, **74**(3), May–June 1996, 86–92.

Yetton, P.W., Johnston, K.D. and Craig, J.F., Computer-aided architects: a case study of IT and strategic change, *Sloan Management Review*, **35**(4), Summer 1994, 57–67.

Index